The Murray Bookchin Reader

We must always be on a quest for the new, for the
potentialities that ripen with the development of the world
and the new visions that unfold with them. An outlook
that ceases to look for what is new and potential in the
name of "realism" has already lost contact with the
present, for the present is always conditioned by the future.
True development is cumulative, not sequential; it is
growth, not succession. The new always embodies the
present and past, but it does so in new ways and more
adequately as the parts of a greater whole.

Murray Bookchin, "On Spontaneity and Organization," 1971

The
Murray Bookchin
Reader

Edited by Janet Biehl

BLACK
ROSE
BOOKS

Montréal/New York
London

Black Rose Books No. BB268
Hardcover ISBN: 1-55164-119-4 (bound)
Paperback ISBN: 1-55164-118-6 (pbk.)
Library of Congress Catalog Card Number: 98-71026

Canadian Cataloguing in Publication Data
Bookchin, Murray, 1921-
Murray Bookchin reader

Includes bibliographical references and index.
ISBN 1-55164-119-4 (bound).—
ISBN 1-55164-118-6 (pbk.)

1. Libertarianism. 2. Environmentalism. 3. Human ecology.
I. Biehl, Janet, 1953- II. Title.

JC585.B593 1998   304.2   C98-900275-6

Designed and typeset by Ben Cracknell Studios

BLACK
ROSE
BOOKS

C.P. 1258	2250 Military Road	99 Wallis Road
Succ. Place du Parc	Tonawanda, NY	London, E9 5LN
Montréal,Québec	14150 USA	England
H2W 2R3 Canada		

To order books in North America: (phone) 1-800-565-9523 (fax) 1-800-221-9985
In Europe: (phone) 44-0181-986-4854 (fax) 44-0181-533-5821

Our Web Site address: http://www.web.net/blackrosebooks

A publication of the Institute of Policy Alternatives of Montréal (IPAM)

Printed in Canada

Contents

Acknowledgments

The idea for this reader initially came from David Goodway, who, one sunny afternoon in May 1992, sat down with Bookchin, Gideon Kossoff, and myself in an attic in Keighley, West Yorkshire, to draft a table of contents. Although the present book bears only the faintest resemblance to the one we sketched that afternoon, its origins do lie in this meeting. Goodway has my warm thanks for setting the wheels in motion.

I am immensely grateful to Dimitri Roussopoulos for his permission to reprint from works issued by his press, Black Rose Books; and to Ramsey Kanaan for his permission to use the materials published under the auspices of A.K. Press. Heartfelt thanks as well to Steve Cook and Jane Greenwood of Cassell for their support for this project. Peter Zegers commented helpfully on the manuscript.

My greatest debt, however, is to Murray Bookchin himself, my companion, who encouraged me to take on this project. Rereading his writings, for this book, has reminded me yet again that it is a privilege to be associated with him.

List of Sources

1 An Ecological Society
Decentralization: Selected from *Our Synthetic Environment*, under the pseudonym Lewis Herber (New York: Alfred A. Knopf, 1962), pp. 237–45. The British edition of this book was published by Jonathan Cape (London, 1963); a revised paperback edition was published by Harper Colophon Books, under the name Murray Bookchin (New York, 1974).

Anarchism and Ecology: From "Ecology and Revolutionary Thought," under the pseudonym Lewis Herber, *Comment* [NY] (1964). This essay was republished in *Anarchy* [UK] 69, vol. 6 (1966); and in Murray Bookchin, *Post-Scarcity Anarchism* (San Francisco: Ramparts Books, 1971; London: Wildwood House, 1974; and Montreal: Black Rose Books, 1986). This selection comes from *Post-Scarcity Anarchism*, pp. 76–82.

The New Technology and the Human Scale: From "Towards a Liberatory Technology," in *Comment* [N.Y.] (1965). Republished in *Anarchy* [UK] 78, vol. 7 (1967) and in *Post-Scarcity Anarchism* (1971, 1974, 1986), from which this selection comes, pp. 106–12. I have removed most of the (often dated) technical material from this and the following selection.

Ecological Technology: From ibid., pp. 113–30.

Social Ecology: From Murray Bookchin, *The Ecology of Freedom* (Palo Alto, CA: Cheshire Books, 1982), pp. 20–5. Second edition published by Black Rose Books (Montreal, 1991).

2 Nature, First and Second

Images of First Nature: From "What Is Social Ecology?" in Murray Bookchin, *The Modern Crisis* (Philadelphia: New Society Publishers, 1986; and Montreal: Black Rose Books, 1987), pp. 52, 55–62. This essay was originally a seminar lecture presented at the University of Frankfurt (Germany) in 1984.

Participatory Evolution: From "Freedom and Necessity in Nature," in Murray Bookchin, *The Philosophy of Social Ecology*, revised edition (Montreal: Black Rose Books, 1995), pp. 77–81. This essay was originally published in *Alternatives*, vol. 13, no. 4 (November 1986); it was heavily revised for the 1995 edition of *The Philosophy of Social Ecology*.

Society as Second Nature: From Murray Bookchin, *Remaking Society: Pathways to a Green Future* (Montreal: Black Rose Books, 1989; Boston: South End Press, 1990), pp. 25–30, 35–9.

On Biocentrism: From Murray Bookchin, *Re-enchanting Humanity* (London: Cassell, 1995), pp. 100–4.

3 Organic Society

Usufruct, Complementarity, and the Irreducible Minimum: From *The Ecology of Freedom* (1982), pp. 48–9, 50–2, and 143–5.

Romanticizing Organic Society: From "Twenty Years Later . . . ," the introduction to the revised edition of *The Ecology of Freedom* (1991), pp. xvii–xix, xxxviii, xxxix–xliv, xlv–xlvii, xlviii, il–li.

4 The Legacy of Domination

The Emergence of Hierarchy: From *The Ecology of Freedom* (1982), pp. 74–87.

The Rise of the State: From Murray Bookchin, *The Rise of Urbanization and the Decline of Citizenship* (San Francisco: Sierra Club Books, 1987), pp. 138–46. Republished in Canada as *Urbanization Without Cities* by Black Rose Books (Montreal, 1992); and republished with revisions as *From Urbanization to Cities* by Cassell (London, 1995). This selection is taken from pp. 129–36 of the latter edition.

The Rise of Capitalism: From *Urbanization* (1987 and 1992), pp. 201–7; in the 1995 Cassell edition, pp. 181–6.

The Market Society: From *The Ecology of Freedom* (1982), pp. 135–9.

5 Scarcity and Post-Scarcity
Conditions of Freedom: From "Post-Scarcity Anarchism" (1967), in *Post-Scarcity Anarchism* (1971), pp. 33–5, 37–40.

The Problem of Want and Work: From "Toward a Liberatory Technology" (1965), in *Post-Scarcity Anarchism* (1971), pp. 89–94.

Cybernation and Automation: From "Toward a Liberatory Technology" (1965), in *Post-Scarcity Anarchism* (1971), pp. 95–105.

Technology for Life: From "Toward a Liberatory Technology" (1965), in *Post-Scarcity Anarchism* (1971), pp. 130–9.

The Fetishization of Needs: From *The Ecology of Freedom* (1982), pp. 67–72.

6 Marxism
Marxism and Domination: This selection combines excerpts from *The Ecology of Freedom* (1982), pp. 64–5, and from "Marxism as Bourgeois Sociology" *Comment* [ns], vol. 1, no. 2 (Feb. 1979). Republished in *Toward an Ecological Society* (Montreal: Black Rose Books, 1980), pp. 203–6.

Marxism and Leninism: From "Listen, Marxist!" (1969), in *Post-Scarcity Anarchism* (1971), pp. 181–5, 198–208.

7 Anarchism
The Two Traditions – Anarchism: From "Listen, Marxist!" (1969), in *Post-Scarcity Anarchism* (1971), pp. 208–20.

Anarchy and Libertarian Utopias: From *Remaking Society* (1989, 1990), pp. 117–22, 124–6.

Cultures of Revolt: From *From Urbanization to Cities* (1987), pp. 211–15; in the 1995 Cassell edition, pp. 189–92.

Spanish Anarchism – The Collectives: This selection combines excerpts from "Overview of the Spanish Libertarian Movement" (1974) and "After Fifty Years" (1985), both in Murray Bookchin, *To Remember Spain* (Edinburgh and San Francisco: A.K. Press, 1995), pp. 9–14, 26–7, 43–4. "Overview" was originally published as "Reflections on Spanish Anarchism" in *Our Generation*, vol. 10, no. 1 (Spring 1974); it was republished (in part) as the introductory essay to Sam Dolgoff, *The Anarchist Collectives: Workers Self-Management in the Spanish Revolution 1936–39* (New York: Free Life Editions, and Montreal: Black Rose Books, both 1974). "After Fifty Years" was originally published as "The Spanish Civil War, 1936," in *New Politics* 1 (Spring 1986).

Critique of Lifestyle Anarchism: From "Social Anarchism versus Lifestyle Anarchism," in Murray Bookchin *Social Anarchism versus Lifestyle Anarchism* (Edinburgh and San Francisco: A.K. Press, 1995), pp. 8–9, 49–54, 56–61.

8 Libertarian Municipalism

The New Municipal Agenda: This selection comes primarily from Chapter 8 of *Urbanization* (1987, 1992, 1995), *passim*; with some interpolations from "Radical Politics in an Era of Advanced Capitalism," *Green Perspectives,* no. 18 (November 1989); "The Meaning of Confederalism," *Green Perspectives,* no. 20 (November 1990); and "Libertarian Municipalism: An Overview," *Green Perspectives,* no. 24 (October 1991). On some occasions, such as while writing *Urbanization,* Bookchin referred to his political ideas as "confederal municipalism" rather than as "libertarian municipalism." In this selection, at his request, I have changed "confederal municipalism" to his preferred "libertarian municipalism."

9 Dialectical Naturalism

Objectively Grounded Ethics: From "Rethinking Ethics, Nature, and Society" (written in 1985), in *The Modern Crisis* (1986), pp. 7–13.

A Philosophical Naturalism: From the introduction to *The Philosophy of Social Ecology,* revised edition (1995), pp. 3–11, 13–15, 16–24, 26–7, 28–33.

Ecologizing the Dialectic: From "Thinking Ecologically: A Dialectical Approach," in *The Philosophy of Social Ecology,* revised edition (1995), pp. 119, 120, 124, 125–6, 127–31, 133–6, 140–1. This article was originally published in *Our Generation,* vol. 18, no. 2 (Spring–Summer 1987).

10 Reason and History

History, Civilization, and Progress: From "History, Civilization, and Progress: Outline for a Criticism of Modern Relativism," in *The Philosophy of Social Ecology,* revised edition (1995), pp. 147–8, 157–79. Originally published in *Green Perspectives,* no. 29 (March 1994).

Introduction

In the aftermath of the cold war, in a world that glorifies markets and commodities, it sometimes seems difficult to remember that generations of people once fought to create a very different kind of world. To many, the aspirations of this grand tradition of socialism often seem archaic today, or utopian in the pejorative sense, the stuff of idle dreams; others, more dismissive, consider socialism to be an inherently coercive system, one whose consignment to the past is well-deserved.

Yet for a century preceding World War I, and for nearly a half century thereafter, various kinds of socialism – statist and libertarian; economistic and moral; industrial and communalistic – constituted a powerful mass movement for the transformation of a competitive society into a cooperative one – and for the creation of a generous and humane system in which emancipated human beings could fulfill their creative and rational potentialities. People are ends in their own right, the socialist tradition asserted, not means for one another's use; and they are substantive beings, with considered opinions and deep feelings, not mass-produced things with artificially induced notions and wants. People can and should throw away the economic shackles that bind them, socialists argued, cast off the fictions and unrealities that mystify them, and plan and construct, deliberately and consciously, a truly enlightened and emancipated society based on freedom and cooperation, reason and solidarity. Material aims would be secondary to ethical concerns, people would have rich, spontaneous social relationships with one another, and they would actively and responsibly participate in making all decisions about their lives, rather than subject themselves to external authoritarian control.

After 1917 a general enthusiasm for the stunning accomplishment of the Bolshevik Revolution pervaded almost all sectors of the international left, so much so that the humanistic ideals of socialism came to be attached to the Communist movement. In the 1930s young American intellectuals growing up under Depression conditions, especially in the vibrant radical political culture of New York City, cut their teeth on the version of socialism that the Communist movement taught them. Their minds brimming with revolutionary strategies and Marxian dialectics, their hopes and passions spurred by life-endangering battles against a capitalist system that seemed on the brink of collapse, they marshaled all their abilities to achieve the century-old socialist ideal.

Tragically, international Communism defiled that ideal. It committed monstrous abuses in the name of socialism, and when these abuses became too much to bear – the show trials of 1936–8, the betrayal of the Spanish Revolution, and the Hitler–Stalin pact – hopes that the Communist movement could usher in a socialist world were shipwrecked. Many radicals, reeling from these blows, withdrew into private life; others accommodated themselves to the capitalist system in varying degrees, even to the point of supporting the United States in the cold war. Still others, who did remain on the left politically, turned their attention to more limited arenas: aesthetics, or "new class" theory, or Frankfurt School sociology. Meanwhile, outside the academy, what remained of the Marxian left persisted in small groups, defying the prevailing "consensus" in favor of capitalism and accommodation.

Among the young intellectuals who had emerged from the 1930s Communist movement, relatively few responded to its failure by attempting to keep the centuries-old revolutionary tradition alive, by advancing a libertarian alternative to Marxism, one better suited to pursue a humane socialist society in the postwar era. It is a distinction of Murray Bookchin that in these years of disillusion, disenchantment, and retreat, he attempted to create just such an alternative.

Born in January 1921 in New York City to Russian Jewish immigrants, Bookchin was raised under the very shadow of the Russian Revolution, partaking of the excitement that it aroused among his immigrant and working-class neighbors. At the same time, from his earliest years, he imbibed libertarian ideas from his maternal grand-mother, who had been a member of the Socialist Revolutionaries, a quasi-anarchistic populist movement, in czarist Russia. In the early 1930s, as the United States plunged deeper into the Depression, he entered the Communist movement's youth organizations, speaking at streetcorner meetings, participating in rent strikes, and helping to organize the unemployed, even as an adolescent, eventually running the educational program for his branch of the Young Communist League. After breaking with Stalinism – initially, in 1935, because of its class-collaborationist policies (the so-called Popular Front), then conclusively in 1937 during the Spanish Civil War – he turned to Trotskyism and later to libertarian socialism, joining a group surrounding the exiled German Trotskyist Josef Weber in the mid-1940s; his earliest works were published in this group's periodical, *Contemporary Issues*.

In the meantime, Bookchin was deeply involved in trade union organizing in northern New Jersey, where he worked for years as a foundryman and an autoworker. (Due to his family's poverty, he went to work in heavy industry directly after high school.) In whatever factory he worked, he engaged in union activities as a member of the burgeoning and intensely militant Congress of Industrial Organizations, particularly the United Automobile Workers.

During the 1930s, Marxian precepts had seemed to explain conclusively the Great Depression and the turbulent labor insurgency that arose during the decade, seeming to challenge the very foundations of the capitalist system. But Marxist prognoses about the 1940s were glaringly unfulfilled. These predictions had it that World War II, like World War I, would end in proletarian revolutions among the belligerent countries. But the proletariat, far from making a revolution in any Western country under the banner of internationalism, fought out the war under the banner of nationalism. Even the German working class abandoned the class consciousness of its earlier socialist history and fought on behalf of Hitler to the very end. Far from collapsing, capitalism emerged from the war unscathed and strengthened, with more stability than ever before.

The Soviet Union, for its part, was clearly far from a socialist society, let alone a communist one. Far from playing a revolutionary role during the war, it was actively involved in suppressing revolutionary movements in its own national interests. Finally, American industrial workers, far from challenging the capitalist system, were becoming assimilated into it. When a major General Motors strike in 1946 ended with his co-workers placidly accepting company pension plans and unemployment benefits, Bookchin's disillusionment with the workers' movement as a uniquely revolutionary force was complete, and his years as a union activist came to an end. The revolutionary tradition, he concluded, would have to dispense with the notion of proletarian hegemony as the compelling force for basic social change. With the consolidation of capitalism on a massive international scale, the idea that conflict between wage labor and capital would bring capitalism to an end had to be called into serious question.

To his credit, Bookchin, faced with these dispiriting conditions, nonetheless refused to relinquish his commitment to revolution. Rather, the revolutionary tradition, he felt, had to explore new possibilities for creating a free cooperative society and reclaim nonauthoritarian socialism in a new form. Anarchism, whose history had long intertwined with that of Marxian socialism, argued that people could manage their own affairs without benefit of a state, and that the object of revolution should be not the seizure of state power but its dissolution. In 1950s America, in the aftermath of the McCarthy period, the left generally – especially the anarchist movement – was small, fragmented, and seemingly on the wane. Yet anarchism's libertarian ideals – "a stateless, decentralized society, based on the communal ownership of the means of production"[1] – seemed to be the basis, in Bookchin's mind, for a viable revolutionary alternative in the postwar era.

Moving decisively toward this left–libertarian tradition in the middle of the decade, Bookchin tried to free anarchism of its more dated nineteenth-century aspects and recast its honorable principles in contemporary terms. "The future of the anarchist movement will depend upon its ability to apply basic libertarian principles to new historical situations," he wrote in 1964.

> . . . Life itself compels the anarchist to concern himself increasingly with the quality of urban life, with the reorganization of society along humanistic lines, with the subcultures created by new, often indefinable strata – students, unemployables, an immense bohemia of intellectuals, and above all a youth which began to gain social awareness with the peace movement and civil rights struggles of the early 1960s.[2]

Even as he embraced the anarchist tradition, however, Bookchin never entirely abandoned Marx's basic ideas. In effect, he drew on the best of both Marxism and anarchism to synthesize a coherent hybrid political philosophy of freedom and cooperation, one that drew on both intellectual rigor and cultural sensibility, analysis and reconstruction. He would call this synthesis social ecology.

Even as Bookchin was moving toward an anarchist outlook, the American economy of the early 1950s was undergoing enormous expansion, with unprecedented economic advances that catapulted even industrial workers into the booming middle class. It was not only military spending that propelled this growth: with government support, science and industry had combined to spawn a wide array of new technologies, suitable for civilian as well as military use. These new technologies, so it was said, seemed poised to cure all social ills of the time, if not engineer an entirely new civilization.

Automobiles, fast becoming a standard consumer item, were promising mobility, suburbs, and jobs – giving plausibility, in the eyes of many Americans, to the slogan, "What's good for GM is good for America." Nuclear power, it was avowed, would meet US energy needs more or less for free; indeed, Lewis Strauss, the former Wall Street investment banker who first chaired the Atomic Energy Commission, predicted that electricity from nuclear power plants would become "too cheap to meter." Miracle grains would feed humanity, and new pharmaceuticals would control formerly intractable diseases. Petrochemicals and petrochemical products – including plastics, food additives, detergents, solvents, and abrasives – would make life comfortable and provide labor-saving convenience for everyone. As for pesticides, as environmental historian Robert Gottlieb observes, they were "being touted as a kind of miracle product, supported by advertising campaigns ('Better Things for Better Living Through Chemistry'), by government policies designed to increase agricultural productivity, and a media celebration of the wonders of the new technology." Most of the American public welcomed these new technologies, seeming to agree with the director of the US Geological Survey, Thomas Nolan, that the new technological resources were "inexhaustible."[3]

It was just at this moment of collective anticipation that Bookchin audaciously suggested that an ecological crisis lay on the horizon. "Within recent years," he wrote in a long 1952 essay, "the rise of little known and even unknown infectious diseases, the increase of degenerative illnesses and finally the high incidence of cancer suggests some connection between the growing use of chemicals in food and human diseases."[4] The chemicals being used in food additives, he insisted in "The Problem of Chemicals in Food," could well be carcinogenic. The new economic and technological boom, despite all its rosy promises, could also have harmful environmental consequences.

Little environmentalist writing existed in the United States in these years, apart from neo-Malthusian tracts that issued dire warnings about overpopulation, like Fairfield Osborn's *Our Plundered Planet* and William Vogt's *The Road to Survival* (both published in 1948). Although a conservation movement existed, it worked primarily for the preservation of wilderness areas in national parks and showed little interest in social or political analysis. The existing literature on chemical pollution, for its part, was silent on the driving role that modern capitalism was playing in the development and application of chemicals.

So it was that before most Americans even realized that an environmental crisis was in the offing, Bookchin was telling them it was. Even more striking, he was already probing its sources. "The principal motives for chemicals," he warned, and the "demands imposed upon [farm] land" are "shaped neither by the needs of the public nor by the limits of nature, but by the exigencies of profit and competition."[5] The use of carcinogenic chemicals was rooted in a profit-oriented society; "profit-minded businessmen" have produced "ecological disturbances . . . throughout the American countryside. For decades, lumber companies and railroads were permitted a free hand in destroying valuable forest lands and wildlife."[6] Bookchin had not only rooted environmental dislocations in modern capitalism – he had found a new limit to capitalist expansion, one that held the potential to supersede the misery of the working class as a source of fundamental social change: environmental destruction.

Amid the McCarthyite intolerance of all social radicalism in 1952, it required considerable courage to write and publish a radical social analysis of environmental problems. Yet not only did Bookchin write such an analysis, he advanced, albeit in rudimentary terms, an anarchist solution to the problems he explored, calling for the decentralization of society to countervail the looming ecological crisis, in passages that presage the marriage of anarchism and ecology that he would expound more fully twelve years later:

> In decentralization exists a real possibility for developing the best traditions of social life and for solving agricultural and nutritional difficulties that have thus far been delivered to chemistry. Most of the food problems of the world would be solved today by well-balanced and rounded communities, intelligently urbanized, well-equipped with industry and with easy access to the land. . . . The problem has become a social problem – an issue concerning the misuse of industry as a whole.[7]

For almost half a century, this assertion of the social causes of ecological problems, and the insistence on their solution by a revolutionary decentralization of society have remained consistent in Bookchin's writings. He elaborated these ideas further in *Our Synthetic Environment,* a pioneering 1962 work that was published five months before Rachel Carson's *Silent Spring;* unlike Carson's book, *Our Synthetic Environment* did not limit its focus to pesticides. A comprehensive overview of ecological degradation, it addressed not only the connections between food additives and cancer but the impact of X-radiation, radionuclides from fallout, and the stresses of urban life, giving a social elaboration of what in those days was called "human ecology."[8]

The freer political atmosphere of the 1960s allowed Bookchin to express more clearly his revolutionary perspective. His 1964 essay "Ecology and Revolutionary Thought," the first manifesto of radical ecology, overtly called for revolutionary change as a solution to the ecological crisis. It advanced a conjunction of anarchism and ecology to create an ecological society that would be humane and free, libertarian and decentralized, mutualistic and cooperative.

In its range and depth, Bookchin's dialectical synthesis of anarchism and ecology, which he called social ecology, had no equal in the postwar international Left. The first major effort to fuse ecological awareness with the need for fundamental social change, and to link a philosophy of nature with a philosophy of social revolution, it remains the most important such effort to this day.

Social ecology, drawing on multiple domains of knowledge, traces the roots of the ecological crisis to dislocations in society. As Bookchin put it in "Ecology and Revolutionary Thought": "The imbalances man has produced in the natural world are caused by the imbalances he has produced in the social world."[9] This inextricable relation between society and ecology remains a pillar of social ecology.

But social ecology has not only a critical dimension but a reconstructive one as well. Since the causes of the ecological crisis are social in nature, we can avert the present danger of ecological disaster only by fundamentally transforming the present society into a rational and ecological one. In this same 1964 article, in "Toward a Liberatory Technology" (written the following year), and in many subsequent works, Bookchin described his version of the truly libertarian socialist society. It would be a decentralized and mutualistic one, free of hierarchy and domination. Town and country would no longer be opposed to each other but would instead be integrated. Social life would be scaled to human dimensions. Politics would be directly democratic at the community level, so that citizens can manage their own social and political affairs on a face-to-face basis, forming confederations to address larger-scale problems. Economic life would be cooperative and communal, and technology would eliminate onerous and tedious labor.

Bookchin would elaborate and refine many aspects of this society – and the means to achieve it – over subsequent decades. But its earliest outlines were sketched as early as 1962 and developed in 1964 and 1965. Here Bookchin also proposed that an ecological society could make use of solar and wind power as sources of energy, replacing fossil fuels. At that time renewable energy sources – solar and wind power – were subjects of some research and experimentation, but they had essentially been abandoned as practical alternatives to fossil and nuclear fuels; nor did the existing environmental literature pay much attention to them. Not only did Bookchin show their relevance to the solution of ecological problems, he stood alone in demonstrating their integral importance to the creation of an ecological society:

> To maintain a large city requires immense quantities of coal and petroleum. By contrast, solar, wind, and tidal energy can reach us mainly in small packets; except for spectacular tidal dams, the new devices seldom provide more than a few thousand kilowatt-hours of electricity. . . . To use solar, wind, and tidal power effectively, the megalopolis must be decentralized. A new type of community, carefully tailored to the characteristics and resources of a region, must replace the sprawling urban belts that are emerging today.[10]

These renewable sources of energy, in effect, had far-reaching anarchistic as well as ecological implications.

The list of Bookchin's innovations in ecological politics does not stop here. To take another example – warnings of a greenhouse effect were hardly common in the early 1960s, yet Bookchin issued just such a warning in 1964:

> It can be argued on very sound theoretical grounds that this growing blanket of carbon dioxide, by intercepting heat radiated from the earth,

will lead to rising atmospheric temperatures, a more violent circulation of air, more destructive storm patterns, and eventually a melting of the polar ice caps (possibly in two or three centuries), rising sea levels, and the inundation of vast land areas.[11]

Bookchin underestimated only the time frame – and it is testimony to the enormity of the ecological problem that the damage that he anticipated would take centuries to develop has actually developed in only a matter of decades.

Bookchin spent much of the 1960s criss-crossing the United States and Canada, indefatigably educating the counterculture and New Left about ecology and its revolutionary significance. The first Earth Day in 1970, followed by the publication of *The Limits to Growth* in 1972, signaled the arrival of ecology as a popular issue. But in the following years a less radical, more technocratic approach to ecological issues came to the fore, one that, in Bookchin's view, represented mere environmental tinkering: instead of proposing to transform society as a whole, it looked for technological solutions to specific environmental problems.

Calling this approach reformistic rather than revolutionary, Bookchin labeled it "environmentalism," in contradistinction to his more radical "ecology." Although some histories of the ecological and environmental movements now assert that Norwegian philosopher Arne Naess was the first to distinguish between environmentalism and ecology (in a paper on deep ecology, presented as a lecture in 1972[12]), Bookchin made this distinction in November 1971, in "Spontaneity and Organization," anchoring it, as always, in a social and political matrix:

> I speak, here, of *ecology,* not environmentalism. Environmentalism deals with the serviceability of the human habitat, a passive habitat that people *use,* in short, an assemblage of things called "natural resources" and "urban resources." Taken by themselves, environmental issues require the use of no greater wisdom than the instrumentalist modes of thought and methods that are used by city planners, engineers, physicians, lawyers – and socialists.
>
> Ecology, by contrast, . . . is an outlook that interprets all interdependencies (social and psychological as well as natural) nonhierarchically. Ecology denies that nature can be interpreted from a hierarchical viewpoint. Moreover, it affirms that diversity and spontaneous development are ends in themselves, to be respected in their own right. Formulated in terms of ecology's "ecosystem approach," this means that each form of life has a unique place in the balance of nature and its removal from the ecosystem could imperil the stability of the whole.[13]

Bookchin's core political program remained far too radical to gain general social acceptance in those decades. But many of his remarkably prescient insights have by now become commonplaces, not only in ecological thought but in mainstream popular culture, while their originating source has been forgotten or obscured. By advancing these ideas when he did, Bookchin exercised a strong and steady influence on the international development of radical ecological thought.

As significant as Bookchin's prescient insights are, they are only part of what is actually a large theoretical corpus. Over the course of five decades, the ideas of social ecology have grown steadily in richness. Encompassing anthropology and history, politics and social criticism, philosophy and natural science, Bookchin's works evoke the grand tradition of nineteenth-century generalists, who could write knowledgeably on a multiplicity of subjects – a tradition that is, lamentably, fast disappearing in the present age of scholarly specialization and postmodernist fragmentation.

Drawing on anthropology and history, Bookchin explored the libertarian and democratic traditions that could contribute to the creation of an ecological and rational society. A "legacy of freedom," he believes, has run like an undercurrent within Western civilization and in other parts of the world, with certain social virtues and practices that are relevant to the socialist ideal. In its nascent form this legacy appears in the "organic society" of prehistoric Europe, with a constellation of relatively egalitarian social relations. These societies were destroyed by the rise of hierarchy and domination and ultimately by the emergence of states and the capitalist system.

Hierarchy and domination, it should be noted, are key concepts in Bookchin's political work, for although in his view the ecological crisis has stemmed proximately from a capitalist economy, its ultimate roots lie in social hierarchies. The ideology of dominating the natural world, he has long maintained, is an anthropomorphic projection of human social domination onto the natural world. It could only have stemmed historically from the domination of human by human, and not the other way around. During the late 1960s and 1970s Bookchin's anthropological, historical, and political explorations of the "legacy of freedom" and the "legacy of domination," as he called it, percolated through radical social movements – not only the ecology movement but the feminist, communitarian, and anarchist movements as well. The concept of hierarchy in particular, assimilated by the counterculture into conventional wisdom, has become essential to radical thought due largely to Bookchin's insistence on its nature and importance in many lectures in the late 1960s.

Bookchin's ideas have retained an underlying continuity over the decades, and it is precisely by upholding his original principles that he has maintained his stalwart opposition to the existing capitalist and hierarchical system. As could be expected of any writer engaged in concrete political activity, his ideas have also changed over time; yet they have done so not to effect a compromise with the existing social order but to sustain a revolutionary position in response to regressive developments both in the larger society and within social movements for change. Often he has initiated intramural debates by objecting to tendencies that he considered out of place in a revolutionary movement, due to their opportunism, their accommodation to the system, or their quietism; his frequently polemical style stems from an earnest attempt to preserve the revolutionary impulse in movements that hold potential for radical social transformation. To his credit, he raised such objections even when the tendencies to which he objected were the more popular ones and when acquiescence would have enhanced his own popularity. Still, even as the key concepts of social ecology remain fundamentally unchanged since the 1960s, the many debates in which he has been engaged have primarily defined and sharpened them. If anything, his ideas have become more sophisticated over time as a result of these debates.

It is typical of Bookchin that his ideas should become honed as a result of practical movement experience. Despite his large body of theoretical writing, he is no mere armchair theorist. Throughout his life he has consistently maintained an active political practice: his union and protest activities in the Depression decade, his libertarian activities of the 1950s and 1960s, his mobilization of opposition to a nuclear power plant proposed for Queens in 1964, his civil rights activities, his participation in endless demonstrations and actions in the 1960s against the Vietnam war and in support of ecology and anarchism, his 1970s involvement in the antinuclear Clamshell Alliance, his efforts to preserve and expand democracy in his adopted state of Vermont, and finally his influence, in the 1980s, on the development of Green movements in the United States and abroad, trying – often unsuccessfully – to keep them on a radical course. Only in his eighth decade have physical infirmities – especially a nearly crippling arthritis – obliged him to withdraw from organized political activity.

Yet withdrawal from active political work has not meant that Bookchin has put down his pen. On the contrary, in an era of reaction, he continues to denounce tendencies that compromise the radicalism of the ecological and anarchist movements, be it a mystical "deep ecology" or an individualistic "lifestyle anarchism," both of which he sees as personalistic and irrationalistic departures from the social, rational, and democratic eco-anarchism and socialism he has championed for decades. With the emergence of ecological–political tendencies that embraced irrationalism, he emphasized that an ecological society would neither renounce nor denigrate reason, science, and technology. So crucial is this point that he today prefers the phrase "rational society" to other labels for a free society, since a rational society would necessarily be one that is ecological. His commitment to longstanding socialist ideals, informed by Marx as well as by social anarchist thinkers, remains firm: for Murray Bookchin, the socialist utopia is still, as he once said, "the only reality that makes any sense."

To all his writing, Bookchin brings a passionate hatred of the capitalist social order, expressed in the cadences of six decades of radical oratory. He brings the grim hatred of the grueling toil that he experienced in factories, and the acerbic intensity of one who has looked down the barrel of a gun during 1930s labor protests. At the same time he brings the originality and creativity of a thinker who is largely self-taught, and the love of coherence of one who studied dialectics with Marxists as a youth. He brings to it, in this age of diminished expectations, the outrage of one who consistently chooses morality over realpolitik, and he serves as the lacerating conscience of those who once held revolutionary sentiments but have since abandoned them.

A thorough understanding of his project would require a reading of his most important books. *Post-Scarcity Anarchism* (1971) contains the two pivotal mid-1960s essays mentioned in this introduction, which encapsulate so many ideas that he later developed more fully and that, in their uncompromising intensity, remain fresh to this day. *The Ecology of Freedom* (1982) is an anthropological and historical account not only of the rise of hierarchy and domination but of the "legacy of freedom," including the cultural, psychological, and epistemological components of both. Although *The Ecology of Freedom* has been heralded in some quarters as Bookchin's *magnum opus*, it has been followed by several books of at least equal importance. *The Philosophy of Social Ecology*, especially its revised edition (1995), is a collection of five philosophical essays on dialectical naturalism, the nature philosophy that underpins his political and social thought; he himself regards it as his most important work to date. *Remaking Society* (1989) is a summary overview of his ideas, with emphasis on their anarchist roots. *From Urbanization to Cities* (which has previously appeared under the titles *Urbanization without Cities* and *The Rise of Urbanization and the Decline of Citizenship*) is a wide-ranging exposition of libertarian municipalism, Bookchin's political program, giving much attention to popular democratic institutional forms in European and American history. *Re-enchanting Humanity* (1995) is his defense of the Enlightenment against a variety of antihumanistic and irrationalistic trends in popular culture today. Finally, his three-volume *The Third Revolution* (of which the first volume is already in print at the time of writing) traces the history of popular movements within Euro–American revolutions, beginning with the peasant revolts of the fourteenth century and closing with the Spanish Revolution of 1936–7.

The present Reader brings together selections from Bookchin's major writings, organized thematically. Even as I have tried to show the development of his ideas over time, I have emphasized those works that have stood the test of time and that are most in accordance with his views today, at the expense of works that, generated in the heat of polemic, sometimes verged on one-sidedness. All of the selections are excerpted from larger works, and all have been pruned in some way, be it to achieve conciseness, to eliminate repetition among the selections in this book, or to produce a thematic balance among them. I have very lightly edited a few of the selections, but only where the need for it was distracting. Regrettably, but necessarily for reasons of space, I have had to cut all textual footnotes, retaining only those that cite a specific source. Except for these notes, I have indicated all cuts in the text with ellipsis points. I have provided the sources for all the selections in the listing that appears before this introduction.

Janet Biehl

NOTES

1 Murray Bookchin, "Ecology and Revolutionary Thought," 1964; as reprinted in *Anarchy* 69, vol. 6 (1966), p. 18. The section "Observations on Classical Anarchism" appeared in the original essay, as it was published in *Comment* in 1964 and in *Anarchy* in 1966, but it was cut from the reprinting in *Post-Scarcity Anarchism* (San Francisco: Ramparts Press, 1971; Montreal: Black Rose Books, 1977).

2 Ibid., pp. 18, 21.

3 Robert Gottlieb, *Forcing the Spring: The Transformation of the American Environmental Movement* (Washington, DC and Covelo, CA: Island Press, 1993), p. 83; Nolan is quoted on p. 37.

4 Lewis Herber (pseud. for Murray Bookchin), "The Problem of Chemicals in Food," *Contemporary Issues*, vol. 3, no. 12 (June–August 1952), p. 235.

5 Ibid., pp. 206, 211.

6 Ibid., p. 209.

7 Ibid., p. 240.

8 Lewis Herber (pseud. for Murray Bookchin), *Our Synthetic Environment* (New York: Alfred A. Knopf, 1962). For a comparison with *Silent Spring*, see Yaakov Garb, "Change and Continuity in Environmental World-View," in *Minding Nature: The Philosophers of Ecology*, edited by David Macauley (New York: Guilford, 1996), pp. 246–7.

9 "Ecology and Revolutionary Thought," in *Post-Scarcity Anarchism*, p. 62.

10 Ibid., p. 74–5.

11 "Ecology and Revolutionary Thought," as it appeared in *Anarchy*, p. 5. Some of the words from this passage were cut when the essay was republished in *Post-Scarcity Anarchism*; see p. 60 of that book.

12 Arne Naess, "The Shallow and the Deep, Long-Range Ecology Movement," *Inquiry*, vol. 16 (1973), pp. 95–100.

13 Murray Bookchin, "Spontaneity and Organization," lecture delivered at *Telos* conference, Buffalo, NY, 1971; published in *Anarchos*, no. 4 (1973) and in *Liberation* (March 1972); republished in *Toward an Ecological Society* (Montreal: Black Rose Books, 1980), where this quotation is on pp. 270–1.

CHAPTER ONE

An Ecological Society

Introduction

Bookchin's interest in ecology arose primarily from his boyhood curiosity about natural phenomena, from his studies of biology in high school, and from his love of green spaces in the environs of his native New York City, as well as from his dismay at their diminution with the buildup of urban streets and buildings.

Yet another source of inspiration for his thinking about ecology were the writings of Karl Marx and Friedrich Engels. In scattered passages the two progenitors of Marxian socialism had alluded provocatively to a conflicted relationship between town and country. "The greatest division of material and mental labour," they wrote, "is the separation of town and country. The antagonism between town and country begins with the transition from barbarism to civilisation, from tribe to State, from locality to nation, and runs through the whole history of civilisation to the present day."[1] Engels, writing alone, lamented the spread of industrial capitalist towns into the countryside. "The present poisoning of the air, water and land can be put to an end only by the fusion" of town and country:

> and only such fusion will change the situation of the masses now languishing in the towns. . . . The abolition of the separation between town and country is . . . not utopian, even in so far as it presupposes the most equal distribution possible of large-scale industry over the whole country. It is true that in the huge towns civilisation has bequeathed us a heritage to rid ourselves of which will take much time and trouble. But this heritage must and will be got rid of, however protracted the process may be.[2]

Such unsystematic but suggestive statements, reinforced by discussions in the *Contemporary Issues* group, gave Bookchin a rough framework for interpreting the environmental changes that

no

he was observing. He began to explore the origins of this cleavage between town and country, between human society and the natural world, and he speculated about how it could be annulled – that is, how town and country could be reintegrated.

It is significant that from his earliest writings on environmental issues, Bookchin did not interpret the ecological crisis as the consequence of a rift between pristine natural world and human culture as such, or as a basic antithesis that could be overcome only by exalting wilderness over civilization. Rather, from the outset he thought in terms of attaining a reconciliation between human and nonhuman nature in a particular kind of society, in which "rounded" human communities would be sensitively embedded in nonhuman nature. This integrative approach contrasts markedly with the romantic nature-worship of later mystical ecologies that would reject civilization with a militancy that sometimes passes over into antihumanism and misanthropy. From their standpoint the very notion of an "ecological society" would be a contradiction in terms: the antidote to ecological crisis is, for them, the veneration of nature, understood as wilderness. Bookchin's integrative approach, by contrast, has been fundamental to his thought from the outset. A legacy of Enlightenment humanism, which he early absorbed from Marxian socialism, it compelled him to look for ecological solutions that would enhance human creativity, not deny it.

The society capable of performing such an integration, Bookchin argued, would be not a strictly Marxist one, focused primarily on economic facts, but an anarchist one, decentralized and mutualistic, nonhierarchical and cooperative. Over the decades he would flesh out this concept more fully, with a social-political program as well as a nature philosophy. Yet even his earliest writings express its major points: its ecological humanism, its technological infrastructure, and especially its ethical outlook, based on principles beneficial to both the social and natural worlds, like unity in diversity and complementarity, differentiation, and development. And he has consistently held to the idea that achieving the integration of human and nonhuman nature requires, as a precondition, changing human social relations – creating a society of freedom and cooperation.

Decentralization
(from *Our Synthetic Environment*, 1962)

Without having read any books or articles on human ecology, millions of Americans have sensed the overall deterioration of modern urban life. They have turned to the suburbs and "exurbs" as a refuge from the burdens of the metropolitan milieu. From all accounts of suburban life, many of these burdens have followed them into the countryside. Suburbanites have not adapted to the land; they have merely adapted a metropolitan manner of life to semirural surroundings. The metropolis remains the axis around which their lives turn. It is the source of their livelihood, their food staples, and in large part their tensions. The suburbs have branched away from the city, but they still belong to the metropolitan tree.

It would be wise, however, to stop ridiculing the exodus to the suburbs and to try to understand what lies behind this phenomenon. The modern city has reached its limits. Megalopolitan life is breaking down – psychically, economically, and biologically. Millions of people have acknowledged this breakdown by "voting with their feet": they have picked up their belongings and left. If they have not been able to sever their connections with the metropolis, at least they have tried. As a social symptom, the effort is significant. The reconciliation of man with the natural world is no longer merely desirable; it has become a necessity. It is a compelling need that is sending millions of people into the countryside. The need has created a new interest in camping, handicrafts, and horticulture. In ever-increasing numbers, Americans are acquiring a passionate interest in their national parks and forests, in their rural landscape, and in their small-town agrarian heritage.

Despite its many shortcomings, this trend reflects a basically sound orientation. The average American is making an attempt, however confusedly, to reduce his environment to a human scale. He is trying to recreate a world that he can cope with as an individual, a world that he correctly identifies with the freedom, gentler rhythms, and quietude of rural surroundings. His attempts at gardening, landscaping, carpentry, home maintenance, and other so-called suburban "vices" reflect a need to function within an intelligible, manipulable, and individually creative sphere of human activity. The suburbanite, like the camper, senses that he is working with basic, abiding things that have slipped from his control in the metropolitan world – shelter, the handiwork that enters into daily life, vegetation, and the land. He is fortunate, to be sure, if these activities do not descend to the level of caricature. Nevertheless, they are important, not only because they reflect basic needs of man but because they also reflect basic needs of the things with which he is working. The human scale is also the natural scale. The soil, the land, the living things on which man depends for his nutriment and recreation are direly in need of individual care.

For one thing, proper maintenance of the soil not only depends upon advances in our knowledge of soil chemistry and soil fertility; it also requires a more personalized approach to agriculture. Thus far, the trend has been the other way; agriculture has become depersonalized and overindustrialized. Modern farming is suffering from gigantism.

The average agricultural unit is getting so big that the finer aspects of soil performance and soil needs are being overlooked. If differences in the quality and performance of various kinds of soil are to receive more attention, American farming must be reduced to a more human scale. It will become necessary to bring agriculture within the scope of the individual, so that the farmer and the soil can develop together, each responding as fully as possible to the needs of the other.

The same is true for the management of livestock. Today food animals are being manipulated like a lifeless industrial resource. Normally, large numbers of animals are collected in the smallest possible area and are allowed only as much movement as is necessary for mere survival. Our meat animals have been placed on a diet composed for the most part of medicated feed high in carbohydrates. Before they are slaughtered, these obese, rapidly matured creatures seldom spend more than six months on the range and six months on farms, where they are kept on concentrated rations and gain about two pounds daily. Our dairy herds are handled like machines; our poultry flocks, like hothouse tomatoes. The need to restore the time-honored intimacy between man and his livestock is just as pronounced as the need to bring agriculture within the horizon of the individual farmer. Although modern technology has enlarged the elements that enter into the agricultural situation, giving each man a wider area of sovereignty and control, machines have not lessened the importance of personal familiarity with the land, its vegetation, and the living things it supports. Unless principles of good land use permit otherwise, a farm should not become smaller or larger than the individual farmer can command. If it is smaller, agriculture will become inefficient; if larger, it will become depersonalized.

With the decline in the quality of urban life, on the one hand, and the growing imbalance in agriculture, on the other, our times are beginning to witness a remarkable confluence of human interests with the needs of the natural world. Men of the nineteenth century assumed a posture of defiance toward the forests, plains, and mountains. Their applause was reserved for the engineer, the technician, the inventor, at times even the robber baron, and the railroader, who seemed to offer the promise of a more abundant material life. Today we are filled with a vague nostalgia for the past. To a large degree this nostalgia reflects the insecurity and uncertainty of our times, in contrast with the echoes of a more optimistic and perhaps more tranquil era. But it also reflects a deep sense of loss, a longing for the free, unblemished land that lay before the eyes of the frontiersman and early settler. We are seeking out the mountains they tried to avoid and we are trying to recover fragments of the forests they removed. Our nostalgia springs neither from a greater sensitivity nor from the wilder depths of human instinct. It springs from a growing need to restore the normal, balanced, and manageable rhythms of human life – that is, an environment that meets our requirements as individuals and biological beings.

Modern man can never return to the primitive life he so often idealizes, but the point is that he doesn't have to. The use of farm machinery as such does not conflict with sound agricultural practices; nor are industry and an urbanized community incompatible with a more agrarian, more natural environment. Ironically, advances in technology itself have largely overcome the industrial problems that once justified the huge concentrations of people and facilities in a few urban areas. Automobiles, aircraft, electric power, and electronic devices have eliminated nearly all the problems of transportation, communication, and social isolation that burdened man in past eras. We can now communicate with one another over a distance of thousands of miles in a matter of seconds, and we can travel to the most remote areas of the world in a few hours. The obstacles created by space and time are essentially gone. Similarly, size need no longer be a problem. Technologists have developed remarkable small-scale alternatives to many of the giant facilities that still dominate modern industry. The smoky steel town, for example, is an anachronism. Excellent steel can be made and rolled with installations that occupy about two or three city blocks. Many of the latest machines are highly versatile and compact. They lend themselves to a large variety of manufacturing and finishing operations. Today the more modern plant, with its clean, quiet, versatile, and largely automated facilities, contrasts sharply with the huge, ugly, congested factories inherited from an earlier era.

Thus, almost without realizing it, we have been preparing the material conditions for a new type of human community – one that constitutes neither a complete return to the past nor a suburban accommodation to the present. It is no longer fanciful to think of man's future environment in terms of a decentralized, moderate-sized city that combines industry with agriculture, not only in the same civic entity but in the occupational activities of the same individual. The "urbanized farmer" or the "agrarianized townsman" need not be a contradiction in terms. This way of life was achieved for a time by the Greek *polis*, by early Republican Rome, and by the Renaissance commune. The urban centers that became the well-springs of Western civilization were not strictly cities in the modern sense of the term. Rather, they brought agriculture together with urban life, synthesizing both into a rounded human, cultural, and social development.

Whether modern man manages to reach this point or travels only part of the way, some kind of decentralization will be necessary to achieve a lasting equilibrium between society and nature. Urban decentralization underlies any hope of achieving ecological control of pest infestations in agriculture. Only a community well integrated with the resources of the surrounding region can promote agricultural and biological diversity. With careful planning, man could use plants and animals not only as a source of food but also, by pitting one species of life against another, as a means of controlling pests, thus eliminating much of his need for chemical methods. What is equally important, a decentralized community holds the greatest promise for conserving natural resources, particularly as it would promote the use of local sources of energy. Instead of relying primarily on concentrated sources of fuel in distant regions of the continent, the community could make maximum use of its own energy resources, such as wind power, solar energy, and hydroelectric power. These sources of energy, so often overlooked because of an almost exclusive reliance on a national division of labor, would help greatly to conserve the remaining supply of high-grade petroleum and coal. They would almost certainly postpone, if not eliminate, the need for turning to radioactive substances and nuclear reactors as major sources of industrial energy. With more time at his disposal for intensive research, man might learn either to employ solar energy and wind power as the principal sources of energy or to eliminate the hazard of radioactive contamination from nuclear reactors.

It is true, of course, that our life lines would become more complex and, from a technological point of view, less "efficient." There would be many duplications of effort. Instead of being concentrated in two or three areas of the country, steel plants would be spread out, with many communities employing small-scale facilities to meet regional or local needs. But the word *efficiency*, like the word *pest,* is relative. Although duplication of facilities would be somewhat costly, many local mineral sources that are not used today because they are too widely scattered or too small for the purposes of large-scale production would become economical for the purposes of a smaller community. Thus, in the long run, a more localized or regional form of industrial activity is likely to promote a more efficient use of resources than our prevailing methods of production.

It is also true that we will never entirely eliminate the need for a national and international division of labor in agriculture and industry. The Midwest will always remain our best source of grains; the East and Far West, the best sources of lumber and certain field crops. Our petroleum, high-grade coal, and certain minerals will still have to be supplied, in large part, by a few regions of the country. But there is no reason why we cannot reduce the burden that our national division of labor currently places on these areas by spreading the agricultural and industrial loads over wider areas of the country. This seems to be the only approach to the task of creating a long-range balance between man and the natural world and of remaking man's synthetic environment in a form that will promote human health and fitness.

An emphasis on agriculture and urban regionalism is somewhat disconcerting to the average city dweller. It conjures up an image of cultural isolation and social stagnation, of a journey backward in history to the agrarian societies of the medieval and ancient worlds. Actually, the urban dweller today is more isolated in the big city than his ancestors were in the countryside. The city man in the modern metropolis has reached a degree of anonymity, social atomization, and spiritual isolation that is virtually unprecedented in human history. Today man's alienation from man is almost absolute. His standards of cooperation, mutual aid, simple human hospitality, and decency have suffered an appalling erosion in the urban milieu. Man's civic institutions have become cold, impersonal agencies for the manipulation of his destiny, and his culture has increasingly accommodated itself to the least common denominator of intelligence and taste. He has nothing to lose even by a backward glance; indeed, in this way he is likely to place his present-day world and its limitations in a clearer perspective.

But why should an emphasis on agriculture and urban regionalism be regarded as an attempt to return to the past? Can we not develop our environment more selectively, more subtly, and more rationally than we have thus far, combining the best of the past and present and bringing forth a new synthesis of man and nature, nation and region, town and country? Life would indeed cease to be an adventure if we merely elaborated the present by extending urban sprawl and by extending civic life until it completely escapes from the control of its individual elements. To continue along these lines would serve not to promote social evolution but rather to "fatten" the social organism to a point where it could no longer move. Our purpose should be to make individual life a more rounded experience, and this we can hope to accomplish at the present stage of our development only by restoring the complexity of man's environment and by reducing the community to a human scale.

Is there any evidence that reason will prevail in the management of our affairs? It is difficult to give a direct answer. Certainly we are beginning to look for qualitative improvements in many aspects of life; we are getting weary and resentful of the shoddiness in goods and services. We are gaining a new appreciation of the land and its problems, and a greater realization of the social promise offered by a more manageable human community. More and more is being written about our synthetic environment, and the criticism is more pointed than it has been in almost half a century. Perhaps we can still hope, as Mumford did more than two decades ago in the closing lines of *The Culture of Cities*:

> We have much to unbuild, and much more to build: but the foundations are ready: the machines are set in place and the tools are bright and

keen: the architects, the engineers, and the workmen are assembled. None of us may live to see the complete building, and perhaps in the nature of things the building can never be completed: but some of us will see the flag or the fir tree that the workers will plant aloft in ancient ritual when they capt the topmost story.

Anarchism and Ecology
(from "Ecology and Revolutionary Thought," 1964)

An anarchist society, far from being a remote ideal, has become a precondition for the practice of ecological principles. To sum up the critical message of ecology: If we diminish variety in the natural world, we debase its unity and wholeness; we destroy the forces making for natural harmony and for a lasting equilibrium; and, what is even more significant, we introduce an absolute retrogression in the development of the natural world that may eventually render the environment unfit for advanced forms of life. To sum up the reconstructive message of ecology: If we wish to advance the unity and stability of the natural world, if we wish to harmonize it, we must conserve and promote variety. To be sure, mere variety for its own sake is a vacuous goal. In nature, variety emerges spontaneously. The capacities of a new species are tested by the rigors of climate, by its ability to deal with predators, and by its capacity to establish and enlarge its niche. *Yet the species that succeeds in enlarging its niche in the environment also enlarges the ecological situation as a whole.* To borrow E. A. Gutkind's phrase, it "expands the environment," both for itself and for the species with which it enters into a balanced relationship.[3]

How do these concepts apply to social theory? To many readers, I suppose, it should suffice to say that, inasmuch as man is part of nature, an expanding natural environment enlarges the basis for social development. But the answer to the question goes much deeper than many ecologists and libertarians suspect. Again, allow me to return to the ecological principle of wholeness and balance as a product of diversity. Keeping this principle in mind, the first step toward an answer is provided by a passage in Herbert Read's "The Philosophy of Anarchism." In presenting his "measure of progress," Read observes: "Progress is measured by the degree of differentiation within a society. If the individual is a unit in a corporate mass, his life will be limited, dull, and mechanical. If the individual is a unit on his own, with space and potentiality for separate action, then he may be more subject to accident or chance, but at least he can expand and express himself. He can develop – develop in the only real meaning of the word – develop in consciousness of strength, vitality, and joy."[4]

Read's thought, unfortunately, is not fully developed, but it provides an interesting point of departure. What first strikes us is that both the ecologist and the anarchist place a strong emphasis on spontaneity. The ecologist, insofar as he is more than a technician, tends to reject the notion of "power over nature." He speaks instead of "steering" his way through an ecological situation, of *managing* rather than *recreating* an ecosystem. The anarchist, in turn, speaks in terms of social spontaneity, of releasing the potentialities of society and humanity, of giving free and unfettered rein to the creativity of people. Each in its own way regards authority as inhibitory, as a weight limiting the creative potential of a natural and social situation. Their object is not to *rule* a domain, but to *release* it. They regard insight, reason, and knowledge as a means for fulfilling the potentialities of a situation, as facilitating the working out of the logic of a situation, not as replacing its potentialities with preconceived notions or distorting their development with dogmas.

Returning to Read's words, what strikes us is that like the ecologist, the anarchist views differentiation as a measure of progress. The ecologist uses the term *biotic pyramid* in speaking of biological advances; the anarchist, the word *individuation* to denote social advances. If we go beyond Read, we will observe that, to both the ecologist and the anarchist, an ever-increasing unity is achieved by growing differentiation. *An expanding whole is created by the diversification and enrichment of its parts.*

Just as the ecologist seeks to expand the range of an ecosystem and promote a free interplay between species, so the anarchist seeks to expand the range of social experience and remove all fetters from its development. Anarchism is not only a stateless society but a harmonized society that exposes man to the stimuli provided by both agrarian and urban life, to physical activity and mental activity, to unrepressed sensuality and self-directed spirituality, to communal solidarity and individual development, to regional uniqueness and worldwide brotherhood, to spontaneity and self-discipline, to the elimination of toil and the promotion of craftsmanship. In our schizoid society, these goals are regarded as mutually exclusive, indeed as sharply opposed. They appear as dualities because of the very logistics of present-day society – the separation of town and country, the specialization of labor, the atomization of man – and it would be preposterous to believe that these dualities could be resolved without a general idea of the *physical* structure of an anarchist society. We can gain some idea of what such a society would be like by reading William Morris's *News From Nowhere* and the writings of Peter Kropotkin. But these works provide us with mere glimpses. They do not take into account the post-World War II developments of technology and the contributions made by the development of ecology. This is not the place to embark on a discussion of "utopian writing," but certain guidelines can be presented. And in presenting these guidelines, I am eager to emphasize not only the more obvious ecological premises that support them but also the humanistic ones.

An anarchist society should be a decentralized society, not only to establish a lasting basis for the harmonization of man and nature *but also to add new dimensions to the harmonization of man and man.* The Greeks, we are often reminded, would have been horrified by a city whose size and population precluded face-to-face, familiar relationships among citizens. Today there is plainly a need to reduce the dimensions of the human community – partly to solve our pollution and transportation problems, partly also to create *real* communities. In a sense, we must *humanize* humanity. Electronic devices such as telephones, telegraphs, radios, and television receivers should be used as little as possible to mediate the relations between people. In making collective decisions – the ancient Athenian ecclesia was, in some ways, a model for making social decisions – all members of the community should have an opportunity to acquire in full the measure of anyone who addresses the assembly. They should be in a position to absorb his attitudes, study his expressions, and weigh his motives as well as his ideas in a direct personal encounter and through face-to-face discussion.

Our small communities should be economically balanced and well rounded, partly so that they can make full use of local raw materials and energy resources, partly also to enlarge the agricultural and industrial stimuli to which individuals are exposed. The member of a community who has a predilection for engineering, for instance, should be encouraged to steep his hands in humus; the man of ideas should be encouraged to employ his musculature; the "inborn" farmer should gain a familiarity with the workings of a rolling mill. To separate the engineer from the soil, the thinker from the spade, and the farmer from the industrial plant promotes a degree of vocational overspecialization that leads to a dangerous measure of social control by specialists. What is equally important, professional and vocational specialization prevents society from achieving a vital goal: the humanization of nature by the technician and the naturalization of society by the biologist.

I submit that an anarchist community would approximate a clearly definable ecosystem – it would be diversified, balanced, and harmonious. It is arguable whether such an ecosystem would acquire the configuration of an urban entity with a distinct center, such as we find in the Greek *polis,* or the medieval commune, or whether, as Gutkind proposes, society would consist of widely dispersed communities without a distinct center. In any case, the ecological scale for any of these communities would be determined by the smallest ecosystem capable of supporting a population of moderate size.

A relatively self-sufficient community, visibly dependent on its environment for the means of life, would gain a new respect for the organic interrelationships that sustain it. In the long run, the attempt to approximate self-sufficiency would, I think, prove more efficient than the exaggerated national division of labor that prevails today. Although there would doubtless be many duplications of small industrial facilities from community to community, the familiarity of each group with its local environment and its ecological roots would make for a more intelligent and more loving use of its environment. I submit that, far from producing provincialism, relative self-sufficiency would create a new matrix for individual and communal development – a oneness with the surroundings that would vitalize the community.

The rotation of civic, vocational, and professional responsibilities would stimulate the senses in the being of the individual, creating and rounding out new dimensions in self-development. In a complete society we could hope to create complete men; in a rounded society, rounded men. In the Western world, the Athenians, for all their shortcomings and limitations, were the first to give us a notion of this completeness. "The *polis* was made for the amateur," H.D.F. Kitto tells us. "Its ideal was that every citizen (more or less, according as the *polis* was democratic or oligarchic) should play his part in all of its many activities – an ideal that is recognizably descended from the generous Homeric conception of *arete* as an all-round excellence and an all-round activity. It implies a respect for the wholeness or the oneness of life, and a consequent dislike of specialization. It implies a contempt for efficiency – or rather a much higher ideal of efficiency; an efficiency which exists not in one department of life, but in life itself."⁵ An anarchist society, although it would surely aspire to more, could hardly hope to achieve less than this state of mind.

If the ecological community is ever achieved in practice, social life would yield a sensitive development of human and natural diversity, falling together into a well-balanced, harmonious whole. Ranging from community through region to entire continents, we would see a colorful differentiation of human groups and ecosystems, each developing its unique potentialities and exposing members of the community to a wide spectrum of economic, cultural, and behavioral stimuli. Falling within our purview would be an exciting, often dramatic variety of communal forms – here marked by architectural and industrial adaptations to semiarid ecosystems, there to grasslands, elsewhere by adaptation to forested areas. We would witness a creative interplay between individual and group, community and environment, humanity and nature. Freed from an oppressive routine, from paralyzing repressions and insecurities, from the burdens of toil and false needs, from the trammels of authority and irrational compulsion, individuals would finally, for the first time in history, be in a position to realize their potentialities as members of the human community and the natural world.

The New Technology and the Human Scale
(from "Toward a Liberatory Technology," 1965)

To the degree that material production is decentralized and localized, the primacy of the community is asserted over national institutions. In these circumstances the popular assembly of the local community, convened in a face-to-face democracy, would take over the full management of social life. The question is whether a future society would be organized around technology, or whether technology is now sufficiently malleable that it can be organized around society. To answer this question we must further examine certain features of the new technology. . . .

[Since 1945, computer technology has undergone a startling miniaturization, from vacuum tubes to microcircuits. Where computers were once enormous, advanced units now occupy the size of an office desk.] Paralleling the miniaturization of computer components is the remarkable sophistication of more traditional forms of technology. Ever-smaller machines are beginning to replace large ones. Continuous hot-strip steel rolling mills, which are among the largest and costliest facilities in modern industry, . . . are geared to a national division of labor, to highly concentrated sources of raw materials (generally located a great distance from the complex), and to large national and international markets. Even if the complex were totally automated, its operating and management needs would far transcend the capabilities of a small, decentralized community. The type of administration it requires tends to foster centralized social forms.

Fortunately, we now have a number of alternatives – more efficient alternatives in many respects – to the modern steel complex. . . . A future steel complex based on electric furnaces, continuous casting, a planetary mill, and a small continuous cold-reducing mill would require only a fraction of the acreage occupied by a conventional installation. It would be fully capable of meeting the steel needs of several moderate-sized communities with low quantities of fuel. This complex would not have to meet the needs of a national market. On the contrary, it is suited only for meeting the steel requirements of small and moderate-sized communities and industrially undeveloped countries. . . . The very scale of our hypothetical steel complex constitutes one of its most attractive features. Also, the steel it produces is more durable, so the community's rate of replenishing its steel products would be appreciably reduced. Since the smaller complex requires ore, fuel, and reducing agents in relatively small quantities, many communities could rely on local resources for their raw materials, thereby conserving the more concentrated resources of centrally located sources of supply, strengthening the independence of the community itself vis-à-vis the traditional centralized economy and reducing the expense of transportation. What would at first glance seem to be a costly, inefficient duplication of effort would prove, in the long run, to be more efficient as well as socially more desirable than a few centralized complexes.

The new technology has produced not only miniaturized electronic components and smaller production facilities but highly versatile, multipurpose machines. For more than a century, the trend in machine design moved increasingly toward technological specialization and single-purpose devices, underpinning the intensive division of labor required by the factory system. Industrial operations were subordinated entirely to the product. In time, this narrow pragmatic approach has "led industry far from the rational line of development in production machinery," observe Eric W. Leaver and John J. Brown.

> It has led to increasingly uneconomic specialization. . . . Specialization of machines in terms of end product requires that the machine be thrown away when the product is no longer needed. Yet the work the production machine does can be reduced to a set of basic functions – forming, holding, cutting, and so on – and these functions, if correctly analyzed, can be packaged and applied to operate on a part as needed.[6]

. . . A small or moderate-sized community using multipurpose machines could satisfy many of its limited industrial needs without being burdened with underused industrial facilities. There would be less loss in scrapping tools and less need for single-purpose plants. The community's economy would be more compact and versatile, more rounded and self-contained, than anything we find in the communities of industrially advanced countries. The effort that goes into retooling machines for new products would be enormously reduced. Finally, multipurpose machines with a wide operational range are relatively easy to automate. The changes required to use these machines in a cybernated industrial facility would generally be in circuitry and programming rather than in machine form and structure. . . .

I do not claim that all of man's economic activities can be completely decentralized, but the majority can surely be scaled to human and communitarian dimensions. This much is certain: we can shift the center of economic power from national to local scale and from centralized bureaucratic forms to local, popular assemblies. This shift would be a revolutionary change of vast proportions, for it would create powerful economic foundations for the sovereignty and autonomy of the local community.

Ecological Technology
(from "Toward a Liberatory Technology," 1965)

In our own time, the development of technology and the growth of cities have brought man's alienation from nature to the breaking point. Western man finds himself confined to a largely synthetic urban environment, far removed physically from the land, and his relationship to the natural world is mediated entirely by machines. He lacks familiarity with how most of his goods are produced, and his foods bear only the faintest resemblance to the animals and plants from which they were derived. Boxed into a sanitized urban milieu (almost institutional in form and appearance), modern man is denied even a spectator's role in the agricultural and industrial systems that satisfy his material needs. He is a pure consumer, an insensate receptacle. It would be unfair, perhaps, to say that he is disrespectful toward the natural environment; the fact is, he scarcely knows what ecology means or what his environment requires to remain in balance.

The balance between man and nature must be restored. Unless we establish some kind of equilibrium between man and the natural world, the viability of the human species will be placed in grave jeopardy. The new technology can be used ecologically to reawaken man's sense of dependence upon the environment; by reintroducing the natural world into the human experience, we can contribute to the achievement of human wholeness.

The classical utopians fully realized that the first step toward wholeness must be to remove the contradiction between town and country. "It is impossible," wrote Fourier nearly a century and a half ago, "to organize a regular and well balanced association without bringing into play the labors of the field, or at least gardens, orchards, flocks and herds, poultry yards, and a great variety of species, animal and vegetable." Shocked by the social effects of the Industrial Revolution, Fourier added: "They are ignorant of this principle in England, where they experiment with artisans, with manufacturing labor alone, which cannot by itself suffice to sustain social union."

To argue that the modern urban dweller should once again enjoy "the labors of the field" may well seem like gallows humor. A restoration of the peasant agriculture that was prevalent in Fourier's day is neither possible nor desirable. Charles Gide is surely correct when he observes that agricultural labor "is not necessarily more attractive than industrial labor; to till the earth has always been regarded . . . as the type of painful toil, of toil which is done with 'the sweat of one's brow.'"[7] . . . If our vision were to extend no further than land management, the only alternative to peasant agriculture would seem to be highly specialized and centralized farming, its techniques paralleling the methods used in present-day industry. Far from achieving a balance between town and country, we would be faced with a synthetic environment that had totally assimilated the natural world.

If the land and community are to be reintegrated physically, and if the community is to exist in an agricultural matrix that renders man's dependence upon nature explicit, the problem is how to achieve this transformation without imposing "painful toil" on the community. How, in short, can husbandry, ecological forms of food cultivation, and farming on a human scale be practiced and, at the same time, toil be eliminated?

Some of the most promising technological advances in agriculture made since World War II are as suitable for small-scale ecological forms of land management as they are for the immense, industrial-type commercial units that have become prevalent over the past few decades. The augermatic feeding of livestock illustrates a cardinal principle of rational farm mechanization – the deployment of conventional machines and devices in a way that virtually eliminates arduous farm labor. By linking a battery of silos with augers, different nutrients can be mixed and transported to feed pens merely by pushing some buttons and pulling a few switches. A job that may once have required the labor of five or six men working half a day with pitchforks and buckets can now be performed by one man in a few minutes. This type of mechanization is intrinsically neutral: it can be used to feed immense herds or just a few hundred head of cattle; the silos may contain natural feed or synthetic, hormonized nutrients; the feeder can be employed on relatively small farms with mixed livestock, or on large beef-raising ranches, or on dairy farms of all sizes. In short, augermatic feeding can be placed in the service either of the most abusive kind of commercial exploitation, or of the most sensitive applications of ecological principles. This holds true for most of the farm machines that have been designed (in many cases, simply redesigned to achieve greater versatility) in recent years. . . .

Let us pause at this point to envision how our free community might be integrated with its natural environment. The community has been established after a careful study was made of its natural ecology – its air and water resources, its climate, its geological formations, its raw materials, its soils, and its natural flora and fauna. Land management by the community is guided entirely by ecological principles, so that an equilibrium is maintained between the environment and its human inhabitants. Industrially rounded, the community forms a distinct unit within a natural matrix; it is socially and aesthetically in balance with the area it occupies.

Agriculture is highly mechanized in the community, but as mixed as possible with respect to crops, livestock, and timber. Variety of flora and fauna is promoted as a means of controlling pest infestations and enhancing scenic beauty. Large-scale farming is practiced only where it does not conflict with the ecology of the region. Owing to the generally mixed character of food cultivation, agriculture is pursued by small farming units, each demarcated from the others by tree belts, shrubs, pastures, and meadows. In rolling, hilly, or mountainous country, land with sharp gradients is covered by timber to prevent erosion and conserve water. The soil on each acre is studied carefully and committed only to those crops for which it is most suited. Every effort is made to blend town and country without sacrificing the distinctive contribution that each has to offer to the human experience. The ecological region forms the living social, cultural, and biotic boundaries of the community or of the several communities that share its resources. Each community contains many vegetable and flower gardens, attractive arbors, park land, even streams and ponds that support fish and aquatic birds. The countryside, from which food and raw materials are acquired, not only constitutes the immediate environs of the community, accessible to all by foot, but invades the community. Although town and country retain their identity and the uniqueness of each is highly prized and fostered, nature appears everywhere in the town, while the town seems to have caressed and left a gentle human imprint on nature. . . .

There is a kind of industrial archaeology that reveals in many areas evidence of a once-burgeoning economic activity long abandoned by our precapitalist predecessors. In the Hudson Valley, the Rhine Valley, the Appalachians, and the Pyrenees are relics of mines and once highly developed metallurgical crafts, the fragmentary remains of local industries, and the outlines of long-deserted farms – all vestiges of flourishing communities based on local raw materials and resources. These communities declined because the products they once furnished were elbowed out by the large-scale national industries based on mass production techniques and concentrated sources of raw materials. Their old infrastructure is often still available as a resource for use by each locality; "valueless" in a highly urbanized society, it is eminently suitable for use by decentralized communities, and it awaits the application of industrial techniques adapted for small-scale quality production. If we were to take a careful inventory of the resources available in many depopulated regions of the world, the possibility that communities could satisfy many of their material needs locally would likely be much greater than we suspect. . . .

It is not that we lack energy per se, but we are only just beginning to learn how to use energy sources that are available in almost limitless quantity. The gross radiant energy striking the earth's surface from the sun is estimated to be more than three thousand times the annual energy consumed by mankind today. Although a portion of this energy is converted into wind or used for photosynthesis by vegetation, a staggering quantity is available for human use. The problem is how to collect it to satisfy a portion of our energy needs. If solar energy could be collected for house heating, for example, twenty to thirty percent of the conventional energy resources we normally employ could be redirected to other purposes. If we could collect solar energy for most or all of our cooking, water heating, smelting, and power production, we would have relatively little need for fossil fuels. Solar devices have been designed for nearly all of these functions. We can heat houses, cook food, boil water, melt metals, and produce electricity with devices that use the sun's energy exclusively, but we can't do it efficiently in every latitude of the earth, and we are still confronted with a number of technical problems that can be solved only by crash research programs. . . .

The ocean's tides are still another untapped resource to which we could turn for electric power. We could trap the ocean's waters at high tide in a natural basis – say, a bay or the mouth of a river – and release them through turbines at low tide. A number of places exist where the tides are high enough to produce electric power in large quantities. . . . We could use temperature differences in the sea or in the earth to generate electric power in sizable quantities. A temperature differential as high as seventeen degrees centigrade is not uncommon in the surface layers of tropical waters; along coastal areas of Siberia, winter differences of thirty degrees exist between water below the ice crust and the air. The interior of the earth becomes progressively warmer as we descend, providing selective temperature differentials with respect to the surface. Heat pumps could be used to avail ourselves of these differentials. . . . If we could acquire electricity or direct heat from solar energy, wind power, or temperature differentials, the heating system of a home or factory would be completely self-sustaining; it would not drain valuable hydrocarbon resources or require external sources of supply.

Winds could also be used to provide electric power in many areas of the world. About one-fortieth of the solar energy reaching the earth's surface is converted into wind. Although much of this goes into the making of the jet stream, a great deal of wind energy is available a few hundred feet above the ground. A United Nations report, using monetary terms to gauge the feasibility of wind power, finds that efficient wind plants in many areas could produce electricity at an overall cost of five mills per kilowatt-hour, a figure that approximates the price of commercially generated electric power. . . .

There should be no illusions about the possibilities of extracting trace minerals from rocks, of solar and wind power, and the use of heat pumps [as alternative sources of energy and raw materials]. Except perhaps for tidal power and the extraction of raw materials from the sea, these sources cannot supply man with the bulky quantities of raw materials and large blocks of energy needed to sustain densely concentrated populations and highly centralized industries. Solar devices, wind turbines, and heat pumps will produce relatively small quantities of power. Used locally and in conjunction with each other, they could probably meet all the power needs of small communities, but we cannot foresee a time when they will be able to furnish electricity in the quantities currently used by cities the size of New York, London, and Paris.

Limitation of scope, however, could represent a profound advantage from an ecological point of view. The sun, the wind, and the earth are experiential realities to which men have responded sensuously and reverently from time immemorial. Out of these primal elements man developed his sense of dependence on – and respect for – the natural environment, a dependence that kept his destructive activities in check. The Industrial Revolution and the urbanized world that followed obscured nature's role in human experience – hiding the sun with a pall of smoke, blocking the winds with massive buildings, desecrating the earth with sprawling cities. Man's dependence on the natural world became invisible; it became theoretical and intellectual in character, the subject matter of textbooks, monographs, and lectures. True, this theoretical dependence supplied us with insights (although partial ones at best) into the natural world, but its one-sidedness robbed us of all sensuous dependence on, and all visible contact and unity with nature. In losing these, we lost a part of ourselves as feeling beings. We became alienated from nature. Our technology and environment became totally inanimate, totally synthetic – a purely inorganic physical milieu that promoted the deanimization of man and his thought.

To bring the sun, the wind, the earth, indeed the world of life back into technology, into the means of human survival, would be a revolutionary renewal of man's ties to nature. To restore this dependence in a way that evoked a sense of regional uniqueness in each community – a sense not only of generalized dependence but of dependence on a specific region with distinct qualities of its own – would give this renewal a truly ecological character. A real ecological system would emerge, a delicately interlaced pattern of local resources, honored by continual study and artful modification. With a true sense of regionalism every resource would find its place in a natural, stable balance, an organic unity of social, technological, and natural elements. Art would assimilate technology by becoming social art, the art of the community as a whole. The free community would be able to rescale the tempo of life, the work patterns of man, its architecture, and its systems of transportation and communication to human dimensions. The electric car, quiet, slow-moving, and clean, would become the preferred mode of urban transportation, replacing the noisy, filthy, high-speed automobile. Monorails would link community to community, reducing the number of highways that scar the countryside. Crafts would regain their honored position as supplements to mass manufacture; they would become a form of domestic, day-to-day artistry. A high standard of excellence, I believe, would replace the strictly quantitative criteria of production that prevail today; a respect for the durability of goods and the conservation of raw materials would replace the shabby, huckster-oriented criteria that result in built-in obsolescence and an insensate consumer society. The community would become a beautifully molded arena of life, a vitalizing source of culture, and a deeply personal, ever-nourishing source of human solidarity.

Social Ecology
(from *The Ecology of Freedom*, 1982)

In almost every period since the Renaissance, a very close link has existed between radical advances in the natural sciences and upheavals in social thought. In the sixteenth and seventeenth centuries, the emerging sciences of astronomy and mechanics, with their liberating visions of a heliocentric world and the unity of local and cosmic motion, found their social counterparts in equally critical and rational social ideologies that challenged religious bigotry and political absolutism. The Enlightenment brought a new appreciation of sensory perception and the claims of human reason to divine a world that had been the ideological monopoly of the clergy. Later, anthropology and evolutionary biology demolished traditional static notions of the human enterprise, along with its myths of original creating and history as a theological calling. By enlarging the map and revealing the earthly dynamics of social history, these sciences reinforced the new doctrines of socialism, with its ideal of human progress, that followed the French Revolution.

In view of the enormous dislocations that now confront us, our own era needs a more sweeping and insightful body of knowledge – scientific as well as social – to deal with our problems. Without renouncing the gains of earlier scientific and social theories, we must develop a more rounded critical analysis of our relationship with the natural world. We must seek the foundations for a more reconstructive approach to the grave problems posed by the apparent contradictions between nature and society. We can no longer afford to remain captive to the tendency of the more traditional sciences to dissect phenomena and examine their fragments. We must combine them, relate them, and see them in their totality as well as their specificity.

In response to these needs, we have formulated a discipline unique to our age: *social ecology*. The more well-known term *ecology* was coined by Ernst Haeckel a century ago to denote the investigation of the interrelationships between animals, plants, and their inorganic environment. Since Haeckel's day, the term has been expanded to include ecologies of cities, of health, and of the mind. This proliferation of a word into widely disparate areas may seem particularly desirable to an age that fervently seeks some kind of intellectual coherence and unity of perception. But it can also prove to be extremely treacherous. Like such newly arrived words as *holism, decentralization,* and *dialectics,* the term *ecology* runs the peril of merely hanging in the air without any roots, context, or texture. Often it is used as a metaphor, an alluring catchword, that loses the potentially compelling internal logic of its premises.

Accordingly, the radical thrust of these words is easily neutralized. *Holism* evaporates into a mystical sigh, a rhetorical expression for ecological fellowship and community that ends with such in-group greetings and salutations as "holistically yours." What was once a serious philosophical stance has been reduced to environmentalist kitsch. *Decentralization* commonly means logistical alternatives to gigantism, not the human scale that would make an intimate and direct democracy possible. *Ecology* fares even worse. All too often it becomes a metaphor, like the word *dialectics,* for any kind of integration and development.

Perhaps even more troubling, the word in recent years has been identified with a very crude form of natural engineering that might well be called *environmentalism.* . . . To distinguish ecology from environmentalism and from abstract, often obfuscatory definitions of the term, I must return to its original usage and explore its direct relevance to society. Put quite simply, ecology deals with the dynamic balance of nature, with the interdependence of living and nonliving things. Since nature also includes human beings, the science must include humanity's role in the natural world – specifically, the character, form, and structure of humanity's relationship with other species and with the inorganic substrate of the biotic environment. From a critical viewpoint, ecology opens to a wide purview the vast disequilibrium that has emerged from humanity's split with the natural world. One of nature's unique species, *homo sapiens,* has slowly and painstakingly developed from the natural world into a unique social world of its own. As both worlds interact with each other through highly complex phases of evolution, it has become as important to speak of a social ecology as to speak of a natural ecology.

Let me emphasize that to ignore these phases of human evolution – which have yielded a succession of hierarchies, classes, cities, and finally states – is to make a mockery of the term *social ecology.* Unfortunately, the discipline has been beleaguered by adherents who try to collapse all the phases of natural and human development into a universal "oneness" (not wholeness) – a yawning "night in which all cows are black," to borrow one of Hegel's caustic phrases. If nothing else, our common use of the word *species* to denote the wealth of life around us should alert us to the fact of *specificity*, of *particularity* – the rich abundance of *differentiated* beings and things that enter into the very subject-matter of natural ecology. To explore these differentiae, to examine the phases and interfaces that enter into their making and into humanity's long development from animality to society – a development latent with problems and possibilities – is to make social ecology one of the most powerful disciplines from which to draw our critique of the present social order.

But social ecology provides more than a critique of the split between humanity and nature; it also poses the need to heal it. Indeed, it poses the need to radically transcend them. As E. A. Gutkind pointed out, "the goal of Social Ecology is wholeness, and not mere adding together of innumerable details collected at random and interpreted subjectively and insufficiently." The science deals with social and natural relationships in communities or "ecosystems." In conceiving them holistically – that is to say, in terms of their mutual interdependence – social ecology seeks to unravel the forms and patterns of interrelationships that give intelligibility to a community, be it natural or social. Holism, here, is the result of a conscious effort to discern how the particulars of a community are arranged, how its "geometry" (as the ancient Greeks might have put it) makes the whole more than the sum of its parts. Hence, the wholeness to which Gutkind refers is not to be mistaken for a spectral oneness that yields cosmic dissolution in a structureless nirvana; it is a richly articulated structure with a history and internal logic of its own.

History, in fact, is as important as form or structure. To a large extent, the history of a phenomenon *is* the phenomenon itself. We are, in a real sense, everything that existed before us, and in turn, we can eventually become vastly more than what we are. Surprisingly, very little in the evolution of life-forms has been lost in natural and social evolution – indeed in our very bodies, as our embryonic development attests. Evolution lies within us (as well as around us) as parts of the very nature of our beings.

For the present, it suffices to say that wholeness is not a bleak undifferentiated "universality" that involves the reduction of a phenomenon to what it has in common with everything else. Nor is it a celestial, omnipresent "energy" that replaces the vast material differentiae of which the natural and social realms are composed. To the contrary, wholeness comprises the variegated structures, the articulations, and the mediations that impart to the whole a rich variety of forms and thereby add unique qualitative properties to what a strictly analytical mind often reduces to "innumerable" and "random" details.

Terms like *wholeness, totality,* and even *community* have perilous nuances for a generation that has known fascism and other totalitarian ideologies. The words evoke images of a "wholeness" achieved through homogenization, standardization, and a repressive coordination of human beings. These fears are reinforced by a "wholeness" that seems to provide an inexorable finality to the course of human history – one that implies a suprahuman, narrowly teleological concept of social law and that denies the ability of human will and individual choice to shape the course of social events. Such notions of social law and teleology have been used to achieve a ruthless subjugation of the individual to suprahuman forces beyond human control. Our century has been afflicted by a plethora of totalitarian ideologies that, placing human beings in the service of history, have denied them a place in the service of their own humanity.

Actually, such a totalitarian concept of "wholeness" stands sharply at odds with what ecologists denote by the term. Ecological wholeness is not an immutable homogeneity but rather the very opposite – a dynamic *unity of diversity*. In nature, balance and harmony are achieved by ever-changing differentiation, by ever-expanding diversity. Ecological stability, in effect, is a function not of simplicity and homogeneity but of complexity and variety. The capacity of an ecosystem to retain its integrity depends not on the uniformity of the environment but on its diversity.

A striking example of this tenet can be drawn from experiences with ecological strategies for cultivating food. Farmers have repeatedly met with disastrous results because of the conventional emphasis on single-crop approaches to agriculture – or *monoculture,* to use a widely accepted term for those endless wheat and corn fields that extend to the horizon in many parts of the world. Without the mixed crops that normally provide both the countervailing forces and mutualistic support that come with mixed populations of plants and animals, the entire agricultural situation in an area has been known to collapse. Benign insects become pests because their natural controls, including birds and small mammals, have been removed. The soil, lacking earthworms, nitrogen-fixing bacteria, and green manure in sufficient quantities, is reduced to mere sand – a mineral medium for absorbing enormous quantities of inorganic nitrogen salts, which were originally supplied more cyclically and timed more appropriately for crop growth in the ecosystem. In reckless disregard for the complexity of nature and for the subtle requirements of plant and animal life, the agricultural situation is crudely simplified; its needs must now be satisfied by highly soluble synthetic fertilizers that percolate into drinking water and by dangerous pesticides that remain as residues in food. A high standard of food cultivation that was once achieved by a diversity of crops and animals, one that was free of lasting toxic agents and probably more healthful nutritionally, is now barely approximated by single crops whose main supports are toxic chemicals and highly simple nutrients.

If the thrust of natural evolution has been toward increasing complexity, and if the colonization of the planet by life has been made possible only as a result of biotic variety, a prudent rescaling of man's hubris should call for caution in disturbing natural processes. That living things, emerging ages ago from their primal aquatic habitat to colonize the most inhospitable areas of the earth, have created the rich biosphere that now covers it has been possible only because of life's incredible mutability and the enormous legacy of life-forms inherited from its long development. Many of these life-forms, even the most primal and simplest, have never disappeared – however much they have been modified by evolution. The simple algal forms that marked the beginnings of plant life and the simple invertebrates that marked the beginnings of animal life still exist in large numbers. They comprise the preconditions for the existence of the more complex organic beings to which they provide sustenance, the sources of decomposition, and even atmospheric oxygen and carbon dioxide. Although they may antedate the "higher" plants and mammals by over a billion years, they interrelate with their more complex descendants in often unravelable ecosystems.

To assume that science commands this vast nexus of organic and inorganic interrelationships in all its details is worse than arrogance: it is sheer stupidity. If unity in diversity forms one of the cardinal tenets of ecology, the wealth of biota that exists in a single acre of soil leads us to still another basic ecological tenet: the need to allow for a high degree of natural spontaneity. The compelling dictum "respect for nature" has concrete implications. To assume that our knowledge of this complex, richly textured, and perpetually changing natural kaleidoscope of life-forms lends itself to a degree of "mastery" that allows us free rein in manipulating the biosphere is sheer foolishness.

Thus, a considerable amount of leeway must be permitted for natural spontaneity – for the diverse biological forces that yield a variegated ecological situation. "Working with nature" requires that we foster the biotic variety that emerges from a spontaneous development of natural phenomena. I hardly mean that we must surrender ourselves to a mystical "Nature" that is beyond all human comprehension and intervention – a Nature that demands human awe and subservience. Perhaps the most obvious conclusion we can draw from these ecological tenets is Charles Elton's sensitive observation: "The world's future has to be managed, but this management would not be just like a game of chess – more like steering a boat." What ecology, both natural and social, can hope to teach us is how to find the current and understand the direction of the stream.

NOTES

1 Karl Marx and Friedrich Engels, *The German Ideology* (Moscow: Progress Publishers, 1964), p. 64.
2 Friedrich Engels, *Herr Eugen Dühring's Revolution in Science (Anti-Dühring)*, trans. Emile Burns (New York: International Publishers, 1939), pp. 323–4.
3 E. A. Gutkind, *The Expanding Environment* (London: Freedom Press, n.d.); later incorporated into *The Twilight of Cities* (Glencoe, NY: Free Press, 1962), pp. 55–144.
4 Herbert Read, "The Philosophy of Anarchism," in *Anarchy and Order: Essays in Politics* (1954; Boston: Beacon Press, 1971), p. 37.
5 H.D.F. Kitto, *The Greeks* (Chicago: Aldine, 1951), p. 16.
6 Eric W. Leaver and John J. Brown, "Machines Without Men," *Fortune* (November 1946).
7 Charles Gide, introduction to F.M.C. Fourier, *Selections from the Works of Fourier* (London: S. Sonnenschein and Co., 1901), p. 14.

Nature, First and Second

Introduction

Amid the technological enchantment of the 1950s, proponents of organic farming, like Bookchin himself, had to defend organic agricultural techniques against the scorn of federal agencies and the chemical industry, both of which were busily making pesticides into agricultural commonplaces. Unlike today, when the value of organic farming is recognized, in those years its value had to be fought for.

As part of that struggle to defend organic farming, Bookchin borrowed the concept "unity in diversity" from the German idealist philosopher G.W.F. Hegel. Recast as a principle of organic agriculture, the concept suggested an alternative farming technique that was able to rid crops of pests, without the use of carcinogenic pesticides. Unlike the monocultures that demanded pesticide use, a diversity of crops in one field could play off potential pests against one another, leaving the crops themselves pest-free. And unlike monocultures, which are susceptible to complete destruction with one pest infestation, ecosystems that are highly diversified yield optimal stability. "Unity in diversity" became a catchword for stability, not only in organic agriculture but in ecosystems generally; it entered the vocabulary of the ecology movement as a concept underpinning the value of diverse species in an ecosystem.

Once organic agriculture gained a measure of acceptance, however, Bookchin himself began to use the phrase "unity in diversity" in a different sense, giving it a more dynamic inter-pretation. While stability can strengthen an ecosystem, he main-tained, it cannot make for species variegation. Diversity plays an important role in producing not only stability but change and innovation. Indeed, without diversification natural evolution could not occur. Today, Bookchin uses the phrase "unity in diversity" to refer to the increasing differentiation that a self-formative biosphere undergoes, within the natural continuum of evolutionary processes.

This evolutionary emphasis is what markedly distinguishes Bookchin's philosophy of nature from that of other schools of ecological-political thought today. Natural evolution, he has long argued, encompasses not only a strictly biological realm (or "first nature") but also a social realm (or "second nature").[1] Far from being inherently antagonistic to each other, first and second nature are actually two aspects of one continuum, Bookchin maintains – at once separate from each other but also mutually imbricated in a shared evolutionary process. Human beings and human society, with their potentialities for self-consciousness and freedom, differ in profound respects from first nature yet emerge from and incorporate it in a graded development.

Perhaps of most interest to social ecology, the evolutionary processes in first nature generate increasing complexity and subject-ivity in life-forms. Consciousness has evolved in a cumulative process, from the simple reactivity of unicellular organisms, to the neuro-logical activity of mammals and reptiles, to a culmination in human intellection. As life-forms attain higher levels of subjectivity, they are able to exercise greater choice in selecting and even improving their own ecological niches.

The dim, emergent subjectivity in first nature can make only rudimentary "choices," but in second nature human beings, possessed of the highest level of subjectivity, are capable of actively and consciously altering their environments, of shaping the societies in which they live – and of creating the ecological society that integrates town and country, or first and second nature, in what Bookchin would later call "free nature."

At first glance, the great significance Bookchin attaches to human consciousness would seem to represent a sharp demarcation between human and nonhuman nature in his thought, one that sets human beings on an entirely different plane from the rest of the natural world. And it is true that he considers humanity as a radically new development in natural evolution, manifesting the potentiality for self-consciouseness, freedom, and innovation. He does regard human consciousness as qualitatively different from that of other life-forms. But by his use of the categories of first and second nature, he also emphasizes the rootedness of human beings in nonhuman nature.

In the mid-1980s a tendency arose within the ecology movement that denigrated the notion that human beings are in any way superior or more advanced than other life-forms in the biosphere. Blaming human-centeredness, or "anthropocentrism," as the cause of the ecological crisis, deep ecology – with its fundamental precept of biocentrism – advanced a notion of "biospheric democracy," which saw human beings as having "intrinsic worth" equal to that of any other species. Bookchin's sharp criticism of this tendency is rooted in two conflicting views of humanity's relationship to the rest of the natural world. Where biocentrism would reduce human beings into "plain citizens" of the biosphere, morally interchangeable with other life-forms, social ecology asserts that human beings are unique in natural evolution. By virtue of their powers of thought and communication, they have the ability to create and even the responsibility to achieve a harmonious, indeed creative relationship with the first nature.

The nineteenth-century philosopher Johann Fichte once remarked that humanity is nature rendered self-conscious. Although this view has sometimes been attributed to Bookchin as well, he actually maintains that second nature has thus far fallen short of realizing humanity's potentiality for creating a liberatory society and an integrative relationship with the nonhuman world. "Where Fichte patently erred was in his assumption that a possibility is a fact," he wrote in *The Ecology of Freedom.*

> We are no more nature rendered self-conscious than we are humanity rendered self-conscious. Reason may give us the capacity to play this role, but we and our society are still totally irrational – indeed, we are cunningly dangerous to ourselves and all that lives around us.[2]

He therefore modifies Fichte's statement to argue that humanity is *potentially* nature rendered self-conscious – that it would actualize that potential only if it were to create an ecological society.

Images of First Nature
(from "What Is Social Ecology?" 1984)

More than any single notion in the history of religion and philosophy, the image of a blind, mute, cruel, competitive, and stingy nature has opened a wide, often unbridgeable chasm between the social world and the natural world and, in its more exotic ramifications, between mind and body, subject and object, reason and physicality, technology and "raw materials," indeed the whole gamut of dualisms that have fragmented not only the world of nature and society but the human psyche and its biological matrix. . . .

What distinguishes social ecology is that it negates the traditionally harsh image of the natural world and its evolution. And it does so not by dissolving the social into the natural, like sociobiology, or by imparting mystical properties to nature that place it beyond the reach of human comprehension and rational insight. Instead, social ecology places the human mind, like humanity itself, within a natural context and explores it in terms of its own natural history, so that the sharp cleavage between thought and nature, subject and object, mind and body, and the social and natural are overcome, and the traditional dualisms of western culture are transcended by an evolutionary interpretation of consciousness with its rich wealth of gradations over the course of natural history.

Social ecology "radicalizes" nature – or more precisely, our understanding of natural phenomena – by questioning, from an ecological standpoint, the prevailing marketplace image of nature: nature not as a constellation of communities that are blind or mute, cruel or competitive, stingy or necessitarian, but, freed of all anthropocentric moral trappings, as a *participatory* realm of interactive life-forms whose most outstanding attributes are fecundity, creativity, and directiveness, marked by a complementarity that renders the natural world the *grounding* for an ethics of freedom rather than domination.

From an ecological standpoint, life-forms are related in an ecosystem not by the "rivalries" and competitive attributes imputed to them by Darwinian orthodoxy, but by the mutualistic attributes emphasized by a growing number of contemporary ecologists – an image pioneered by Peter Kropotkin. Indeed, social ecology challenges the very premises of the "fitness" that enters into the Darwinian drama of evolutionary development, with its fixation on survival rather than differentiation and fecundity. As William Trager has emphasized in his insightful work on symbiosis:

> The conflict in nature between different kinds of organisms has been popularly expressed in phrases like the "struggle for existence" and the "survival of the fittest." Yet few people have realized that mutual cooperation between organisms – symbiosis – is just as important, and that the "fittest" may be the one that helps another to survive.[3]

It is tempting to go beyond this pithy and highly illuminating judgment to explore an ecological notion of natural evolution based on the development of *ecosystems,* not merely individual species. This is a concept of evolution as the dialectical development of ever-variegated, complex, and increasingly fecund contexts of plant–animal communities, as distinguished from the traditional notion of biological evolution based on the atomistic development of single life-forms, a characteristically entrepreneurial concept of the isolated "individual," be it animal, plant, or bourgeois – a creature that fends for itself and either survives or perishes in a marketplace "jungle." As ecosystems become more complex and open a greater variety of evolutionary pathways, due to their own richness of diversity, increasingly flexible species themselves, in mutualistic complexes as well as singly, introduce a dim element of "choice" – by no means intersubjective or willful in the human meaning of these terms.

Concomitantly, these ensembles of species alter the environment of which they are part and exercise an increasingly *active* role in their own evolution. Life, in this *ecological* conception of evolution, ceases to be the passive *tabula rasa* on which eternal forces that we loosely call "the environment" inscribe the destiny of a "species," an atomistic term that is meaningless outside the context of an ecosystem and other species.

Life is active, interactive, procreative, relational, and contextual. It is not a passive lump of "stuff," a form of metabolic matter that awaits the action of forces external to it and that is mechanically shaped by them. Ever striving and always producing new life-forms, there is a sense in which life is self-directive in its own evolutionary development, not passively reactive to an inorganic or organic world that impinges upon it from outside and determines its destiny in isolation from the ecosystem that it constitutes and of which it is a part.

Our studies of "food webs" (a not quite satisfactory term for describing the interactivity that occurs in an ecosystem or, more properly, an ecological *community*) demonstrate that the complexity of biotic interrelationships, their diversity, and their intricacy are crucial in an ecosystem's stability. In contrast to biotically complex temperate zones, relatively simple desert and arctic ecosystems are very fragile and break down easily with the loss or numerical decline of only a few species. The thrust of biotic evolution over greater eras of organic evolution has been toward the increasing diversification of species and their interlocking into highly complex, basically mutualistic relationships, without which the widespread colonization of the planet by life would have been impossible.

Unity in diversity (a concept deeply rooted in the western philosophical tradition) is not only the determinant of an ecosystem's stability; it is the source of an ecosystem's fecundity, of its innovativeness, of its evolutionary potential to create newer, still more complex life-forms and biotic interrelationships, even in the most inhospitable areas of the planet. Ecologists have not sufficiently stressed the fact that a multiplicity of life-forms and organic interrelationships in a biotic community opens new evolutionary pathways of development, a greater variety of evolutionary interactions, variations, and degrees of flexibility in the capacity to evolve, and is hence crucial not only in the community's stability but also in its innovativeness in the natural history of life.

The ecological principle of unity in diversity grades into a richly mediated social principle; hence my use of the term *social* ecology. Society, in turn, attains its "truth," its self-actualization, in the form of richly articulated, mutualistic networks of people based on community, roundedness of personality, diversity of stimuli and activities, an increasing wealth of experience, and a variety of tasks.

Is this grading of ecosystem diversity into social diversity, based on humanly scaled decentralized communities, merely analogical reasoning? My answer would be that it is not a superficial analogy but a deep-seated continuity between nature and society that social ecology recovers from traditional nature philosophy, without its archaic dross of cosmic hierarchies, static absolutes, and cycles. In the case of social ecology, it is not in the *particulars* of differentiation that plant–animal communities are ecologically united with human communities; rather, it is the *logic* of differentiation that makes it possible to relate the mediations of nature and society into a continuum.

What makes unity in diversity in nature more than a suggestive ecological metaphor for unity in diversity in society is the underlying fact of wholeness. By wholeness I do not mean any finality of closure in a development, any "totality" that leads to a terminal "reconciliation" of all "Being" in a complete identity of subject and object or a reality in which no further development is possible or meaningful. Rather, I mean varying degrees of the actualization of potentialities, the organic unfolding of the wealth of particularities that are latent in the as-yet-undeveloped potentiality. This potentiality can be a newly planted seed, a newly born infant, a newly formed community, a newly emerging society. Given their radically different specificity, they are all united by a processual reality, a shared "metabolism" of development, a unified catalysis of growth as distinguished from mere "change" that provides us with the most insightful way of *understanding* them that we can possibly achieve.

Wholeness is literally the unity that finally gives order to the particularity of each of these phenomena; it is what has emerged from the process, what integrates the particularities into a unified form, what renders the unity an operable reality and a "being" in the literal sense of the term – an order as the actualized *unity* of its diversity from the flowing and emergent process that yields its self-realization, the fixing of its directiveness into a clearly contoured form, and the creation in a dim sense of "self" that is identifiable with respect to "others" with which it interacts. Wholeness is the *relative* completion of a phenomenon's potentiality, the fulfillment of latent possibility as such, all its concrete manifestations aside, to become more than the realm of *mere* possibility and attain the "truth" or fulfilled reality of possibility. To think this way – in terms of potentiality, process, mediation, and wholeness – is to reach into the most underlying nature of things, just as to know the biography of a human being and the history of a society is to know them in their authentic reality and depth.

The natural world is no less encompassed by this processual dialectic and developmental ecology than the social, although in ways that do not involve will, degrees of choice, values, ethical goals, and the like. Life itself, as distinguished from the nonliving, however, emerges from the inorganic latent with all the potentialities and particularities that it has immanently produced from the logic of its own nascent forms of self-organization. Obviously, so does society as distinguished from biology, humanity as distinguished from animality, and individuality as distinguished from humanity in the generic sense of the word. But these distinctions are not absolutes. They are the unique and closely interrelated phases of a shared continuum, of a process that is united precisely by its own differentiations, just as the phases through which an embryo develops are both distinct from and incorporated into its complete gestation and its organic specificity.

This continuum is not simply a philosophical construct. It is an earthy anthropological fact that lives with us daily as surely as it explains the emergence of humanity out of mere animality. Individual socialization is the highly nuanced "biography" of that development in everyday life and in everyone, as surely as the anthropological socialization of our species is part of its history. I refer to the biological basis of all human socialization: the protracted infancy of the human child that renders its cultural development possible, in contrast to the rapid growth of nonhuman animals, a rate of growth that quickly forecloses their ability to form a culture and develop sibling affinities of a lasting nature; the instinctual drives that extend feelings of care, sharing, intimate consociation, and finally love and a sense of responsibility for one's own kin into the institutional forms we call society; and the sexual division of labor, age-ranking, and kin-relationships that, however culturally conditioned and even mythic in some cases, formed and still inform so much of social institutionalization today. These formative elements of society rest on biological facts and, placed in the contextual analysis I have argued for, require ecological analysis.

Participatory Evolution
(from "Freedom and Necessity in Nature," 1986, rev. 1994)

Ecologists generally treat diversity as a source of ecological stability, in the belief that while the vulnerability to pests of a single crop treated with pesticides can reach alarming proportions, a more diversified crop, in which a number of plant and animal species interact, produces natural checks on pest populations.

But the fact that biotic – and social – evolution has been marked until recently by the development of ever more complex species and ecocommunities raises an even more challenging issue. The diversity of an ecocommunity may be a source of greater stability from an agricultural standpoint; but from an evolutionary standpoint, it may be an ever-expanding, albeit nascent source of freedom within nature, a medium for providing varying degrees of *choice, self-directiveness, and participation by life-forms in their own development.*

I wish to propose that the evolution of living beings is no mere passive process, the product of exclusively chance conjunctions between random genetic changes and "selective" environmental "forces," and that the "origin of species" is no mere result of external influences that determine the "fitness" of a life-form to survive as a result of random factors in which life is simply an object of an indeterminable "selective" process. The increase in diversity in the biosphere *opens new evolutionary pathways,* indeed, alternative evolutionary directions, in which species play an *active* role in their own survival and change.

However nascent, choice is not totally absent from biotic evolution; indeed, it increases as species become structurally, physiologically, and above all neurologically more complex. As the ecological contexts within which species evolve – the communities and interactions they form – become more complex, they open new avenues for evolution and a greater ability of life-forms to act self-selectively, forming the bases for some kind of choice, favoring precisely those species that can participate in ever-greater degrees in their own evolution, basically in the direction of greater complexity. Indeed, species and the ecocommunities in which they interact to create more complex forms of evolutionary development are increasingly the very "forces" that account for evolution as a whole.

"Participatory evolution," as I call this view, is somewhat at odds with the prevalent Darwinian or neo-Darwinian syntheses, in which nonhuman life-forms are primarily "objects" of selective forces exogenous to them. No less is it at odds with Henri Bergson's "creative evolution," with its semimystical *élan vital.* Ecologists, like biologists, have yet to come to terms with the notion that symbiosis (not only "struggle") and participation (not only "competition") factor in the evolution of species. The prevalent view of nature still stresses the exclusively necessitarian character of the natural world. An immense literature, both artistic and scientific, stresses the "cruelty" of a nature that bears no witness to the suffering of life and that is "indifferent" to cries of pain in the "struggle for existence." "Cruel" nature, in this imagery, offers no solace for extinction – merely an all-embracing darkness of meaningless motion to which humanity can oppose only the light of its culture and mind. Such formulations impart a sophisticated ethical dimension to the natural world that is more anthropomorphic than meaningful.

But even if the formulation is anthropomorphic, it bespeaks a presence in natural evolution – subjectivity, and specifically *human* consciousness – that cannot be ignored in formulating an evolutionary theory. We may reasonably claim that human will and freedom, at least as self-consciousness and self-reflection, have their own natural history in potentialities of the natural world – in contrast to the view that they are *sui generis*, the product of a rupture with the whole of development so unprecedented and unique that it contradicts the gradedness of all phenomena from the antecedent potentialities that lie behind and within every processual "product." Such claims are intended to underwrite our efforts to deal with the natural world as we choose – indeed, as Marx put it in the *Grundrisse*, to regard nature merely as "an object for mankind, purely a matter of utility."

The dim choices that animals exercise in their own evolution should not be confused with the will and degree of intentionality that human beings exhibit in their social lives. Nor is the nascent freedom that is rendered possible by natural complexity comparable to the ability of humans to make rational decisions. The differences between the two are qualitative, however much they can be traced back to the evolution of all animals. . . .

Despite the monumental nature of his work, Darwin did not fully organicize evolutionary theory. He brought a profound evolutionary sensibility to the "origin of species," but in the minds of his acolytes species still stood somewhere between inorganic machines and mechanically functioning organisms. No less significant are the empirical origins of Darwin's own work, which are deeply rooted in the Lockean atomism that nourished nineteenth-century British science as a whole. Allowing for the nuances that appear in all great books, *The Origin of Species* accounts for the way in which *individual* species originate, evolve, adapt, survive, change, or pay the penalty of extinction as if they were fairly isolated from their environment. In that account, any one species stands for the world of life as a whole, in isolation from the life-forms that normally interact with it and with which it is interdependent. Although predators depend upon their prey, to be sure, Darwin portrays the strand from ancestor to descendant in lofty isolation, such that early *eohippus* rises, step by step, from its plebeian estate to attain the aristocratic grandeur of a sleek racehorse. The paleontological diagramming of bones from former "missing links" to the culminating beauty of *Equus caballus* more closely resembles the adaptation of Robinson Crusoe from an English seafarer to a self-sufficient island dweller than the reality of a truly emerging being.

This reality is contextual in an ecological sense. The horse lived not only among its predators and food but in creatively interactive relationships with a great variety of plants and animals. It evolved not alone but in ever-changing ecocommunities, such that the "rise" of *Equus caballus* occurred conjointly with that of other herbivores that shared and maintained their grasslands and even played a major role in creating them. The string of bones that traces *eohippus* to *Equus* is evidence of the succession of ecocommunities in which the ancestral animal and its descendants interacted with other life-forms.

One could more properly modify *The Origin of Species* to read as the evolution of ecocommunities as well as the evolution of species. Indeed, placing the community in the foreground of evolution does not deny the integrity of species, their capacity for variation, or their unique lines of development. Species become vital participants in their own evolution – active beings, not merely passive components – taking full account of their nascent freedom in the natural process.

Nor are will and reason *sui generis*. They have their origins in the growing choices conferred by complexity and in the alternative pathways opened by the growth of complex ecocommunities and the development of increasingly complex neurological systems – in short, processes that are both internal and external to life-forms. To speak of evolution in very broad terms tends to conceal the specific evolutionary processes that make up the overall process.

Many anatomical lines of evolution have occurred: the evolution of the various organs that freed life-forms from their aquatic milieu; of eyes and ears, which sophisticated their awareness of the surrounding environment; and of the nervous system, from nerve networks to brains. Thus, mind too has its evolutionary history in the natural world, and as the neurological capability of life-forms to function more actively and flexibly increases, so too does life itself help create new evolutionary directions that lead to enhanced self-awareness and self-activity. Selfhood appears germinally in the communities that life-forms establish as *active agents in their own evolution,* contrary to conventional evolutionary theory.

Society as Second Nature
(from *Remaking Society*, 1989)

Society itself in its most primal form stems very much *from* nature. Every social evolution, in fact, is virtually an extension of natural evolution into a distinctly human realm. As the Roman orator and philosopher Cicero declared some two thousand years ago: "by the use of our hands we bring into being within the realm of Nature, a second nature for ourselves." Cicero's observation, to be sure, is very incomplete: the primeval, presumably untouched "realm of Nature" or "first nature," as it has been called, is reworked in whole or part into "second nature" not only by the use of our hands. Thought, language, and complex, very important biological changes also play a crucial and, at times, a decisive role in developing a second nature within first nature.

I use the term *reworking* advisedly to focus on the fact that second nature is not simply a phenomenon that develops outside of first nature – hence the special value that should be attached to Cicero's expression "*within* the realm of Nature." To emphasize that second nature, or more precisely society (to use this word in its broadest possible sense), emerges from *within* primeval first nature is to reestablish the fact that social life always has a naturalistic dimension, however much society is pitted against nature in our thinking. *Social* ecology clearly expresses the fact that society is not a sudden eruption into the world. Social life does not necessarily face nature as a combatant in an unrelenting war. The emergence of society is a *natural* fact that has its origins in the biology of human socialization.

The human socialization process from which society emerges – be it in the form of families, bands, tribes, or more complex types of human intercourse – has its source in parental relationships, particularly mother and child bonding. The biological mother, to be sure, can be replaced in this process by many surrogates, including fathers, relatives, or for that matter, all members of a community. It is when *social* parents and *social* siblings – that is, the human community that surrounds the young – begin to participate in a system of care, that is ordinarily undertaken by biological parents, that society begins to truly come into its own.

Society thereupon advances beyond a mere reproductive group toward institutionalized human relationships, and from a relatively formless animal community into a clearly structured social *order.* But at the very inception of society, it seems more than likely that human beings were socialized into second nature by means of deeply ingrained blood ties, specifically maternal ties. . . . Reproduction and family care remain the abiding biological bases for every form of social life as well as the originating factor in the socialization of the young and the formation of a society. As Robert Briffault observed in the early half of this century, the "one known factor which establishes a profound distinction between the constitution of the most rudimentary human group and all other animal groups [is the] association of mothers and offspring which is the sole form of true social solidarity among animals. Throughout the class of mammals, there is a continuous increase in the duration of that association, which is the consequence of the prolongation of the period of infantile dependence,"[4] a prolongation that Briffault correlates with increases in the period of fetal gestation and advances in intelligence.

The biological dimension that Briffault adds to society and socialization cannot be stressed too strongly. It is a decisive presence, not only in the origins of society over ages of animal evolution, but in the daily recreation of society in our everyday lives. The appearance of a newly born infant and the highly extended care it receives for many years reminds us that it is not only a human being that is being reproduced, but society itself. By comparison with the young of other species, children develop slowly and over a long period of time. Living in close association with parents, siblings, kin groups, and an ever-widening community of people, they retain a plasticity of mind that makes for creative individuals and ever-formative social groups. Although nonhuman animals may approximate human forms of association in many ways, they do not create a second nature that embodies a cultural tradition; nor do they possess a complex language, elaborate conceptual powers, or an impressive capacity to restructure their environment purposefully according to their own needs.

A chimpanzee, for example, remains an infant for only three years and a juvenile for seven. By the age of ten, it is a full-grown adult. Children, by contrast, are regarded as infants for approximately six years and juveniles for fourteen. A chimpanzee, in short, grows mentally and physically in about half the time required by a human being, and its capacity to learn, or at least to think, is already fixed by comparison with a human being, whose mental abilities may expand for decades. By the same token, chimpanzee associations are often idiosyncratic and fairly limited. Human associations, on the other hand, are basically stable, highly institutionalized, and marked by a degree of solidarity, indeed by a degree of creativity, that has no equal in nonhuman species as far as we know.

This prolonged degree of human mental plasticity, dependency, and social creativity yields two results that are of decisive importance. First, early human association must have fostered a strong predisposition for *interdependence* among members of a group – not the "rugged individualism" we associate with independence. The overwhelming mass of anthropological evidence suggests that participation, mutual aid, solidarity, and empathy were the social virtues early human groups emphasized within their communities. The idea that people are dependent upon each other for the good life, indeed for survival, followed from the prolonged dependence of the young upon adults. Independence, not to mention competition, would have seemed utterly alien, if not bizarre, to a creature reared over many years in a largely dependent condition. Care for others would have been seen as the perfectly natural outcome of a highly acculturated being that was, in turn, clearly in need of extended care. Our modern version of individualism, more precisely of egotism, would have cut across the grain of early solidarity and mutual aid – traits, I may add, without which such a physically fragile animal as a human being could hardly have survived as an adult, much less as a child.

Second, human interdependence must have assumed a highly structured form. There is no evidence that human beings normally relate to each other through the fairly loose systems of bonding found among our closest primate cousins. That human social bonds can be dissolved or deinstitutionalized in periods of radical change or cultural breakdown is too obvious to argue here. But during relatively stable conditions, human society was never the "horde" that anthropologists of the last century presupposed as a basis for rudimentary social life. On the contrary, the evidence points to the fact that all humans, perhaps even our distant hominid ancestors, lived in some kind of structured family groups, and later in bands, tribes, villages, and other forms. In short, they bonded together (as they still do), not only emotionally and morally but also structurally in contrived, clearly definable, and fairly permanent institutions.

Nonhuman animals may form loose communities and even take collective protective postures to defend their young from predators. But such communities can hardly be called structured, except in a broad, often ephemeral sense. Humans, by contrast, create highly formal communities that tend to become increasingly structured over the course of time. In effect, they form not only communities but a new phenomenon called *societies.*

If we fail to distinguish animal communities from human societies, we risk minimizing the unique features that distinguish human social life from animal communities – notably, the ability of society to *change* for better or worse and the factors that produce these changes. By the same token, if we reduce a complex society to a mere community, we risk ignoring how societies differed from each other over the course of history, and understanding how simple differences in status were elaborated into firmly established hierarchies, or hierarchies into economic classes. Indeed, we risk misunderstanding the very meaning of the term *hierarchy,* which actually refers to highly organized systems of command and obedience – as distinguished from personal, individual, and often short-lived differences in status that in many cases involve no acts of compulsion. We tend, in effect, to confuse the strictly institutional creations of human will, purpose, conflicting interests, and traditions, with community life in its most fixed forms, as though we were dealing with inherent, unalterable features of society rather than fabricated structures that can be modified, improved, worsened – or simply abandoned.

The trick of every ruling elite from the beginning of history to modern times has been to identify its own socially created hierarchical systems of domination with community life *as such,* with the result that human-made institutions acquire divine or biological sanction. A given society and its institutions thus tend to become reified into permanent and unchangeable entities that acquire a mysterious life of their own apart from nature – namely, the products of a seemingly fixed "human nature" that is the result of genetic programming at the very inception of social life. When annoying issues like war and social conflict are raised, they are ascribed to the activity of genes. . . .

Social ecology . . . avoids the simplicities of dualism and the crudities of reductionism by trying to show how nature slowly *phases* into society, without ignoring the differences between society and nature on the one hand, and the extent to which they merge with each other, on the other. The everyday socialization of the young by the family is no less rooted in biology than the everyday care of the old by the medical establishment is rooted in the hard facts of society. By the same token, we never cease to be mammals who still have primal natural urges, but we institutionalize these urges and their satisfaction in a wide variety of social forms. Hence the social and the natural continually permeate each other in the most ordinary activities of daily life without losing their identity in a shared process of interaction, indeed of interactivity.

Obvious as this may seem at first in such day-to-day problems as caretaking, social ecology raises questions that have far-reaching importance for the different ways society and nature have interacted over time and the problems these interactions have produced. How did a divisive, indeed seemingly combative relationship between humanity and nature emerge? What were the institutional forms and ideologies that rendered this conflict possible? Given the growth of human needs and technology, was such a conflict really unavoidable? And can it be overcome in a future, ecologically-oriented society?

How would a rational, ecologically-oriented society fit into the processes of natural evolution? Even more broadly, is there any reason to believe that the human mind – itself a product of natural evolution as well as culture – represents a decisive high point in natural development, notably in the long development of subjectivity from the sensitivity and self-maintenance of the simplest life-forms to the remarkable intellectuality and self-consciousness of the most complex?

In asking these highly provocative questions, I am not trying to justify a strutting arrogance toward nonhuman life-forms. Clearly, we must bring humanity's uniqueness as a species, marked by rich conceptual, social, imaginative, and constructive attributes, into synchronicity with nature's fecundity, diversity, and creativity. This synchronicity will not be achieved by opposing nature to society, nonhuman to human life-forms, natural fecundity to technology, or a natural subjectivity to the human mind. Indeed, an important result that emerges from a discussion of the interrelationship of nature to society is the fact that human intellectuality, although distinct, also has a far-reaching natural basis. Our brains and nervous systems did not suddenly spring into existence without a long antecedent natural history. That which we most prize as integral to our humanity – our extraordinary capacity to think on complex conceptual levels – can be traced back to the nerve network of primitive invertebrates, the ganglia of a mollusk, the spinal cord of a fish, the brain of an amphibian, and the cerebral cortex of a primate.

Here too, in the most intimate of our human attributes, we are no less products of natural evolution than we are of social evolution. As human beings we incorporate without ourselves aeons of organic differentiation and elaboration. Like all complex life-forms, we are not only part of natural evolution; we are also its heirs and the products of natural fecundity.

In trying to show how society slowly grows out of nature, however, social ecology is also obliged to show how society itself undergoes differentiation and elaboration. In doing so, social ecology must examine those junctures in social evolution where splits occurred that slowly brought society into opposition to the natural world, and explain how this opposition emerged from its inception in prehistoric times to our own era. Indeed, if the human species is a life-form that can consciously and richly enhance the natural world rather than simply damage it, it is important for social ecology to reveal the factors that have rendered many human beings into parasites on the world of life rather than active partners in organic evolution. This project must be undertaken not in a haphazard way, but with a serious attempt to render natural and social development coherent in terms of each other, and relevant to our times and the construction of an ecological society. . . .

What unites society with nature in a graded evolutionary continuum is the remarkable extent to which human beings, living in a rational, ecologically-oriented society, could *embody* the *creativity* of nature – this, as distinguished from a purely *adaptive* criterion of evolutionary success. The great achievements of human thought, art, science, and technology serve not only to monumentalize culture, *they serve to monumentalize natural evolution itself.* They provide heroic evidence that the human species is a warm-blooded, excitingly versatile, and keenly intelligent life-form – not a cold-blooded, genetically programmed, and mindless insect – that expresses *nature's* greatest powers of creativity.

Life-forms that create and consciously alter their environment, hopefully in ways that make it more rational and ecological, represent a vast and indefinite extension of nature into fascinating, perhaps unbounded lines of evolution that no branch of insects could ever achieve – notably, the evolution of a fully *self-conscious* nature. . . . Natural history is a *cumulative* evolution toward ever more varied, differentiated, and complex forms and relationships.

This *evolutionary* development of increasingly variegated entities, most notably of life-forms, contains exciting, latent possibilities. With variety, differentiation, and complexity, nature, in the course of its own unfolding, opens new directions for still further development along alternative lines of natural evolution. To the degree that animals become complex, self-aware, and increasingly intelligent, they begin to make those elementary choices that influence their own evolution. They are less and less the passive objects of "natural selection" and more and more the subjects of their own development.

A brown hare that mutates into a white one and sees a snow-covered terrain in which to camouflage itself is *acting* on behalf of its own survival, not simply adapting in order to survive. It is not merely being "selected" by its environment; it is selecting its own environment and making a *choice* that expresses a small measure of subjectivity and judgment.

The greater the variety of habitats that emerge in the evolutionary process, the more a given life-form, particularly a neurologically complex one, is likely to play an active and judgmental role in preserving itself. To the extent that natural evolution follows this path of neurological development, it gives rise to life-forms that exercise an ever-wider latitude of choice and a nascent form of freedom in developing themselves.

Given this conception of nature as the cumulative history of more differentiated levels of material organization (especially of life-forms) and of increasing subjectivity, social ecology establishes a basis for a meaningful understanding of humanity and society's place in natural evolution. Natural history is not a "catch as catch can" phenomenon. It is marked by tendency, by direction, and as far as human beings are concerned, by conscious purpose. Human beings and the social worlds they create can open a remarkably expansive horizon for development of the natural world – a horizon marked by consciousness, reflection, and an unprecedented freedom of choice and capacity for conscious creativity. The factors that reduce many life-forms to largely adaptive roles in changing environments are replaced by a capacity for consciously adapting environments to existing and new life-forms.

Adaptation, in effect, increasingly gives way to creativity, and the seemingly ruthless action of "natural law" to greater freedom. What earlier generations called "blind nature" to denote nature's lack of moral direction turns into free nature, a nature that slowly finds a voice and the means to relieve the needless tribulations of life for all species in a highly conscious humanity and an ecological society. . . . The issue, then, is not whether social evolution stands opposed to natural evolution. The issue is *how* social evolution can be situated *in* natural evolution and *why* it has been thrown – needlessly – against natural evolution to the detriment of life as a whole. Our capacity to be rational and free does not assure us that this capacity will be realized. If social evolution is the potentiality for expanding the horizon of natural evolution along unprecedented creative lines, and human beings are the potentiality for nature to become self-conscious and free, the issue we face is *why* these potentialities have been warped and *how* they can be realized.

It is part of social ecology's commitment to natural evolution that these potentialities are indeed real and that they can be fulfilled. . . . Until society can be reclaimed by an undivided humanity that will use its collective wisdom, cultural achievements, technological innovations, scientific knowledge, and innate creativity for its own benefit and for that of the natural world, all ecological problems will have their roots in social problems.

On Biocentrism
(from *Re-enchanting Humanity*, 1995)

> The *intuition* of biocentric equality is that all things in the biosphere have an equal right to live and blossom and to reach their own individual form of unfolding and self-realization within the larger Self-realization. This basic *intuition* is that all organisms and entities in the ecosphere as parts of the interrelated whole, are *equal in intrinsic* worth.[5]

This stunning doctrine literally defines deep ecology. "Deep" it is in every sense – not only in the intuitions that the authors and their acolytes hold, but in the many presuppositions they make. . . . On the other hand, we may decide to agree with Robyn Eckersley, a champion of biocentrism, that no such abilities are necessary, that the "navigational skills of birds" are themselves on a par with the wide-ranging intelligence of people.

> Is there not something self-serving and arrogant in the (unverifiable) claim that first nature is striving to achieve something that has presently reached its most developed form in us – second nature? A more impartial, biocentric approach would be simply to acknowledge that *our* special capabilities (e.g., a highly developed consciousness, language and tool-making capability) are simply one form of excellence alongside the myriad others (e.g., the navigational skills of birds, the sonar capability and playfulness of dolphins, and the intense sociality of ants) rather than *the* form of excellence thrown up by evolution.[6]

Whether birds have "navigation skills" – which assumes conscious agency in negotiating their migratory flights over vast distances with clear geographical goals – or primarily tropistic reactions to changes in daylight and possibly the earth's magnetic fields of force, need not occupy us here. What counts is that Eckersley's state of mind, like that of deep ecologists generally, essentially debases the intellectual powers of people who, over previous centuries, consciously mapped the globe, gave it mathematical coordinates, and invented magnetic compasses, chronometers, radar, and other tools for navigation. They did so with an intellectuality, flexibility, and with techniques that no bird can emulate – that is, with amazing skillfulness, since skill involves more than physical reactions to natural forces and stimuli.

When Eckersley places the largely tropistic reactions of birds on a par with human thought, she diminishes the human mind and its extraordinary abilities. One might as well say that plants have "skills" that are on a par with human intellectuality because plants can engage in photosynthesis, a complex series of biochemical reactions to sunlight. Are such reactions really commensurate with the ability of physicists to understand how solar fusion occurs and of biochemists to understand how photosynthesis occurs? If so, then corals "invented" techniques for producing islands and plants "invented" techniques for reaching to the sun in heavily forested areas. In short, placing human intellectual foresight, logical processes, and innovations on a par with tropistic reactions to external stimuli is to create a stupendous intellectual muddle, not to evoke the "deep" insights that deep ecologists claim to bring to our understanding of humanity's interaction with the natural world.

Eckersley's crude level of argumentation is no accident; Devall and Sessions prepare us for it by approvingly citing Warwick Fox to the effect that we can make "no firm ontological divide in the field of existence: That there is no bifurcation in reality between the human and the non-human realms . . . to the extent that we perceive boundaries, we fall short of deep ecological consciousness."[7]

No one has quite told whales, I assume, about this new evolutionary dispensation. Still less are grizzly bears, wolves, entire rainforest ecosystems, mountains, rivers, "and so on" aware of their community with human beings. Indeed, in this vast panoply of life-forms, ecosystems, mineral matter, "and so on," no creature seems to be capable of *knowing* – irrespective of how they communicate with members of their own kind – about the existence or absence of this "firm ontological divide" *except human beings.* If, as Devall and Sessions seem to believe, there is "no firm ontological divide" between the human and nonhuman realms, it is unknown to every species in the biosphere, let alone entities in the abiotic world – except our own.

In fact, the "ontological divide" between the nonhuman and the human is *very* real. Human beings, to be sure, are primates, mammals, and vertebrates. They cannot, as yet, get out of their animal skins. As products of organic evolution, they are subject to the natural vicissitudes that bring enjoyment, pain, and death to complex life-forms generally. But it is a crucial fact that they alone *know* – indeed, *can* know – that there is a phenomenon called evolution; they alone know that death is a reality; they alone can even formulate such notions as self-realization, biocentric equality, and a "self-in-Self"; they alone can generalize about their existence – past, present, and future – and produce complex technologies, create cities, communicate in a complex syllabic form, "and so on"! To call these stupendous attributes and achievements mere differences in degree between human beings and nonhuman life-forms – and to equate human "consciousness" with the "navigational skills" of migratory birds – is so preposterously naive that one might expect such absurdities from children, not professors.

What apparently worries deep ecologists about this "divide," with all its bifurcations and boundaries, is not so much that its existence is obvious as that it is inconvenient. Beclouding their simplistic monism, we may suppose, is a fear of the dualism of René Descartes, which they feel obliged to dispel. Ironically, they seem incapable of coping with this dualism without taking recourse to a Bambi-style anthropomorphism that effectively transforms all nonhuman beings into precisely what they profess to abhor – namely, anthropomorphisms. If they cannot make human beings into nonhuman animals, they make nonhuman animals into human beings. Accordingly, animals are said to have "skills" in much the same sense that human beings do. The earth has its own "wisdom," wilderness is equated with "freedom," and all life-forms exhibit "moral" qualities that are entirely the product of human intellectual, emotional, and social development.

Put bluntly: If human beings are "equal in intrinsic worth" to nonhuman beings, then boundaries between human and nonhuman are erased, and either human beings are merely one of a variety of animals, or else nonhuman beings are human. . . .

Having entangled the reader with extravagant claims for a set of unsupported personal beliefs, Devall and Sessions proceed in the name of an exclusively human "active deep questioning and meditative process" to reduce readers to the status of "'plain citizens' of the biotic community, not lord or master over all other species."[8]

Devall and Sessions use words with multiple meanings to give the most alienating interpretation to people. Whatever the democracy could possibly mean in the animal world, human beings are not mere "plain citizens" in a biospheric democracy. They are immensely superior to any other animal species, although deep ecologists equate *superiority* with being the "lord and master of all other species," hence an authoritarian concept. But *superior* may mean not only higher in rank, status, and authority but "of great value, excellence; extraordinary," if my dictionary is correct. That superiority can simply mean "having more knowledge, foresight, and wisdom" – attributes we might expect to find in a teacher or even a Zen master – seems to disappear from the highly selective deep ecological lexicon.

Deep ecology's contradictory presuppositions, intuitions, anthropo-morphisms, and naive assertions leave us spinning like tops. We are enjoined to engage in "deep questioning" in order to decide on intuitive grounds that we are *intrinsically* no different in "worth" or "value" from any "entity" in the "ecosphere." Yet the "deep question-ing" so prized by Devall, Sessions, Naess, *et al.*, is something that *no other life-form can do* – besides us. In the vastness of the ecosphere, nothing apart from human beings is capable of even voicing the notion of "biocentric egalitarianism," much less *understanding* any notion of "rights," "intrinsic worth," or "superiority" and "inferiority." It is the ultimate in anthropomorphism to impute a moral sense to animals that lack the conceptual material of abstract thought provided by language and the rich generalizations we form in our minds from our vast repertoire of words.

Strictly speaking, if we were nothing but "plain citizens" in the ecosphere, we should be as furiously *anthropo-centric* in our behavior, just as a bear is Urso-centric or a wolf Cano-centric. That is to say, as "plain citizens" of the ecosphere – and nothing more – we should, like every other animal, be occupied *exclusively* with our own survival, comfort, and safety. As Richard Watson has so astutely noted: "If we are to treat man as part of nature on egalitarian terms with other species, then man's behavior must be treated as morally neutral" – that is, as amoral. In which case, Watson continues, "we should not think there is something morally or ecosophically wrong with the human species dispossessing and causing the extinction of other species."[9]

Yet deep ecologists ask us precisely in the name of a biospheric "citizenship" not to be occupied exclusively with our survival. Put simply: Deep ecologists ask us to be "plain citizens" and at the same time expect – even oblige – us to think and behave as very uncommon, indeed quite extraordinary ones! In a perceptive article, critic Harold Fromm states this contradiction with remarkable pithiness:

> The "intrinsic worth" that biocentrists connect with animals, plants, and minerals is projected by the desiring human psyche in the same way that "the will of God" is projected by human vanity upon a silent universe that never says anything. . . . The "biocentric" notion of "intrinsic worth" is even more narcissistically "anthropocentric" than ordinary self-interest because it hopes to achieve its ends by denying that oneself is the puppeteer–ventriloquist behind the world one perceives as valuable.[10]

As biocentrists, deep ecologists ask us to take the role of the invisible puppeteer – pulling the strings and ignoring the fact that we are pulling them.

NOTES

1 In his earlier writings Bookchin often refers to first nature simply as "nature," following convention. But because the meanings of the word *nature* are so numerous and varied, in his more recent writings he no longer uses the word unmodified.

2 Murray Bookchin, *The Ecology of Freedom* (Palo Alto, CA: Cheshire Books, 1982), pp. 315–16.

3 William Trager, *Symbiosis* (New York: Van Nostrand Reinhold, 1970), p. vii.

4 Robert Briffault, "The Evolution of the Human Species," in *The Making of Man*, edited by V. F. Calverton (New York: Modern Library, 1931), pp. 765–6.

5 Bill Devall and George Sessions, *Deep Ecology: Living as if Nature Mattered* (Salt Lake City: Gibbs M. Smith, 1985), p. 67, emphases added.

6 Robyn Eckersley, "Divining Evolution: The Ecological Ethics of Murray Bookchin," *Environmental Ethics*, vol. 11 (Summer 1989), p. 115.

7 Devall and Sessions, *Deep Ecology*, p. 66. Actually, this quotation from Fox comes from a criticism of deep ecology in *The Ecologist*, vol. 14, no. 5–6 (1984), pp. 194–200 and 201–4, which does not prevent Devall and Sessions from bringing it to the service of deep ecology.

8 Devall and Sessions, *Deep Ecology*, p. 68.

9 Richard Watson, "Eco-Ethics: Challenging the Underlying Dogmas of Environmentalism," *Whole Earth Review* (March 1985), pp. 5–13.

10 Harold Fromm, "Ecology and Ideology," *Hudson Review* (Spring 1992), p. 30.

CHAPTER THREE

Organic Society

Introduction

In Bookchin's view, society and culture must be understood by examining not only what they are at present but their origins and subsequent development over the course of history. Thus, to rescue a tradition of freedom in support of his ecological society, he traces a "legacy of freedom" that has run as an alternative libertarian undercurrent through Western history. In his 1982 book *The Ecology of Freedom* he gave particular attention to what he calls "organic society" – that is, the preliterate band and tribal cultures that preceded recorded history in Europe and America and that persisted far longer in other parts of the world. Insofar as a number of its features hold relevance for the creation of an ecological society, organic society is part of the "legacy of freedom."

Perhaps the most important of these features is the relatively egalitarian nature of individual organic societies in their earliest phases. Initially such groups were internally free of social hierarchy – that is, institutionalized systems of rank based on status distinctions. Lacking social hierarchies, organic societies also lacked domination, or the subordination of one sector of the community to another. Finally, lacking domination, the group also lacked *concepts* of domination, not only of dominating people but of dominating first nature.

As part of this egalitarianism, organic societies had strikingly communistic principles of social organization. An organic community, for example, would compensate for individual handicaps and weaknesses rather than let such individuals fend for themselves, fulfilling what Bookchin calls "the inequality of equals" or "complementarity." To all individuals in the community, it would provide the means necessary to sustain life, regardless of their individual contribution to it; it would guarantee what Bookchin, following anthropologist Paul Radin, calls the "irreducible minimum." And all individuals in the community would have general access to the community's resources based on their need for them, rather than limited access based on ownership or other exclusive rights, in what Bookchin refers to as the principle of "usufruct."

These three principles – complementarity, the irreducible minimum, and usufruct – reflected a high level of cooperation and mutual care within a community. (This description, it should be emphasized, applies only to the internal life of a tribal community and not to its relations with other communities; as Bookchin later emphasized, tribal life in organic society was not only parochial but was characterized by frequent intertribal wars.)

Bookchin also explored a number of religious aspects of the internal life of organic societies in *The Ecology of Freedom*. While writing these chapters in the 1970s, he was influenced by the New Age anthropology that was fashionable at the time. In subsequent years, however, this very anthropology contributed to developments in ecological thought that he would reject as regressive. Neopagan religions, for example, underwent a revival and became popular in the late 1980s as a supposed antidote to an anti-ecological worldview. Aboriginal peoples came to be romanticized as models of ecological thinking, supposedly exemplifying lifeways that are harmonious with first nature from which modern societies could learn. Some parts of the ecology movement adopted as a slogan, "Back to the Pleistocene!"

Bookchin later regretted the influence that this anthropology had on *The Ecology of Freedom*, as he wrote in his introduction to the second edition, published in 1991:

> I examined organic society's various religious beliefs, and cosmologies: its naturalistic rituals, its mythic personalizations of animals and animal spirits, its embodiment of fertility in a Mother Goddess, and its overall animistic outlook. I believed that the Enlightenment's battle against superstition had been long since won in American and European culture, and that no one would mistake me for advocating a revival of animism or Goddess worship. As much as I admired many features of organic cultures, I never believed that we could or should introduce their naïve religious, mythic, or magical beliefs or their cosmologies into the present-day ecology movement.[1]

Bookchin took particular exception, in this 1991 introduction, to the notion that people in organic society are "ecological mentors" for people today to follow. Although the world of preliterate peoples was animistic, he pointed out, they could not have consciously lived in harmony with "nature," since they had no concept of nature as such, as distinguished from culture or society. Thus, they could have held no specific conscious attitudes toward it – neither one of domination or harmony. Moreover, despite their belief in animistic spirits, they still had to kill animals in order to obtain food, clothing, and shelter – and their approach in doing so was primarily instrumental. Nor, finally, were they necessarily restrained by concepts of limit and moderation, Bookchin observes; on the contrary, they appear in numerous cases to have engaged in overkill and hunted species to extinction needlessly.

Insofar as organic society lacked a concept of nature, it lacked a consciousness, as well, of humanity's role in natural evolution. To have gained this self-consciousness has been a major advance in human thinking. If in one sense the demise of organic society represented a "fall from Eden" – the Eden of primitive egalitarianism and complementarity – in another sense it was a major step toward enlightenment. Once humanity gained self-consciousness of itself and of first nature, becoming increasingly innovative and creative, human beings could consciously choose the role they would play in it and adopt those virtues and practices that supported that role. They could begin to do so as a matter of conscious ethical choice – not out of blindness or mystification.

Thus, in a dialectical progression, human society forsook a way of life that was, in some ways, benign, but that lacked the universality and consciousness necessary for men and women to realize their latent human attributes. Indeed, this great sublation of humanity beyond both organic society and a Janus-faced civilization that has legacies of both freedom and domination, into a rational, ecological society that preserves the liberatory aspects of both, is the project of social ecology.

Usufruct, Complementarity, and the Irreducible Minimum
(from *The Ecology of Freedom*, 1982)

It is easy to see that organic society's harmonized view of nature follows directly from the harmonized relations within the early human community. Just as medieval theology structured the Christian heaven on feudal lines, so people of all ages have projected their social structures onto the natural world. To the Algonquians of the North American forest, beavers lived in clans and lodges of their own, wisely cooperating to promote the well-being of the community. Animals also had their magic, their totem ancestors (the elder brother), and were invigorated by the Manitou, whose spirit nourished the entire cosmos. Accordingly, animals had to be conciliated or else they might refuse to provide humans with skins and meat. The cooperative spirit that formed a basis for the survival of the organic community was an integral part of the outlook of preliterate people toward nature and the interplay between the natural world and the social.

We have yet to find a language that adequately encompasses the quality of this deeply embedded cooperative spirit. Expressions like "love of nature" or "communism," not to speak of the jargon favored by contemporary sociology, are permeated by the problematical relationships of our own society and mentality. Preliterate humans did not have to "love" nature; they lived in a kinship relationship with it. They would not distinguish between our "aesthetic" sense on this score, and their own functional approach to the natural world, because natural beauty is there to begin with – in the very cradle of the individual's experience. The poetic language that awakens such admiration among whites who encounter the spokesmen for Indian grievances is rarely "poetry" to the speaker; rather, it is an unconscious eloquence that reflects the dignity of Indian life.

So too with other elements of organic society and its values: cooperation is too primary to be adequately expressed in the language of western society. From the outset of life, coercion in dealing with children is so rare in most preliterate communities that western observers are often astonished by the gentleness with which so-called primitives deal with even the most intractable of their young. Yet in preliterate communities the parents are not "permissive"; they simply respect the personality of their children, much as they do that of the adults. Until age hierarchies begin to emerge, the everyday behavior of parents fosters an almost unbroken continuity in the lives of the young between the years of childhood and adulthood. . . .

The word *property* connotes an individual appropriation of goods, a personal claim to tools, land, and other resources. In this loose sense, property is fairly common in organic societies, even in groups that have a very simple, undeveloped technology. By the same token, cooperative work and the sharing of resources on a scale that could be called communistic is also fairly common. On both the productive side of economic life and the consumptive, appropriation of tools, weapons, food, and even clothing may range widely – often idiosyncratically, in western eyes – from the possessive and seemingly individualistic to the most meticulous and often ritualistic parceling out of a harvest or a hunt among members of a community.

But primary to both of these seemingly contrasting relationships is the practice of *usufruct,* the freedom of individuals in a community to appropriate resources merely by virtue of the fact that they are using them. Such resources belong to the user as long as they are being used. Function, in effect, replaces our hallowed concept of possession – not merely as a loan or even "mutual aid," but as an unconscious emphasis on use itself, on need that is free of psychological entanglements with proprietorship, work, and even reciprocity. The western identification of individuality with ownership and personality with craft – the latter laden with a metaphysics of selfhood as expressed in a crafted object wrested by human powers from an intractable nature – has yet to emerge from the notion of use itself and the guileless enjoyment of needed things. Need, in effect, still orchestrates work to the point where property of any kind, communal or otherwise, has yet to acquire independence from the claims of satisfaction. A collective need subtly orchestrates work, not personal need alone, for the collective claim is implicit in the primacy of usufruct over proprietorship. Hence even the work performed in one's own dwelling has an underlying collective dimension in the potential availability of its products to the entire community.

Communal property, once property itself has become a category of consciousness, already marks the first step toward private property, just as reciprocity, once it too becomes a category of consciousness, marks the first step toward exchange. Proudhon's celebration of "mutual aid" and contractual federalism, like Marx's celebration of communal property and planned production, mark no appreciable advance over the primal principle of usufruct. Both thinkers were captive to the notion of interest, to the rational satisfaction of egotism.

There may have been a period in humanity's early development when interest had not yet emerged to replace complementarity, the disinterested willingness to pool needed things and needed services. There was a time when Gontran de Poncins, wandering into the most remote reaches of the Arctic, could still encounter "the pure, the true Eskimos, the Eskimos who knew not how to lie" – and hence to manipulate, to calculate, to project interest beyond social need. Here community attained a completeness so exquisite and artless that needed things and services fit together in a lovely mosaic with a haunting personality of its own.

We should not disdain these almost utopian glimpses of humanity's potentialities, with their unsullied qualities for giving and collectivity. Preliterate peoples that still lack an "I" with which to replace a "we" are not (as Levy-Bruhl was to suggest) deficient in individuality as much as they are rich in community. This is a greatness of wealth that can yield a lofty disdain for objects. Cooperation, at this point, is more than just a cement between members of the group; it is an organic melding of identities that, without losing individual uniqueness, retains and fosters the unity of consociation. Contract, forced into this wholeness, serves merely to subvert it – turning an unthinking sense of responsibility into a calculating nexus of aid and an unconscious sense of collectivity into a preening sense of mutuality. As for reciprocity, so often cited as the highest evocation of collectivity, it is more significant in forming alliances between groups than in fostering internal solidarity within them.

Usufruct, in short, differs qualitatively from the quid pro quo of reciprocity, exchange, and mutual aid – all of which are trapped within history's demeaning account books with their "just" ratios and their "honest" balance sheets. Caught in this limited sphere of calculation, consociation is always tainted by the rationality of arithmetic. The human spirit can never transcend a quantitative world of "fair dealings" between canny egos whose ideology of interest barely conceals a mean-spirited proclivity for acquisition. To be sure, social forces were to fracture the human collectivity by introducing contractual ties and cultivating the ego's most acquisitive impulses. Insofar as the guileless peoples of organic societies held to the values of usufruct in an *unconscious* manner, they remained terribly vulnerable to the lure, often the harsh imposition, of an emerging contractual world. Rarely is history notable for its capacity to select and preserve the most virtuous traits of humanity. But there is still no reason why hope, reinforced by consciousness and redolent with ancestral memories, may not linger with us as an awareness of what humanity has been in the past and what it can become in the future. . . .

Freedom, an unstated reality in many preliterate cultures, was burdened by constraints, but these constraints were closely related to the early community's material conditions of life. It is impossible to quarrel with famine, with the need for coordinating the hunt of large game, with seasonal requirements of food cultivation, and later with warfare. To violate the Crow hunting regulations was to endanger every hunter and possibly place the welfare of the entire community in jeopardy. If the violations were serious enough, the violator would be beaten so severely that he might very well not survive. The mild-mannered Eskimo would grimly but collectively select an assassin to kill an unmanageable individual who gravely threatened the well-being of the band. But the virtually unbridled "individualism" so characteristic of power brokers in modern society was simply unthinkable in preliterate societies. Were it even conceivable, it would have been totally unacceptable to the community. Constraint, normally guided by public opinion, custom, and shame, was inevitable in the early social development of humanity – not as a matter of will, authority, or the exercise of power, but because it was unavoidable.

Personal freedom was thus clearly restricted from a modern viewpoint. Choice, will, and individual proclivities could be exercised or expressed within confines permitted by the environment. . . . But organic society, despite the physical limitations it faced (from a modern viewpoint), nevertheless functioned unconsciously with an implicit commitment to freedom that social theorists were not to attain until fairly recent times. Paul Radin's concept of the irreducible minimum rests on an unarticulated principle of freedom. To be assured of the material means of life irrespective of one's productive contribution to the community implies that, wherever possible, society will compensate for the infirmities of the ill, handicapped, and old, just as it will for the limited powers of the very young and their dependency on adults. Even though their productive powers are limited or failing, people will not be denied the means of life that are available to individuals who are well-endowed physically and mentally. Indeed, even individuals who are perfectly capable of meeting all their material needs cannot be denied access to the community's common produce, although deliberate shirkers in organic society are virtually unknown.

The principle of the irreducible minimum thus affirms the existence of *inequality* within the group – inequality of physical and mental powers, of skills and virtuosity, psyches and proclivities. It does so not to ignore these inequalities or denigrate them, but on the contrary to *compensate* for them. Equity here is the recognition of inequities that are not the fault of anyone and that must be adjusted as a matter of unspoken social responsibility. To assume that everyone is "equal" is patently preposterous, if their "equality" is to lie in their strength, intellect, training, experience, talent, disposition, and opportunities. Such "equality" scoffs at reality and denies the commonality and solidarity of the community by subverting its responsibilities to compensate for differences between individuals. It is a heartless "equality," a mean-spirited one that is simply alien to the very nature of organic society. As long as the means exist, they must be shared as much as possible according to needs – and needs are unequal insofar as they are gauged according to individual abilities and responsibilities.

Hence, organic society tends to operate unconsciously according to the *equality of unequals* – that is, a freely given, unreflective form of social behavior and distribution that compensates inequalities and does not yield to the fictive claim, yet to be articulated, that everyone is equal. Marx was to put this well when, in opposition to "bourgeois right," with its claim of the "equality of all," he remarked that freedom abandons the very notion of "right" *as such* and "inscribes on its banners: from each according to his ability, to each according to his needs." Equality is inextricably tied to freedom as the recognition of inequality and transcends necessity by establishing a culture and distributive system based on compensation for the stigma of natural "privilege."

The subversion of organic society drastically undermined this principle of authentic freedom. Compensation was restructured into rewards, just as gifts were replaced by commodities. Cuneiform writing, the basis of our alphabetic script, had its origins in the meticulous records the temple clerks kept of products received and products dispersed – in short, the precise accounting of goods, possibly even when the land was "communally owned" and worked in Mesopotamia. Only afterward were these ticks on clay tablets to become narrative forms of script. The early cuneiform accounting records of the Near East prefigure the moral literature of a less giving and more despotic world in which the equality of unequals gave way to mere charity. Thereafter "right" was to supplant freedom. No longer was it the primary responsibility for society to care for its young, elderly, infirm, or unfortunates; their care became a "private matter" for family and friends – albeit very slowly and through various subtly shaded phases. On the village level, to be sure, the old customs still lingered on in their own shadowy world, but this world was not part of "civilization" – merely an indispensable but concealed archaism.

Romanticizing Organic Society
(from "Twenty Years Later . . . ," 1991)

We are faced with the difficulty that few people seem to know how to build or develop ideas anymore. They promiscuously collect intellectual fragments here and there, like so many dismembered artifacts, drawing upon basically contradictory views and traditions with complete aplomb. Indeed, any serious attempt to rationally discuss the very troubling issues of our time in a coherent manner is often treated as a symptom of psychopathology rather than an earnest effort to make sense of the ideological chaos so prevalent today. Ironically, in its own quixotic way, postmodernism often inadvertently works with a rationality of its own that is nonetheless opaque to itself, and it often strives for the very coherence whose existence it denies to its critics.

The intellectual tendencies that celebrate incoherence, antirationalism, and mysticism are not merely symptoms of a waning intellectuality today. They literally *justify* and *foster* it. The massive shift by many people away from serious concerns with the objective conditions of life – such as institutional forms of domination, the use of technology for exploitative purposes, and the everyday realities of human suffering – toward an introverted subjectivism, with its overwhelming focus on psychology and "hidden" motivations, the rise of the culture industry, and the intellectual anxieties over collegiate issues like academic careers and pedagogical eminence – all testify to a sense of disempowerment in both social and personal life.

That the mystical ecologies are becoming popular today is not a mere intellectual aberration, any more than the popularity of postmodernism. To the contrary, their popularity expresses the inability of millions of people to cope with a harsh and demoralizing reality, to control the increasingly oppressive direction in which society is moving. Hence myths, pagan deities, and "Pleistocene" and "Neolithic" belief-systems together with their priests and priestesses provide a surrogate "reality" into which the naïve acolyte can escape. Indeed, when this preening emphasis on the subjective is clothed in the mystical vapors and inchoate vagaries of fevered imaginations, any recognition of reality is dissolved by beliefs in the mythic. The rational is replaced by the intuitional, and palpable social opponents are replaced by their shadows, to be exorcised by rituals, incantations, and magical gymnastics.

All of these practices are merely socially harmless surrogates for the authentic problems of our time. Ghosts from a distant past, the products of our ancestors' own imaginations, in turn, are invoked as objects of our reverence in the name of an "earth wisdom" that is actually as ineffectual as we are in our everyday lives. The new surrogate "reality" that is becoming a widespread feature in our time percolates through the mass media and the publishing industry, which are only too eager to nourish, even celebrate the proliferation of wiccan covens, Goddess-worshipping congregations, assorted pantheistic and animistic cults, "wilderness" devotees, and ecofeminist acolytes – to which I can add a new "deep ecology" professoriat that is increasingly prepared to feed a gullible public with "biocentric" pablum. . . .

These ideologies, from postmodernism to ecofeminism, subtly enchant the new human commodities with the mental fireworks, amulets, charms, and brightly tinted garments that provide them with a mystical patina to conceal their empty lives. Capitalism has nothing whatever to fear from mystical and "biocentric" ecologies, or their many high-priced artifacts. The bourgeoisie easily guffaws at these absurdities and is only too eager to commodify them into new sources of profit. Indeed, to state the issue bluntly, it is profit, power, and economic expansion that primarily concerns the elites of the existing social order, not the antics or even the protests of dissenters who duel with ghosts instead of institutionalized centers of power, authority, and wealth.

. . . It has become all too fashionable among many mystical ecologists to condemn human intervention into first nature, except to meet the minimal needs of life and survival. We are enjoined to "let nature take its course," to avoid any alteration of first nature except for what is "necessary" – a word that often remains ill-defined – to keep human beings alive and well. Such noninterventionist attitudes are commonly imputed to prehistoric and aboriginal peoples, who presumably lived in total "Oneness" with first nature and the wildlife around them. Taking Aldo Leopold's phrase "not man apart" to its most extreme conclusion, mystical ecologists call for a complete integration to first nature – by "returning to the Pleistocene," as many "biocentrists" demand. . . .

These forebears of our species and our own ancestors lived in a climatically turbulent era, marked by advances and retreats of glaciers, wide swings in temperature, and a feast-or-famine diet. Their lives were often very precarious, despite the periodic abundance of game. Nor were they fully equipped with the means to deal with the natural vicissitudes that white middle-class people today take so readily for granted, such as the certainty of warmth in cold weather, adequate shelter, and the ordinary creature comforts to which middle-class people are wedded – leaving all luxuries and pleasures aside. They lacked a written body of knowledge by which a complex tradition of ideas could be handed down; the writing materials with which to express thoughts and reflections that were more complex than those involved in meeting the needs of everyday life; the libraries in which to meditate, research, and gather the wisdom of past ages – in short, the vast array of intellectual and spiritual materials to sensitize their outlook and sensibilities.

It might seem more plausible for deep ecologists to call for a return to the *sensibility* of these distant times, rather than an actual physical return. But here too we are besieged by a barrage of unanswered questions. We would want to know what kind of sensibility Pleistocene and Paleolithic hunters had in their dealings with the multitude of animals they encountered in the "Great Age of Mammals," as the two periods have been called. After all, Paleolithic hunter-gatherers developed the stone-tipped spear, the all-important spear-thrower – which made it possible to effectively pierce very tough hides and muscles – and the bow and arrow, which could inflict mortal damage over a sizable distance. The more sophisticated and lethal their hunting kit, the greater an impact these humans must have had on the large mammals of the late Pleistocene and the Paleolithic. If we are to return to the sensibility of these epochs, we would want to know if they really viewed the animals they killed "reverentially," as so many mystical ecologists claim, or if they had a more pragmatic attitude toward them, using magic to propitiate a "bison spirit" or "bear spirit" in rituals before and after kills. We would want to know if they really did feel themselves to be absorbed into an all-encompassing "Oneness" with the animals around them, or whether they had any sense of human self-identity that involved feelings of "apartness" from those animals. We would want to know if they really chose not to intervene in first nature any more than was absolutely necessary, as mystical ecologists believe, or if they significantly altered their surroundings. We would want to know if they really did behave toward wildlife as "tender carnivores" in pursuit of "sacred game," as Paul Shepard's evocative book on hunter-gatherer sensibility is titled, or if they held a more mundane attitude toward animals as means for satisfying their very material as well as subjective needs.

Actually, we will never know with certainty the answers to these questions of sensibility. The outlook that today's mystical ecologists cultivate toward the Pleistocene, the Paleolithic, and the Neolithic is often highly romanticized and certainly does not correspond to many things that we *do* know about those eras. If I am to examine the nature of aboriginal sensibilities, I must do so as honestly as possible and decide which characterizations *probably* apply better to our ancestors of the distant past. This much is clear: much of the archaeological evidence does not support the ecological–romantic view of early peoples, however unpleasant the data may be. Researchers have argued with good reason, for example, that effective human hunters in the Pleistocene may have played a major role in killing off some, if not most, of the great Pleistocene and Paleolithic mammals. Which is not to deny that others have claimed that climatic changes, with important ecological consequences in the Pleistocene and Paleolithic, are more likely to have ended forever the lives of mammoths, mastodons, woolly rhinoceroses, cave bears, and giant sloths, among others. . . . [Much] evidence throws factual weight on the side of the "overkill," as distinguished from the primarily climatic approach, and supports the view that early hunter-gatherers contributed to exterminating or may have exterminated many Pleistocene animals.

After so much has been written by romantics of the last century and mystical ecologists today about the "Oneness" that preliterate peoples felt for the game they hunted, should we be shocked by this conclusion? I believe not – unless we choose to simplify the complex dialectic involved in what we regard as an "ecological sensibility." Indeed, that early hunters – whose "ecological sensibility" is so revered by mystical ecologists – would try to satisfy their needs *in any way they could* should not surprise us. In fact, these hunters were predatory opportunists, no less than wolves or coyotes, *precisely* because they were *very* much part of "Nature" (to invoke that much-abused word), just as were all the life-forms around them. Early hunters did not live in Disneyland, where sociable "mice" and gleeful "rabbits" jostle with human visitors in a pseudo-animistic, cartoonlike world.

Another area in dispute is the extent to which preliterate peoples altered the wild environments in which they lived. We know that early hunters were clearly not devout conservers of the original forests, for example. As Stephen J. Pyne emphasizes in his informative study *Fire in America,* "the virgin forest was not encountered in the sixteenth and seventeenth centuries; it was invented in the late eighteenth and early nineteenth centuries. For this condition Indian fire practices were largely responsible."[2] Hunter-gatherer foragers, in fact, used fire on a global scale to create grasslands for herbivores. The great prairies of the Midwest were literally created by Indian torches, which were systematically applied, long before those lands were expropriated by

Europeans. Since humanity's discovery of fire, few forests that we can call "virgin" remain today, however large the girth or height of their individual trees. Great forests of the eighteenth century were often restorations of trees that had been cleared and reduced to parkland and prairies in pre-Columbian times. The "forest primeval" that Longfellow celebrated in his poetry was often made up of trees that European settlers had permitted to come back after Indians had turned the forests and the areas they occupied into parklands. That European settlers permitted the trees to return in order to use them to build ships and homes does not alter the fact that these forests were anything but "primeval," or that Indian communities were anything but reluctant to "tamper" with "Nature." . . .

It is *not* my intention to defame aboriginal hunters or to place their behavior on a par with that of lumber companies or the meat-packing industry. No Paleo-Indian and Indian overkills and deforestation compares even remotely to the terrifying ecological devastation and the genocide practiced by Euro-American settlers on the New World and its native people. The greed and exploitation that has destroyed Indian cultures over the past five centuries can in no way be justified morally or culturally. The interaction of European settlers and Native Americans could have opened a new opportunity for a sensitive integration of both cultures, but that opportunity was lost in an orgy of bloodletting and plunder by European settlers, particularly land speculators, railroaders, lumber barons, and capitalist entrepreneurs generally.

But with all due regard to the many remarkable features of Native American cultures, pre-Columbian hunters took a large toll in wildlife, often showing few, if any, concerns for conservation. From such overkills, game animals took years to regenerate. Nor was this regeneration helped by their hunters' fertility rituals, unless we are to naïvely believe, like modern believers in magic, that they served to increase animal fertility. "Thanks to their hunting prowess," observes Alston Chase in his superbly researched and well-written book, *Playing God in Yellowstone,* "the Indians of the Yellowstone region – the Shoshone and their cousins, the Bannock and Lemhi – had eaten themselves out of house and home. When Lewis and Clark first met the Shoshone in 1805, they were starving. Their chief told the explorers that they had 'nothing but berries to eat.'"[3] . . .

Far from seeking to defame aboriginal peoples, I think we must examine the *rationale* for their seeming "insensitivity" to animal life and forests. Hunter-gatherers were not motivated by a desire for profit, like competitive rivals in a capitalist marketplace whose behavior is guided by the maxim "grow or die." As I have emphasized, these hunters were living beings like other life-forms, and as any life-form would, they tried to survive by any means possible. At the same time, the needs of these humans were greater and more complex than those of other life-forms. As creatures endowed by natural evolution with highly intelligent minds, they would not only have required animal and vegetable food to meet their immediate needs; they would also have wanted a secure supply of food once they knew how to preserve meat and plants. Owing to their *naturally* endowed intelligence, they would have wanted good clothing, even "luxuries" such as comfortable bedding, sturdy skins for homes, plumage and carved bone amulets, beadlike teeth for ornaments, magical artifacts, an assortment of tools and medicines, and coloring matter for aesthetic purposes. That the needs of these humans were greater and more complex than those of other life-forms was due not to any perverse traits on their part but to endowments that stemmed from their evolution as unique animals. These wants, in short, shaped their behavior, as they would have for any nonhuman being. And these wants were a product of an intelligence that had been formed as a result of aeons of evolutionary development, not any demonic or mysterious impulse that is vaguely "unnatural."

Inasmuch as preliterate people were human, moreover, they were capable of reasoning conceptually, of speaking fluently, and of feeling abiding insecurities. Early humanity can hardly be faulted for behaving more intelligently than bears, foxes, and wolves; *natural evolution* endowed them with larger brains and a capacity for making tools and weapons to enhance their powers of survival and for changing their environment to abet their well-being. They had amazing memories, and of extreme importance, they possessed vivid imaginations. They decorated their weapons, painted animals and designs on rocks and caves, engaged in analogical thinking, created myths, and felt passions incomparably more compelling than any that are discernable in animals.

Yet they were also truly part of "Nature." In the late Pleistocene and early Paleolithic, it was their very "closeness" to first nature, coupled with their emerging second nature, that would have caused them to act in ways that contradict our present-day romanticized notions of their behavior. They were undergoing a major transition from the domain of biological evolution to that of social evolution. As such, they could variously exhibit utter indifference to the pain they inflicted on animals and a strong affinity for them in their rituals – contradictory forms of behavior that occurred almost simultaneously. In these respects, their sensibility was shaped by animalistic as well as cultural needs, indeed by their very "Oneness" with first nature. In turn, their sense of "Oneness" with first nature was shaped by a mental repertoire that could make for what we today would regard as cruelty *as well as* empathy toward nonhuman life, depending upon the extent to which they identified themselves with it and the kind of society they created, which led to a sense of "apartness" from it – a thoroughly dialectical tension in their outlook. . . .

Looking back to the very beginnings of second nature, it should be emphasized that humanity's consciousness of first nature, as distinguished from a consciousness of its specific, narrow ecological niches, *presupposes* that it separate itself from a purely nichelike animal existence. Human beings at some point had to at least *begin* to see first nature generally as an "other" if their self-identity and self-consciousness as human beings were to emerge. Without a sense of contrast between the human and nonhuman, people are limited to the bedrock existence of seeking mere survival, to a way of life so undifferentiated from that of other living things that they know little more than the unmediated confines of their limited ecological community. This way of life is bereft of purpose, meaning, or orientation, apart from what people create in their imagination. And it is a way of life that no human being could endure except by *ceasing* to think.

Which is to say that, epistemologically at least, differentiation would not exist and the evolution of a human psyche would never get under way. In order for human beings to differentiate themselves in natural evolution, there must be *duality,* such as dualities between self and other and between the human and the nonhuman. Here, duality must not be confused with *dualism.* Today, in fact, the danger that confronts ecological thinking is less a matter of a dualistic sensibility – a dualism that mystical ecologists have criticized to the point of pulverization – than of *reductionism,* an intellectual dissolution of *all* difference into an undefinable "Oneness" that excludes the possibility of creativity and turns a concept like "interconnectedness" into the bonds of a mental and emotional straitjacket. Without otherness, duality, and differentiation, "interconnectedness" dissolves psychological and personal heterogeneity into a "night in which all cows are black." Without "otherness," duality, and differentiation, all heterogeneity of life-forms would have been limited to a deadening homogeneity, and organic evolution would not have occurred. In terms of natural history, the biosphere would indeed still be a "Gaia" covered by Lynn Margulis's soup of prokaryotic cells.

Today, to follow a mystical path to "Oneness" is to sink back into the timeless, ahistorical, misty island of the Lotus Eaters, who in Homer's *Odyssey* have no recollection of a past and no vision of a future but vegetate in an unperturbable existence that consists of eating, digesting, and defecating, like animals that live on a strictly day-by-day basis. This is a world that has no sense of "otherness," no sense of self, no sense of consciousness – indeed, no sensibility at all beyond the mere maintenance of life, presumably in the bosom of an equally vacuous "cosmic Self." To understand early sensibilities and their development, we must acknowledge that humanity *had* to break with the purely animalistic sensibility – if sensibility it can be called at all – that had confined it to a mere ecological niche, if it was to enter into and know the larger world around it. Human beings had to regard first nature as "other," however much romantics of all sorts bemoan the loss of a universal "Oneness" in a golden Pleistocene, Paleolithic, or Neolithic past. Given their naturally endowed potentialities, humans had to go beyond a realm of mere survival into one of creativity and innovation, and satisfy their naturally endowed capacity to adapt environments to meet their own needs.

The terrible psychological upheavals produced by the twentieth century have made us truly wary of social history, of "otherness," of the dualities of separation from nonhuman nature. But "separation" and "otherness" are *human* facts of life, if only because natural evolution has produced a life-form – humanity – whose very specificity is premised on a *conscious* sense of "separation" that can increasingly distinguish human from nonhuman reality. "Otherness" must be conceived of as a *graded* phenomenon, to be sure, one that may result in any of several kinds of society. It may eventuate in very destructive relationships characterized by *opposition, domination,* and *antagonism,* as we know today – the results of which stain the social history that lies behind us and possibly the precarious future that lies before us.

But "otherness" may also take the form of *differentiation,* of *articulation,* of *complementarity, as it did in the early history of humanity.* As human beings began to emerge from first nature, possibly in the Pleistocene and certainly in the Paleolithic, their relationship to animals as "others" was largely *complementary.* Hunters know that they are dealing with a nonhuman "other," but animism may have been a form of solicitation rather than coercion. Early animism imparted a cooperative impulse to these cultures, despite the fact that animal spirits had to be propitiated. Game, it was assumed, could then be *lured* to "accept" the hunters' spears and arrows, as Paleolithic cave paintings suggest. Even the overkills of the late Pleistocene and early Paleolithic may have arisen not from a sense of the "other" as an opponent or foe, but from a naïve ignorance of the ecological impact these overkills would have on the great Pleistocene megafauna. In this respect, early hunters merely combined the behavior of an ordinary animal predator with that of an increasingly socialized, animistic human being. . . .

I regard it as a form of ahistorical arrogance, so characteristic of recent times, to look back at preliterate peoples' behavior and cast it in forms that suit modern standards of ecological morality, or respond with pious disappointment to their cruelty or indifference to other living beings. It is a form of modern ahistorical arrogance to expect that they would *not* use their environments up to the hilt or change them as they needed to. What we should properly ask, if we are not to sink into the fatuities of romanticism and mysticism, is not whether humans *should* intervene into nature – for nothing will stop them from trying to fulfill their most basic "natural" potentialities – but *how* they should intervene and toward what *ends*. These are really the profoundly ethical questions that we must ask, and they can only be answered in a *thinking* way – by unscrambling the virtues and vices of humanity's social development, by determining if evolution has any meaningful thrust toward increased subjectivity and consciousness in the great evolutionary parade of life-forms, and by bringing greater mind to bear on the pivotal role of social development in all of these issues. . . .

Natural evolution, given its marvelous creativity, its fecundity, its growing subjectivity, and its capacity for innovation, deserves our respect and love for its own attributes. We do not have to create ideological artifacts like deities – female or male – or use magical arts to appreciate first nature as a wondrous phenomenon – including such wonders as the human mind and humanity's capacity to act morally and self-consciously. An appreciation and love of first nature should properly stem from a clear-sighted and aesthetic naturalism, not from a supernaturalism, with its projection of sovereign humanlike "beings" into the biotic world and its canny use of terms like *immanence* and "earth groundedness." Indeed, whether we truly know and fully appreciate first nature depends very much on having the intellectual and emotional ability *not* to confuse ourselves as human beings with coyotes, bears, or wolves, much less with insensate things like rocks, or rivers, or even more absurdly, with the "cosmos." . . .

For early hunters themselves, their animistic sensibility was a mixed blessing. Clearly, it featured a cooperative spirit in their relations to animals as "others," and it certainly alerted hunters to the attributes of the animals they stalked. Nevertheless, however much preliterate peoples' animism includes a cooperative dimension, we know today that insofar as it rests on a belief in spirits or a supernature, it clearly rests on a false image of the natural world. Besides boxing them into inflexible customs and traditions, animism involves an innocent belief in magic that rendered aboriginal peoples very vulnerable to the technology, particularly the weaponry, of Europeans who awed or, with their bullets, bloodily disabused them of the spells with which their shamans had "protected" them.

To believe that animism has any objective reality, as many mystical ecologists suggest, is simply infantile, not unlike the behavior of a child who angrily kicks a stool over when he or she falls. In view of what we know today about first nature, animistic souls and magical methods of reaching them have no more basis in objective reality than the visions that many North American Indians traditionally induced in themselves by fasting, self-torture, auto-suggestion, and similar techniques that distort the human sensorium. In a preliterate community, inducing a vision of a guardian spirit by warping one's senses might enhance one's own sense of self-worth, courage, and bravado, thereby making one a better hunter, but these visions tell us no more about the reality of first nature than Castaneda's tales about talking coyotes. Mythic knowledge and the belief in magic, so important to animism, are a self-delusion – one that is understandable as the beliefs of preliterate peoples, but among modern people they are explicable only as evidence of the extent to which they are removed from reality, indeed, the extent to which they lack authentic "earth wisdom."

NOTES

1 Murray Bookchin, "Twenty Years Later . . . ," introduction to the second edition of *The Ecology of Freedom* (Montreal: Black Rose Books, 1991), pp. xiv–xv.
2 Stephen J. Pyne, *Fire in America* (Princeton, NJ: Princeton University Press, 1982), p. 71.
3 Alston Chase, *Playing God in Yellowstone: The Destruction of America's First National Park* (New York: Harvest/Harcourt Brace Jovanovich, 1986, 1987), p. 104.

CHAPTER FOUR

The Legacy of Domination

Introduction

According to Marx, "primitive egalitarianism" was destroyed by the rise of social classes, in which those who own wealth and property exploit the labor of those who do not. But from his observations of contemporary history, Bookchin realized that class analysis in itself does not explain the entirety of social oppression. The elimination of class society could leave intact relations of sub-ordination and domination. Engels, in his essay "On Authority," wrote explicitly that he not only would preserve hierarchy in a "classless" society but regarded it as indispensable in industrial production.

In order to attain the broadest possible freedom in an ecological society, Bookchin emphasized that it would be necessary to eliminate not only social classes but social hierarchies as well. Thus, where Marx had worked with categories of class and exploitation, Bookchin developed broader categories of hierarchy and domination – not to replace the Marxist categories, or to deny the reality of class and exploitation, but to subsume them as particulars within more generalized concepts. Hierarchy and domination, in Bookchin's view, historically provided the substrate of oppression out of which class relations were formed.

In *The Ecology of Freedom* Bookchin shows how the rise of hierarchy eroded the complementarity of relatively egalitarian communities long before the appearance of property ownership. Although social and material factors, including population growth and physical force, were deeply involved in generating hierarchical social relations, Bookchin emphasizes the role of changes in consciousness as well. Incipient hierarchies gave rise to a hierarchical sensibility that ranked people as superior or inferior by a given standard and then used that ranking to justify the domination of the latter by the former. Once thinking was reordered along these lines, it would see hierarchy where in reality there was only difference. Mere differences in ability, experience, and knowledge would thereupon become acceptable rationales for domination.

Gradually hierarchical relations came to be elaborated along ever more complex lines, giving rise to the patriarchal domination of wives, sons, daughters, and dependants; the domination of whole communities by shamanistic and priestly guilds; the domination of one community by another; and later the domination of peoples by elite rulers. Ultimately status distinctions phased into outright class structures based on the exploitation of serfs, slaves, and the industrial proletariat.

Once a hierarchical sensibility had been established in this way, it could be projected out onto first nature, as people could begin to think in terms of dominating the natural world. Indeed, the idea of dominating first nature could not have existed unless human beings already had gained it from their experience of social domination.

Once the idea of dominating nature was formed, it became a basic assumption of Western culture that the creation of wealth depended upon it. Indeed, the supposed necessity of dominating first nature became a rationale for the further domination of human by human.

> It remains one of the most widely accepted notions, from classical times to the present, that human freedom from the "domination of man by nature" entails the domination of human by human as the earliest means of production and the use of human beings as instruments for harnessing the natural world. Hence, in order to harness the natural world, it has been argued for ages, it is necessary to harness human beings as well, in the form of slaves, serfs, and workers. That this instrumental notion pervades the ideology of nearly all ruling elites and has provided both liberal and conservative movements with a justification for their accommodation to the status quo requires little if any elaboration. The myth of a "stingy" nature has always been used to justify the "stinginess" of exploiters in their harsh treatment of the exploited.[1]

Ruling classes, in order to legitimate their rule, generally try to expand the domain of what is accepted as biological or natural and therefore inalterable, at the expense of what might otherwise be thought of as social and therefore subject to human alteration. Conversely, it is an emancipatory step to try to expand the realm of what convention holds to be social at the expense of what it defines as biological, precisely to open up possibilities for the transformation of existing social relationships.

Bookchin's contention that the domination of human by human preceded the idea of dominating first nature falls into this second category of ideas. Contrary to necessitarian myths, he argues that human emancipation does not depend on the domination of first nature; rather, a free society can as well be an ecological society. Indeed, since the ecological crisis has its origins in social pathologies, an ecological society can arise only after social hierarchy and domination have been removed.

The Emergence of Hierarchy
(from *The Ecology of Freedom*, 1982)

Organic societies, even the most egalitarian, are not homogeneous social groups. Each member of the community is defined by certain everyday roles based on sex, age, and ancestral lineage. In early organic societies, these roles do not seem to have been structured along hierarchical lines; nor do they seem to have involved the domination of human by human. Generally, they simply define the individual's responsibilities to the community: the raw materials, as it were, for a functional status in the complex nexus of human relationships. Lineage determines who can or cannot marry whom, and families related by marriage are often as obligated to help each other as are kin directly related by blood ties. Age confers the prestige of experience and wisdom. Finally, sexual differences define the community's basic division of labor.

Even before material surpluses began to increase significantly, the roles each individual played began to change from egalitarian relationships into elites based increasingly on systems of obedience and command. To make this assertion raises a number of very provocative questions. Who were these emerging elites? What was the basis of their privileges in early society? How did they rework organic society's forms of community status – forms based on usufruct, a domestic economy, reciprocity, and egalitarianism – into what were later to become class and exploitative societies? These questions are not academic: they deal with emotionally charged notions that lurk to this very day in the unconscious apparatus of humanity, notably the influence of biological facts, such as sex, age, and ancestry on social relationships. Unless these notions are carefully examined and the truths separated from the untruths, we are likely to carry an archaic legacy of domination into whatever social future awaits us. . . .

A careful survey of food-gathering and hunting communities reveals that women enjoyed a higher degree of parity with men than we have been commonly led to believe. Both sexes occupy a distinctly sovereign role in their respective spheres, and their roles are much too complementary economically to make the domination of women by men the comfortable social norm that biased white observers served up generations ago to allay the guilt-feelings of Victorian patriarchs. In daily life, women withdraw into a sorority based on their domestic and food-gathering activities and men into a fraternity of hunters. There both sexes are completely autonomous. The sharply etched distinctions between "home" and the "world" that exist in modern society do not exist in organic communities. There home and world are so closely wedded that a man, shut out from a family, is literally a nonsocial being – a being who is nowhere. Although the male tends, even in many egalitarian communities, to view himself as the "head" of the family, his stance is largely temperamental and accords him no special or domestic power. It is simply a form of boastfulness, for the hard facts of life vitiate his pretenses daily. Woman's food-gathering activities usually provide most of the family's food. She not only collects the food but prepares it, makes the family's clothing, and produces its containers, such as baskets and coiled pottery. She is more in contact with the young than the male and takes a more "commanding" role in their development. If her husband is too overbearing, she can unceremoniously put him out of the hut or simply return to her own family, where she and her children are certain of being provided for, no matter what her family thinks of her decision. As she ages, her experience becomes a revered source of wisdom; she becomes a "matriarch" in many cases, the head of the family in fact if not in form.

What women in preliterate communities distinctly *do* lack is the male's mobility. The human child's protracted development and dependency – a long period of mental plasticity that is vitally necessary for elaborating a cultural continuum – restricts the mother's capacity to move about freely. The primal division of labor that assigned hunting tasks to the male and domestic tasks to the female is based on a hard biological reality: a woman, coupled to a noisy infant, can scarcely be expected to practice the stealth and athleticism needed to hunt large animals. By its very nature, the mother-child relationship limits her to comparatively sedentary lifeways. Moreover, if woman is not weak in terms of her capacity to do hard work, she is certainly the "weaker sex" when pitted against armed, possibly hostile men from an alien community. Women need their men not only as hunters but also as guardians of the family and the group. Men become the community's guardians not by virtue of usurpation, but because they are better equipped muscularly in a materially undeveloped culture to defend their community against hostile marauders. . . .

As bands began to increase in size and number, as they began to differentiate into clans, tribes, and tribal federations and to make war on one another, an ever larger social space emerged that was increasingly occupied by men. Men tended to become the clan headsmen or tribal chiefs and fill the councils of tribal federations. For all of this was "men's work," like hunting and herding animals. They had the mobility and physical prowess to defend their own communities, attack hostile communities, and thereby administer an extrabiological, distinctly social sphere of life.

In communities where matrilineal descent carried considerable cultural weight and woman's horticultural activities formed the basis of economic life, she assumed social roles very similar to those of the man. Usually, she occupied these roles on the clan level, rarely on the tribal one. Moreover, she almost invariably shared her social role with males. In a matricentric society, these males were her brothers, not her husband. What woman's social eminence in matricentric communities reveals, however, is that the male's rising position in social affairs results not from any conscious degradation of woman to a domestic "unworldly" sphere. To the contrary, in the beginning at least, the male did not have to "usurp" power from the female; indeed, social "power" as such did not exist but had yet to be created. The social sphere and the man's position in it emerged naturally. The primordial balance that assigned complementary economic functions to both sexes on the basis of parity slowly tipped toward the male, favoring his social preeminence. . . .

The male, in a hunting community, is a specialist in violence. From the earliest days of his childhood, he identifies with such "masculine" traits as courage, strength, self-assertiveness, decisiveness, and athleticism – traits necessary for the welfare of the community. The community, in turn, will prize the male for these traits and foster them in him. If he becomes a good hunter, he will be highly regarded by everyone; by envious men and admiring women, by respectful children and emulative youths. In a society preoccupied with the problem of survival and obliged to share its resources, a good hunter is an asset to all.

Similarly, the female is a specialist in child-rearing and food-gathering. Her responsibilities focus on nurture and sustenance. From childhood she will be taught to identify with such "feminine" traits as caring and tenderness, and she will be trained in comparatively sedentary occupations. The community, in turn, will prize her for these traits and foster them in her. If she cultivates these traits, she will be highly regarded for her sense of responsibility to her family, her skill and artfulness. In a matricentric society, these traits will be elevated into social norms that could well be described as the temperament of the community. We find this temperament today in many American Indian and Asian villages that practice horticulture, even if the kinship system is patrilineal. Similarly, in a patricentric society, "masculine" traits will be elevated into the norms of a community temperament, although they rarely coexist with matrilineal systems of kinship.

There is no intrinsic reason why a patricentric community, *merely* because it has a "masculine" temperament, must be hierarchical or reduce women to a subjugated position. The economic roles of the two sexes are still complementary; without the support that each sex gives to the other, the community will disintegrate. Moreover, both sexes still enjoy complete autonomy in their respective spheres. In projecting our own social attitudes into preliterate society, we often fail to realize how far removed a primordial domestic community is from a modern political society. . . . As long as the growing civil sphere is a pragmatic extension of the male's role in the division of labor, it is merely that and no more. Even while the civil sphere is expanding, it is still rooted in domestic life and, in this sense, enveloped by it; hence, the numinous power that surrounds woman in the most patricentric of primordial societies.

Only when social life itself undergoes hierarchical differentiation and emerges as a separate terrain to be organized on its own terms do we find a conflict between the domestic and civil spheres – one that extends hierarchy into domestic life and results not only in the subjugation of woman, but in her degradation. Then the distinctively "feminine" traits, which primordial society prizes as a high survival asset, sink to the level of social subordination. The woman's nurturing capacities are degraded into renunciation; her tenderness to obedience. Man's "masculine" traits are also transformed. His courage turns into aggressiveness; his strength is used to dominate; his self-assertiveness is transformed into egotism; his decisiveness into repressive reason. His athleticism is directed increasingly to the arts of war and plunder.

Until these transformations occur, however, it is important to know the raw materials from which hierarchical society will raise its moral and social edifice. The violation of organic society is latent within organic society itself. The primal unity of the early community, both internally and with nature, is weakened merely by the elaboration of the community's social life – its ecological differentiation. Yet the growing civil space occupied by the male is still enveloped in a natural matrix of blood ties, family affinities, and work responsibilities based on a sexual division of labor. Not until distinctly social interests emerge that clash directly with its natural matrix and turn the weaknesses, perhaps the growing tensions, of organic society into outright fractures, will the unity between human and human, and between humanity and nature, finally be broken. Then power will emerge, not simply as a social fact, with all its differentiations, but as a concept – and so will the concept of freedom.

To find what is perhaps the one primary group that, more than any other in preliterate communities, transects kinship lines and the division of labor – that in its own right forms the point of departure for a separate social interest as distinguished from the complementary relations that unite the community into a whole – we must turn to the age group, particularly to the community's elders. To be born, to be young, to mature, and finally to grow old and idle is natural fact – as much as it is to be a woman or a man, or to belong to a blood-lineage group. But the older one becomes, the more one acquires distinct interests that are not "natural." These interests are uniquely social. The later years of life are a period of diminishing physical powers; the declining years, a period of outright dependency. The aging and the aged develop interests that are tied neither to their sexual roles nor to their lineage. They depend for their survival ultimately on the fact that the community is social in the fullest sense of the term; that it will provide for them not because they participate in the process of production and reproduction, but because of the *institutional* roles they can create for themselves in the social realm.

The sexes complement each other economically; the old and the young do not. In preliterate communities, the old are vital repositories of knowledge and wisdom, but this very function merely underscores the fact that their capacities belong largely to the cultural and social sphere. Hence, even more than the boasting self-assertive male who may be slowly gaining a sense of social power, the aging and the aged tend to be socially conscious as such – as a matter of survival. They share a common interest independent of their sex and lineage. They have the most to gain from the institutionalization of society and the emergence of hierarchy, for it is within this realm and as a result of this process that they can retain powers that are denied to them by physical weakness and infirmity. Their need for social power, and for hierarchical social power at that, is a function of their loss of biological power. The social sphere is the only realm in which this power can be created and concomitantly the only sphere that can cushion their vulnerability to natural forces. Thus, they are the architects *par excellence* of social life, of social power, and of its institutionalization along hierarchical lines.

The old can also perform many functions that relieve young adults of certain responsibilities. Old women can care for the children and undertake sedentary productive tasks that would otherwise be performed by their daughters. Similarly, old men can make weapons and teach their sons and grandsons to use them more effectively. But these tasks, while they lighten the burdens of the young, do not make the old indispensable to the community. And in a world that is often harsh and insecure, a world ruled by natural necessity, the old are the most dispensable members of the community. Under conditions where food may be in short supply and the life of the community occasionally endangered, they are the first to be disposed of. The anthropological literature is replete with examples in which the old are killed and expelled during periods of hunger, a practice that changes from the episodic into the customary in the case of communities that normally leave their aged members behind to perish whenever the group breaks camp and moves to a different locale.

Thus, the lives of the old are always clouded by a sense of insecurity. This sense is incremental to the insecurity that people of all ages may feel in materially undeveloped communities. The ambiguity that permeates the outlook of the primordial world toward nature – a shifting outlook that mixes reverence or ecological adaptation with fear – is accented among the aged with a measure of hatred, for insofar as fear is concerned, they have more to fear from nature's vicissitudes than do the young. The nascent ambiguities of the aged toward nature later give rise to western "civilization's" mode of repressive reason. This exploitative rationality pits civil society against domestic society and launches social elites on a quest for domination that, in a later historical context, transforms insecurity into egotism, acquisitiveness, and a craze for rule – in short, the social principle graduated by its own inner dialectic into the asocial principle. Here, too, are the seeds for the hatred of eros and the body, a hatred, in turn, that forms the archetypal matrix for willful aggression and the Thanatic death wish.

Initially, the medium by which the old create a modicum of power for themselves is through their control of the socialization process. Fathers teach their sons the arts of getting food; mothers, their daughters. The adults, in turn, consult their parents on virtually every detail of life, from the workaday pragmatic to the ritual. In a preliterate community, the most comprehensive compendium of knowledge is inscribed on the brains of the elders. However much this knowledge is proffered with concern and love, it is not always completely disinterested; it is often permeated, even if unconsciously, by a certain amount of cunning and self-interest. Not only is the young mind shaped by the adults, as must necessarily be the case in all societies, but it is shaped to respect the wisdom of the adults, if not their authority. The harsh initiation ceremonies that many preliterate communities inflict on adolescent boys may well have the purpose of using pain to "brand" the elders' wisdom on young minds, as a number of anthropologists contend; but I would also suggest that it "brands" a sense of their authority as well. The aged, who abhor natural necessity, become the embodiment of social necessity: the dumb "cruelty" that the natural world inflicts on them is transmitted by social catalysis into the conscious cruelty they inflict on the young. Nature begins to take her revenge on the earliest attempts of primordial society to control her. But this is nature internalized, the nature in humanity itself. The attempt to dominate external nature will come later, when humanity is conceptually equipped to transfer its social antagonisms to the natural world outside. . . .

In fairness to primordial society, we must note that hierarchy founded merely on age is not institutionalized hierarchy. Rather, it is hierarchy in its most nascent form: hierarchy embedded in the matrix of equality. For age is the fate of everyone who does not die prematurely. To the extent that privileges accrue to the elders, everyone in the community is heir to them. Inasmuch as these privileges vary with the fortunes of the community, they are still too tenuous to be regarded as more than compensations for the infirmities that elders must suffer with the aging process. The primordial balance that accords parity to all members of the community, women as well as men, is thereby perpetuated in the privileges accorded to the old. In this sense they cannot be regarded simply as privileges.

What is problematical in the future development of hierarchy is *how* the elders tried to institutionalize their privileges and *what* they finally achieved. Radin, in a perceptive if overly ruthless discussion of age-linked hierarchy, notes that the elders in food-gathering communities "almost always functioned as medicine-men of some kind or another" and, with the development of clan-agricultural societies, acquired their "main strength" from the "rituals and ritualistic societies which they largely controlled." Social power begins to crystallize as the fetishization of magical power over certain forces of nature. In trying to deal with this dialectical twist, we must refocus our perspective to include a unique mode of social sensibility and experience, one that is strikingly modern: the sensibility and experience of the elder cum shaman.

The shaman is a strategic figure in any discussion of social hierarchy because he (and at times she, although males predominate in time) solidifies the privileges of the elders – a general stratum in the primordial community – into the particularized privileges of a special segment of that stratum. He professionalizes power. He makes power the privilege of an elect few, a group that only carefully chosen apprentices can hope to enter, not the community as a whole. His vatic personality essentially expresses the insecurity of the individual on the scale of a social neurosis. If the male hunter is a specialist in violence, and the woman food-gatherer a specialist in nurture, the shaman is a specialist in fear. As magician and divinator combined in one, he mediates between the suprahuman power of the environment and the fears of the community. Weston La Barre observes that in contrast to the priest, who "implores the Omnipotent," the shaman is "psycho-logically and socially the more primitive of the two. . . . External powers invade and leave his body with practiced ease, so feeble are his ego boundaries and so false his fantasies." Perhaps more significant than this distinction is the fact that the shaman is the incipient State personified. As distinguished from other members of the primordial community, who participate coequally in the affairs of social life, the shaman and his associates are professionals in political manipulation. They tend to subvert the innocence and amateurism that distinguishes domestic society from political society. Shamans "banded informally [together] even in the simplest food-gathering civilizations," notes Radin. "As soon as the clan political patterns emerged we find them formally united together, either in one group or separately." Bluntly stated, the shamanistic groups to which Radin alludes were incipient political institutions. . . .

But the shaman's position in primordial society is notoriously insecure. Often highly remunerated for his magical services, he might be vindictively attacked, perhaps assassinated outright, if his techniques fail. Thus, he must always seek alliances and, more significantly, foster the creation of mutually advantageous power centers for his protection from the community at large. As a quasi-religious formulator, a primitive cosmologist, he literally creates the ideological mythos that crystallizes incipient power into actual power. He may do this in concert with the elders, enhancing their authority over the young, or with the younger but more prominent warriors, who tend to form military societies of their own. From them, in turn, he receives the support he so direly needs to cushion the ill effects that follow from his fallibility. That he may compete with these powers and attempt to usurp their authority is irrelevant at this period of development. The point is that the shaman is the demiurge of political institutions and coalitions. He not only validates the authority of the elders with a magico-political aura, but in his need for political power, he tends to heighten the "masculine" temperament of a patricentric community. He exaggerates the aggressive and violent elements of that temperament, feeding it with mystical sustenance and supernatural power.

Domination, hierarchy, and the subordination of woman to man now begin to emerge. But it is difficult to delineate in this development the emergence of organized economic classes and the systematic exploitation of a dominated social stratum. The young, to be sure, are placed under the rule of a clan or tribal gerontocracy; the elders, shamans, and warrior chiefs, in turn, acquire distinct social privileges. But so ingrained in society are the primordial rules of usufruct, complementarity, and the irreducible minimum that the economy of this early world proves to be surprisingly impervious to these sociopolitical changers. "The majority of aboriginal tribes," observes Radin, "possessed no grouping of individuals based on true class distinctions." He adds that "slaves not a few of them had, but, while their lives were insecure because they had no status, they were never systematically forced to do menial work or regarded as an inferior and degraded class in our sense of the term." Men of wealth there were, too, in time, but as Manning Nash observes, "in primitive and peasant economies leveling mechanisms play a crucial role in inhibiting aggrandizement by individuals or by special groups." These leveling mechanisms assume a variety of forms:

> forced loans to relatives or co-residents; a large feast following economic success; a rivalry of expenditures like the potlatch of the Northwest Coast Indians in which large amounts of valuable goods were destroyed; the ritual levies consequent on holding office in civil and religious hierarchies in Meso-America; or the giveaways of horses and goods of the Plains Indians. Most small-scale economies have a way of scrambling wealth to inhibit reinvestment in technical advance, and this prevents crystallization of class lines on an economic base.

In fact, independent wealth, the most precious of personal goals in bourgeois society, tends to be highly suspect in preliterate societies. Often it is taken as evidence that the wealthy individual is a sorcerer who has acquired his riches by a sinister compact with demonic powers. Wealth so acquired is "treasure," bewitched power concretized, the stuff from which mythology weaves its Faustian legends. The very "independence" of this wealth – its freedom from direct social control – implies a breach with the most basic of all primordial rules: the mutual obligations imposed by blood ties. The prevalence of the lineage system, as distinguished from "civilization's" territorial system, implies that, even if hierarchy and differentials in status exist, the community consists of kin; its wealth, as Patrick Malloy observes, must be "used to reinforce or expand social relations," not weaken or constrict them. Wealth can be acquired only within the parameters of the lineage system, and it effectively filters down to the community through the workings of the "leveling system." As Malloy astutely observes: the "richest man" in the community will frequently "be the worst off because he has given all of his material wealth away." He has definite obligations "to provide gifts when requested, take care of bride-wealth, and other important functions critical to the survival of the community."

Thus, nature still binds society to herself with the primal blood oath. This oath validates not only kinship as the basic fact of primordial social life but its complex network of rights and duties. Before hierarchy and domination can be consolidated into social classes and economic exploitation; before reciprocity can give way to the "free exchange" of commodities; before usufruct can be replaced by private property, and the "irreducible minimum" by toil as the norm for distributing the means of life – before this immensely vast complex can be dissolved and replaced by a class, exchange, and propertied one, the blood oath with all its claims must be broken.

Hierarchy and domination remain captive to the blood oath until an entirely new social terrain can be established to support class relations and the systematic exploitation of human by human. We must fix this *pre*class, indeed, *pre*economic, period in social development clearly in our minds because the vast ideological corpus of "modernity" – capitalism, particularly in its Western form – has been designed in large part to veil it from our vision. Even such notions as primitive communism, matriarchy, and social equality, so widely celebrated by radical anthropologists and theorists, play a mystifying role in perpetuating this veil instead of removing it. Lurking within the notion of primitive communism is the insidious concept of a "stingy nature," of a "natural scarcity" that dictates communal relations – as though a communal sharing of things were exogenous to humanity and must be imposed by survival needs to overcome the "innate" human egoism that "modernity" so often identifies with selfhood. Primitive communism also contains the concept of property, however communal in character, that identifies selfhood with ownership. Usufruct, as the transgression of proprietary claims in *any* form, is concealed by property as a public institution. Indeed, communal property is not so far removed conceptually and institutionally from "public property," "nationalized property," or "collectivized property" that the incubus of proprietorship can be said to be removed completely from the sensibility and practices of a communist society. Finally, "matriarchy," the rule of society by women instead of men, merely alters the nature of rule; it does not lead to its abolition. "Matriarchy" merely changes the gender of domination and thereby perpetuates domination as such.

"Natural scarcity," property, and rule thus persist in the very name of the critique of class society, exploitation, private property, and the acquisition of wealth. By veiling the primordial blood oath that constrains the development of hierarchy and domination into class society, economic exploitation, and property, the class critique merely replaces the constraints of kinship with the constraints of economics instead of transcending *both* to a higher realm of freedom. It reconstitutes bourgeois right by leaving property unchallenged by usufruct, rule unchallenged by nonhierarchical relationships, and scarcity unchallenged by an abundance from which an ethical selectivity of needs can be derived. The more critical substrate of usufruct, reciprocity, and the irreducible minimum is papered over *by a less fundamental* critique: the critique of private property, of injustice in the distribution of the means of life, and of an unfair return for labor. Marx's own critique of justice in his remarks on the Gotha Program remains one of the most important contributions he made to radical social theory, but its economistic limitations are evident in the tenor of the work as a whole.

The Rise of the State
(from *From Urbanization to Cities*, 1987)

Contrary to rationalistic and contractual image of the state, state institutions emerged slowly, uncertainly, and precariously out of a social milieu that was distinctly nonstatist in character. In fact, the social and organic sources of the state had to be meticulously reworked before they could give rise to state institutions. The ancient temple corporation, actually a religious legitimation of tribal collectivity and public control of land, seems to have been the most likely source of the Near Eastern state. This was a time when priests commonly became kings or, at least, when the kingship often took on a priestly character. In either case the temple and palace monumentalized as well as deified the tribal community.

Despite the increasing secularization of the state, notably in Greece and Rome, the state never completely lost its religious trappings and its function as the custodian of the collectivistic community. This attribute, whether as an ensemble of feudal nobles or a monarchy and ultimately as an absolutist empire, remained with it well into recent times. The traditional "head of state," be he a lord or a king, always remained the "father of his people," whether by divine right or as a divinity in his own right. Hence, prior to the rise of republican systems of governance, the state always appeared not as a constituted phenomenon but as a reworking of a very traditional, organic, patriarchal, indeed tribalistic body of relationships in which power was not simply conferred by the community, as in the case of elected kingships, but inherited along lineage and blood lines in a manner redolent of the ancient tribalist blood tie. The present always entails a reworking of the past, a transmutation rather than a dissolution of traditional forms to meet new needs and imperatives.

It is notable that the rise of the centralized nation-state in Europe also followed this archaic and highly organic process of transmutation of old into new. Indeed, until "the age of the democratic revolutions," to use the title of R. R. Palmer's distinguished book, it was not through the constitution of new states but the recovery of ancient rights that king and community were thrown into civil war with each other, a conflict that often took the shape of monarchy against municipality. Both parties sought not to innovate new forms of governance but to restore old ones from the past. Characteristically, the earliest form of the European nation-state appears not as the emergence of a national economy, significant as this development proved to be, but as the increasing sovereignty of the kingly household itself – the monarchical *oikos* – and the image of the "nation" as a kingly patrimony. . . .

What makes the English state interesting is the challenge it raises to simplistic theories of state formation and rule. I refer to its organic roots and its evolution out of household offices. The English state was born not out of an administrative body of autonomous departments but rather out of the personal responsibilities of the king's servants – his immediate household coterie – often in opposition to the doubtful loyalties of the king's own feudal barons. Perhaps the foremost of these royal servants was the king's personal secretary, his chancellor, who carried the royal seal and coordinated the emerging departments that comprised the administrative portion of the royal court. In time the chancellor became the pole around which an increasing number of clerks, experts, and specialists in various governmental areas, and overseers of what was to become a fairly complex executive authority, collected to form the all-important English chancery. Almost every aspect of monarchical rule fell within its purview, principally the king's exchequer, who saw to the collection of taxes and Henry II's professional judiciary.

In fact, the English state was formed largely from the king's bedroom, dining table, men-in-waiting, and household clergy, not from constituted principles of government that spoke in the interests of a specific "ruling class." Class theories of the "origins of the state" to the contrary notwithstanding, the English state of the Middle Ages began as the elaboration of a patrimony rather than as the institution-alization of one class's authority over that of another. The English barons, who were to view the formation of this state with suspicion and later with overt hostility, found it difficult to claim it as their own. A continual tension existed – occasionally expressing itself in a violent form – between the baronial infrastructure of English medieval society and the monarchy, which formed the originating impulse of the authentic, fairly complete state. In its patrimonial form, the English state is no exception to the "origins of the state" generally; this mode of state formation is very similar to the way in which the "barbarian" chiefdoms of an earlier tribal society gradually extended their power from networks furnished by their personal retainers and clans. The journey from valet to prime minister, amusing as the juxtaposition may seem, is closer to the truth of state formation than the more sociological idea that the state emerged as an agency of class interest – whatever it was to become later in history.

I have dwelt in some detail on the origins of the English state – in time to be regarded as the prototype of the nation-state *par excellence* – not because of its uniqueness but rather because of its continuity with the ancient past. The organic growth of the English monarchy parallels to a remarkable degree the rise of the *oikos* forms of statehood. Historically, these forms go back to early Egypt, Persia, Babylonia, and even Rome before the empire became heavily bureaucratized. . . .

By the end of the twelfth century, France had already begun to catch up with England by creating *officiers du roi* (officials of the king) who shared power with the French barons in the traditional royal council. By degrees, the French began to outpace their English rivals. Functionaries, emerging from the royal household, acquired expanding administrative roles so that the kingly servants were soon to be royal bureaucrats rather than household administrators. . . . In time, the immense French bureaucracy of the sixteenth and seventeenth centuries, in theory answerable only to the monarchy, acquired a life – indeed, an outlook – of its own. The emergence of a bureaucratic sensibility, permeating all levels of French society, can hardly be emphasized too strongly. A new, almost ubiquitous "nobility of the robe," ennobled more as functionaries of the monarchy than by virtue of birth, began to overshadow the hereditary "nobility of the sword." In contrast to so much of feudal Europe, the sons of the French middle classes began to regard the royal bureaucracy rather than the clerical hierarchy as the avenue toward upward mobility and power, a shift in perspective that linked the French "bourgeoisie," whatever that word meant some two centuries ago, to the monarchy more tightly than historians of "class conflict" would have us believe. The French Revolution, conceived as the "classic bourgeois revolution" of emerging capitalism, was to test this "class analysis" in the fiery crucible of insurrection, with more dismal results than later, nineteenth-century historians suspected. . . .

What is most intriguing is that neither absolutism nor the rise of a nation-state provides us with an adequate explanation for the rise of a "national economy," as Hannah Arendt suggests. . . . Although European nation-states from the sixteenth century onward created the arena for a national economy, they did not necessarily create the forces that shaped it. Absolutism, which sculpted a sense of nationhood out of feudal parochialism, played a very crucial role: it not only supplanted localism with nationalism; it also stifled a highly decentralistic, localistic, and spontaneous society, marked by a rich diversity of cultural, economic and communal attributes, replacing it with increasingly homogenized lifeways, bureaucratized institutions, and centralized state forms. In some cases, this absolutist alternative favored the later expansion of a market economy; in others, it led to state parasitism and outright regression. In all cases, however, it turned localist politics into nationalist statecraft, divesting citizenship of its classical attributes and turning vital, empowered, and strongly etched men and women into passive, disempowered, and obedient "subjects."

This shift from a living people to deadened subjects did not occur without furious resistance. A belief in autonomy, regional and local identity, and citizen empowerment ran very high between the late Middle Ages and fairly recent times. The battle to retain these distinctly political qualities and rights was to be fought not in national political parties or by professional statesmen; rather, it was conducted on the level of village, town, neighborhood, and city life, where the ideals of confederation were to be opposed to demands for a nation-state and the values of decentralization were to be opposed to those of centralization. What lay in the balance was not only the future of the town and countryside but the development of political institutions as opposed to state institutions – and an active citizenry as opposed to a passive "constituency."

The Rise of Capitalism
(from *From Urbanization to Cities*, 1987)

The market society that we call capitalism – a society that tends to reduce all citizens to mere buyers and sellers and debases all the ecologically varied social relationships produced by history to the exchange of objects called commodities – did not "evolve" out of the feudal era. It literally exploded into being in Europe, particularly England, during the eighteenth and especially nineteenth centuries, although it had existed in the ancient world, the Middle Ages, and with growing significance in the mixed economy of the West from the fourteenth century up to the seventeenth. It is still spreading around the world – intensively in its traditional Euro-American center and extensively in the non-European world. Its forms have varied from the largely mercantile (its earliest kind) through the industrial (its more recent eighteenth- and nineteenth-century forms) to the statist, corporate, and multinational forms of our own time. It has slowly penetrated from its special spheres, such as market arenas of exchange and the production of commodities in cottages and later in factories, into domestic life itself, such as the family and neighborhood. This is a fairly recent "advance" that can be dated most strikingly from the midpoint of the twentieth century. Its invasion of neighborhoods, indeed of villages and small towns into the recesses of domestic or familial relationships, has subverted the social bond itself and threatens to totally undermine any sense of community and ecological balance and diversity in social life.

Moreover, the newly gained dominance of the capitalist market relationship over all other forms of production and consociation is a major source of what I have denoted "urbanization" – the explosion of the city itself into vast urban agglomerations that threaten the very integrity of city life and citizenship. What makes the market society we call capitalism unique, even by contrast to its early mercantile form, is that it is an ever-expansive, accumulative, and in this respect cancerous economic system whose "law of life" is to "grow or die." Capitalism in its characteristically modern and "dominant" form threatens not only to undermine every "natural economy" (to use Marx's own term), be it small-scale agriculture, artisanship, or simple exchange relationships; it threatens to undermine every dimension of "organic society," be it the kinship tie, communitarian forms of association, systems of self-governance, and localist allegiances – the sense of home and place. Owing to its metastatic invasion of every aspect of life by means of monetization and what Immanuel Wallerstein calls "commodification," it threatens the integrity of the natural world – soil, flora, fauna, and the complex economies that have made present-day life-forms and relationships possible by turning everything "natural" into an inorganic, essentially synthetic form.[2] Soil is being turned into sand, variegated landscapes into level and simplified ones, complex relationships into more primal forms such that the evolutionary clock is being turned back to a biotically earlier time when life was less varied in form and its range more limited in scope.

The effect of capitalism on the city has been nothing less than catastrophic. The commonly used term "urban cancer" can be taken literally to designate the extent to which the traditional *urbs* of the ancient world has been dissolved into a primal, ever-spreading, and destructive form that threatens to devour city and countryside alike. Growth in the special form that singles out modern capitalism from all earlier forms of economic life, including earlier forms of capitalism itself, has affected what we persist in calling the "city" by leading to the expansion of pavements, streets, houses, and industrial, commercial, and retail structures over the entire landscape, just as a cancer spreads over the body and invades its deepest recesses.

Cities, in turn, have begun to lose their form as distinctive cultural and physical entities, as humanly scaled and manageable political entities. Their functions have changed from ethical arenas with a uniquely humane, civilized form of consociation, free of all blood ties and family loyalties, into immense, overbearing, and anonymous marketplaces. They are becoming centers primarily of mass production and mass consumption, including culture as well as physically tangible objects. Indeed, culture has become objectivized into commodities, as have human relationships, which are increasingly being simplified and mediated by objects. The simplification of social life and the biosphere by a growth-oriented economy in which production and consumption become ends in themselves is yielding the simplification of the human psyche itself. The strong sense of individuation that marked the people of the mixed society preceding capitalism is giving way to a receptive consumer and taxpayer, a passive observer of life rather than an active participant in it, lacking economic roots that support self-assertiveness and community roots that foster participation in social life. Citizenship itself, conceived as a function of character formation, and politics, as part of *paideia* or the education of a social being, tend to wane into personal indifference to social problems. The decline of the citizen, more properly his or her dissolution into a being lost in a mass society – the human counterpart of the mass-produced object – is furthered by a burgeoning of structural gigantism that replaces the human scale and by a growing bureaucracy that replaces all the organic sinews that held precapitalist society together. The counselor is the humanistic counterpart of the indifferent bureaucrat and the counseling chamber is the structural counterpart of the governmental office.

Let it be said that this debasement of the ecological complexity of the city, of its politics, citizens, even of the individuals who people its streets and structures, is of very recent origin. It did not really begin in a manorial society, with its barons and serfs, food cultivators, and artisans, and all the "orders" we denote as feudal. Nor did it follow from those grossly misnamed revolutions, the "bourgeois-democratic" ones of England, America, and France, that ostensibly catapulted capital into political control of a society it presumably "controlled" economically during earlier generations. Rather, this development began to appear with technical innovations that made possible both the mass manufacture of cheap commodities and, what is crucially important, their increasingly rapid transportation into the deepest recesses of western Europe, inexpensive and highly competitive with the products of local artisans who had serviced their localities for centuries. It need hardly be emphasized that this development depended enormously for its success on the opening of colonial markets abroad: the Americas, Africa, and particularly Asia, the area where the English crown found its richest jewel, notably India.

It was the extraordinary combination of technical advances with the existence of a highly variegated society, relatively free of the cultural constraints on trade that prevailed in antiquity, that gave economic ascendancy to the capitalistic component of the mixed economy over all its other components. Neither wealth from the Americas nor the large monetary resources accumulated by port cities from long-distance trade fully explains the rise of industrial capitalism – a form of capitalism that more than any other penetrated into the very inner life of Europe. Had the wealth acquired from the New World been a decisive factor in creating industrial capitalism, Spain rather than England should have become its center, for it was Spanish conquistadores who initially plundered the Aztec and Inca empires and brought their precious metals to Europe. The very wealth these "empires" provided for the ascendant nation-state in Spain served to weaken town life in the Iberian peninsula and provide the means for absolute monarchs to embark on an archaic program of continental empire building that eventually ruined Spanish cities and the countryside alike.

Nor did long-distance trade provide the most important sources for capitalizing industrial development. Rather it fostered consumption more than production, the dissolute lifeway that makes for a diet of luxuries instead of the parsimonious habits that steer investment into new means of production. Indeed, too much state centralization and too much commerce, despite the wealth they initially generated, ultimately led to excessive expenditures for territorial expansion and high living by elite groups in all the orders of a courtly society. That nation-building, increased centralization, or more properly, national consolidation prepared the way for industrial capitalism by opening more "hinterlands" to trade is patently clear. So, too, did the increases in the population of dispossessed, propertyless hands, whether as a result of land enclosures or normal demographic growth, hands that were available for a factory system that had yet to appear on the economic horizon. Europe, in effect, was more open than any part of the world to the expansion of its capitalist component along industrial lines. This was especially true of England. . . . What pushed the capitalist component of this mixed economy into a nation that could regard itself as the "workshop of the world" in the nineteenth century was a series of inventions that made the factory system and the distribution of its wares possible.

Nor need we be concerned with whether the needs of a "rising bourgeoisie" produced the Industrial Revolution or the Industrial Revolution gave rise to the "bourgeoisie," which in any case was *always* a presence in all the major cities of Europe. Factories, in fact, had begun to appear in eighteenth- and even seventeenth-century England long before an industrial technology had emerged. Whether the "bourgeoisie" entered into the productive sphere rather than the commercial, it tried to bring labor together and rationalize output even with tools; hence a strictly technological interpretation of the *rise* of industrial capitalism would be greatly misleading. My concern here is how industrial capitalism managed to gain ascendancy over *other* forms of production, including commercial capitalism, and alter all social relations that encountered its power. Waterwheels had preceded the steam engine as a prime mover, and worksheds organized around simple tools had preceded mechanized factories. But without the inventions that introduced the Industrial Revolution in the late eighteenth and early nineteenth centuries, it is doubtful that industrial capitalism could have impacted so powerfully on Europe and ultimately on the entire world. . . .

Within a span of some two generations, England was transformed on a scale unprecedented in the history of western Europe. Friedrich Engels's *The Condition of the Working Class in England,* a period piece based on personal observations in 1844, could justly call the changes introduced by the new industrial inventions – principally in textiles, metallurgy, and transportation – a historic change of unprecedented proportion. The rapidity of the transformation is what makes these changes so startling in a domain of human endeavor – technology – which had developed over centuries at a slow, piecemeal pace. The social and cultural ramifications of this technological revolution were nothing less than monumental.

The Market Society
(from *The Ecology of Freedom*, 1982)

By the middle of the present century, large-scale market operations had colonized every aspect of social and personal life. The buyer–seller relationship – a relationship that lies at the very core of the market – became the all-pervasive substitute for human relationships at the most molecular level of social, indeed personal life. To "buy cheaply" and "sell dearly" places the parties involved in the exchange process in an inherently antagonistic posture: they are potential rivals for each other's goods. The commodity – as distinguished from the gift, which is meant to create alliances, foster association, and consolidate sociality – leads to rivalry, dissociation, and asociality.

Although philosophers from Aristotle to Hegel articulated their concern for the dissociative role of a commerce and industry organized for exchange, society itself had long buffered exchange with a social etiquette – one that still lingers on in the vestigial face-to-face archaic marketplace of the bazaar. Here one does not voice a demand for goods, compare prices, and engage in the market's universal duel called bargaining. Rather, etiquette requires that the exchange process begin gracefully and retain its communal dimension. It opens with the serving of beverages, an exchange of news and gossip, some personal chit-chat, and, in time, expressions of admiration for the wares at hand. One leads to the exchange process tangentially. The bargain, if struck, is a bond, a compact sealed by time-honored ethical imperatives.

The apparently noncommercial ambience of this exchange process should not be viewed as mere canniness or hypocrisy. It reflects the limits that precapitalist society imposed on exchange to avoid the latent impersonality of trade, as well as its potential meanness of spirit, its insatiable appetite for gain, its capacity to subvert all social limits to private material interest, to dissolve all traditional standards of community and consociation, to subordinate the needs of the body politic to egoistic concerns.

But it was not only for these reasons that trade was viewed warily. Precapitalist society may well have seen in the exchange of commodities a return of the inorganic, of the substitution of things for living human relationships. These objects could certainly be viewed symbolically as tokens of consociation, alliance, and mutuality – which is precisely what the gift was meant to represent. But divested of this symbolic meaning, these mere things or commodities could acquire socially corrosive traits. Left unchecked and unbuffered, they might well vitiate all forms of human consociation and ultimately dissolve society itself. The transition from gift to commodity, in effect, could yield the disintegration of the community into a marketplace, the consanguineous or ethical union between people into rivalry and aggressive egotism.

That the triumph of the commodity over the gift was possible only after vast changes in human social relationships has been superbly explored in the closing portion of *Capital*. I need not summarize Marx's devastating narration and analysis of capitalist accumulation, its "general law," and particularly the sweeping dislocation of the English peasantry from the fifteenth century onward. The gift itself virtually disappeared as the objectification of association. It lingered on merely as a by-product of ceremonial functions. The traditional etiquette that buffered the exchange process was replaced by a completely impersonal, predatory – and today, an increasingly electronic – process. Price came first, quality came later; and the very things that were once symbols rather than mere objects for use and exchange became fetishized, together with the "needs" they were meant to satisfy. Suprahuman forces now seemed to take command over the ego itself. Even self-interest, which Greek social theory viewed as the most serious threat to the unity of the *polis,* seemed to be governed by a market system that divested the subject of its very capacity to move freely through the exchange process as an autonomous buyer and seller.

Ironically, modern industry, having derived from archaic systems of commerce and retailing, has returned to its commercial origins with a vengeful self-hatred marked by a demeaning rationalization of trade itself. The shopping mall with its extravagant areas delivered over to parked motor vehicles, its sparseness of sales personnel, its cooing "muzak," its dazzling array of shelved goods, its elaborate surveillance system, its lack of all warmth and human intercourse, its cruelly deceptive packaging, and its long checkout counters that indifferently and impersonally record the exchange process – all speak to a denaturing of consociation at levels of life that deeply affront every human sensibility and the sacredness of the very goods that are meant to support life itself.

What is crucially important here is that this world penetrates personal as well as economic life. The shopping mall is the agora of modern society, the civic center of a totally economic and inorganic world. It works its way into every personal haven from capitalist relations and imposes its centricity on every aspect of domestic life. The highways that lead to its parking lots and its production centers devour communities and neighborhoods; its massive command of retail trade devours the family-owned store; the subdivisions that cluster around it devour farmland; the motor vehicles that carry worshippers to its temples are self-enclosed capsules that preclude all human contact. Not only does the inorganic return to industry and the marketplace; it calcifies and dehumanizes the most intimate relationships between people in the presumably invulnerable world of the bedroom and nursery. The massive dissolution of personal and social ties that comes with the return of the inorganic transforms the extended family into the nuclear family and finally delivers the individual over to the purveyors of singles' bars.

With the hollowing out of community by the market system, with its loss of structure, articulation, and form, comes the concomitant hollowing out of personality itself. Just as the spiritual and institutional ties that linked human beings together into vibrant social relations are eroded by the mass market, so the sinews that make for subjectivity, character, and self-definition are divested of form and meaning. The isolated, seemingly autonomous ego that bourgeois society celebrated as the highest achievement of "modernity" turns out to be the mere husk of a once fairly rounded individual whose very completeness as an ego was responsible because he or she was rooted in a fairly rounded and complete community.

As the inorganic replaces the organic in nature, so the inorganic replaces the organic in society and personality. The simplification of the natural world has its uncanny parallel in the simplification of society and subjectivity. The homogenization of ecosystems goes hand in hand with the homogenization of the social environment and the so-called individuals who people it. The intimate association of the domination of human by human with the notion of the domination of nature terminates not only in the notion of domination as such; its most striking feature is the *kind* of prevailing nature – an *inorganic* nature – that replaces the organic nature that humans once viewed so reverently.

We can never disembed ourselves from nature – any more than we can disembed ourselves from our own viscera. The technocratic "utopia" of personalized automata remains a hollow myth. The therapies that seek to adjust organic beings to inorganic conditions merely produce lifeless, inorganic, and depersonalized automata. Hence nature always affirms its existence as the matrix for social and personal life, a matrix in which life is always embedded by definition. By rationalizing and simplifying society and personality, we do not divest it of its natural attributes; rather, we brutally destroy its organic attributes. Thus nature never simply coexists with us; it is part of every aspect of our structure and being. To turn back natural evolution from more complex forms of organic beings to simpler ones, from the organic to the inorganic, entails the turning back of society and social development from more complex to simpler forms.

Dispelling the myth that *our* society is more complex than earlier cultures requires short shrift; our complexity is strictly technical, not cultural; our effluvium of "individuality" is more neurotic and psychopathic, not more unique or more intricate. "Modernity" reached its apogee between the decades preceding the French Revolution and the 1840s, after which industrial capitalism fastened its grip on social life. Its career, with a modest number of exceptions, has yielded a grim denaturing of humanity and society. Since the middle of the present century, even the vestiges of its greatness – apart from dramatic explosions like the 1960s – have all but disappeared from virtually every realm of experience.

What has largely replaced the sinews that held community and personality together is an all-encompassing, coldly depersonalizing bureaucracy. The agency and the bureaucrat have become the substitutes for the family, the town and neighborhood, the personal support structures of people in crisis, and the supernatural and mythic figures that afforded power and tutelary surveillance over the destiny of the individual. With no other structures to speak of but the bureaucratic agency, society has not merely been riddled by bureaucracy; it has all but become a bureaucracy in which everyone, as Camus was wont to say, has been reduced to a functionary. Personality as such has become congruent with the various documents, licenses, and records that define one's place in the world. More sacred than such documents as passports, which are the archaic tokens of citizenship, a motor vehicle license literally validates one's identity, and a credit card becomes the worldwide coinage of exchange.

The legacy of domination thus culminates in the growing together of the State and society – and with it, a dissolution of the family, community, mutual aid, and social commitment. Even a sense of one's personal destiny disappears into the bureaucrat's office and filing cabinet. History itself will be read in the microfilm records and computer tapes of the agencies that now form the authentic institutions of society. Psychological categories have indeed "become political categories," as Marcuse observed in the opening lines of his *Eros and Civilization,* but in a pedestrian form that exceeds his most doleful visions. The Superego is no longer formed by the father or even by domineering social institutions; it is formed by the faceless people who preside over the records of birth and death, of religious affiliation and educational pedigree, of "mental health" and psychological proclivities, of vocational training and job acquisition, of marriage and divorce certificates, of credit ratings and bank accounts; in short, of the endless array of licenses, tests, contracts, grades, and personality traits that define the status of the individual in society. Political categories have replaced psychological categories in much the same sense that an electrocardiograph has replaced the heart. Under state capitalism, even economic categories become political categories. Domination fulfills its destiny in the ubiquitous, all-pervasive State; its legacy reaches its denouement in the dissolution, indeed the complete disintegration, of a richly organic society into an inorganic one – a terrifying destiny that the natural world shares with the social.

Reason, which was expected to dispel the dark historic forces to which a presumably unknowing humanity had been captive, now threatens to become one of these very forces in the form of rationalization. It now enhances the efficiency of domination. The great project of Western speculative thought – to render humanity self-conscious – stands before a huge abyss: a yawning chasm into which the self and consciousness threaten to disappear.

NOTES

1 Murray Bookchin, *Remaking Society* (Montreal: Black Rose Books, 1989), p. 32.
2 See Immanuel Wallerstein, *Historical Capitalism* (London: Verso Editions, 1983).

CHAPTER FIVE

Scarcity and Post-Scarcity

Introduction

For all but the privileged few, history has been in great part a chronicle of material scarcity – that is, an insufficiency of the goods and services that people need and value – all too often as a result of an unequal distribution of wealth. At best, people living under conditions of material scarcity must spend an inordinate amount of time working to produce the goods they need for material survival, or else earn a livelihood. This necessity, Bookchin maintains, reduces people to a quasi-animalistic existence; it prevents them from fulfilling their potential for rationality and freedom and thus from becoming fully human.

At the same time, material scarcity has also been an ideology as well as a reality – in particular, ruling elites have used it as a rationale for authoritarianism – both when scarcity is real, and when it has been artificially induced for the benefit of the few. There are not enough goods to meet the needs and desires of everyone, we are told, because resources are scarce – that is, because nature is "stingy." As a result of this "stinginess," an authority such as the state, this ideology holds, is necessary in order to prevent people from struggling against one another, in a war of all against all, to obtain what they can; it is further necessary, they insisted, to organize humanity's domination of nonhuman nature, in order to generate goods. Material scarcity, says Bookchin, thus

> provided the historic rationale of the development of the patriarchal family, private property, class domination, and the state; it nourished the great divisions in hierarchical society that pitted town against country, mind against sensuousness, work against play, individual against society, and finally, the individual against himself.[1]

Because of scarcity's pernicious social and political consequences, its elimination has been a longstanding vision in the socialist tradition. The desire for technologies of production that would reduce toil and create abundance dates back at least to Robert Owen, who in 1818 announced glowingly that an "age of plenty" for humankind was dawning, one in which "new scientific power will soon render human labor of little avail in the creation of wealth."[2]

In the United States of the early 1960s, the postwar technological revolution seemed to fulfill the dream of Owen and others like him. Some New Left commentators, to be sure, took a less sanguine view, warning that the new technologies of automation and cybernation would have negative social consequences, such as unemployment. According to a 1963 paper endorsed by Students for a Democratic Society (SDS):

> Automation has sharply reduced the demand for employment, mass production industries, agriculture, and many trade and service enterprises. During the fifties, for example, manufacturers were able to increase productive output by 70 percent, with no increase whatever in the number of manufacturing workers. Just when the need for workers was being reduced, a radical increase in the number of people needing jobs was taking place. . . . Thus advancing technology and an exploding population create an enormous employment problem.[3]

And Free Speech Movement leader Mario Savio warned that one of the "most crucial problems facing the United States today" was the "problem of automation," in which machines put people out of work.[4]

Herbert Marcuse, for his part, felt that the "objective abundance" of the 1960s would have ambiguous social consequences. On the one hand, it would have the desirable consequence of making possible the liberation of the libido; but it would also generate the artificial satisfactions of consumerism and a new form of imperialism.

But others in the socialist tradition followed Owen and welcomed the advent of automation and cybernation, and the revolution in production they created, as a crucial step in ending the age-old problem of scarcity. Bookchin was one of them; in contrast to Marcuse's pessimism, he emphasized the possibilities of abundance, not only for erotic liberation but for social and political revolution. These technologies, he argued, held the potential, for the first time in human history, to abolish scarcity and want on a worldwide basis and usher in a life of plenty for all. In effect, he argued that they were rendering material scarcity obsolete.

Significantly, by bringing about the end of material scarcity, he argued, these technologies are depriving the ruling classes of a critical rationale for their authority. Equally important, by enabling humanity to pass to abundance, they are making possible a reduction of onerous and tedious toil, thus providing people with the free time they need in order to participate fully in political and social life.

Capitalism, Bookchin acknowledges, is perverting the use of cybernation and automation, like all other technologies, for oppressive rather than liberatory ends. But if they could be appropriated for liberatory ends, the material abundance and reduction in toil they generate could undergird a society of what he calls "post-scarcity." That is, they could constitute the technical means for the creation of utopia.

"Post-scarcity," as Bookchin uses the word, does not mean material abundance alone; rather, the technological means for utopia have to be set in the context of a society that is itself utopian: an ecological, rational society.

> The human relationships and psyches of the individual in a post-scarcity society must fully reflect the freedom, security, and self-expression that this abundance makes possible. Post-scarcity society, in short, is the fulfillment of the social and cultural potentialities latent in a technology of abundance.[5]

Bookchin's ecological society would depend on at least two types of technology: the ecological technologies of renewable energy, and the productive technologies that would eliminate scarcity. The judicious application of both would make possible a free society without toil or material want, without hierarchy or domination, and even without repression or guilt. In such a society people would finally have the material base to fulfill their potentialities for freedom and rationality as human beings.

Conditions of Freedom
(from "Post-Scarcity Anarchism," 1967)

All the successful revolutions of the past have been particularistic revolutions of minority classes seeking to assert their specific interests over those of society as a whole. The great bourgeois revolutions of modern times offered an ideology of sweeping political reconstitution, but in reality they merely certified the social dominance of the bourgeoisie, giving formal political expression to the economic ascendancy of capital. The lofty notions of the "nation," the "free citizen," of "equality before the law," concealed the mundane reality of the centralized state, the atomized isolated man, the dominance of bourgeois interest. Despite their sweeping ideological claims, the particularistic revolutions replaced the rule of one class with that of another, one system of exploitation with another, one system of toil with another, and one system of psychological repression with another.

What is unique about our era is that the particularistic revolution has now been subsumed by the possibility of the generalized revolution – complete and totalistic. Bourgeois society, if it achieved nothing else, revolutionized the means of production on a scale unprecedented in history. This technological revolution, culminating in cybernation, has created the objective, quantitative basis for a world without class rule, exploitation, toil, or material want. The means now exist for the development of the rounded man, the total man, freed of guilt and the workings of authoritarian modes of training, and given over to desire and the sensuous apprehension of the marvelous. It is now possible to conceive of man's future experience in terms of a coherent process in which the bifurcations of thought and activity, mind and sensuousness, discipline and spontaneity, individuality and community, man and nature, town and country, education and life, work and play are all resolved, harmonized, and organically wedded in a qualitatively new realm of freedom. Just as the particularized revolution produced a particularized, bifurcated society, so the generalized revolution can produce an organically unified, many-sided community. The great wound opened by propertied society in the form of the "social question" can now be healed.

That freedom must be conceived of in human terms, not in animal terms – in terms of life, not of survival – is clear enough. Men do not remove their ties of bondage and become fully human merely by divesting themselves of social domination and obtaining freedom in its *abstract* form. They must also be free *concretely*: free from material want, from toil, from the burden of devoting the greater part of their time – indeed, the greater part of their lives – to the struggle with necessity. To have seen these material preconditions for human freedom, to have emphasized that freedom presupposes free time and the material abundance for abolishing free time as a social privilege, is the great contribution of Karl Marx to modern revolutionary theory.

By the same token, the *preconditions* for freedom must not be mistaken for the *conditions* of freedom. The *possibility* of liberation does not constitute its *reality*. Along with its positive aspects, technological advance has a distinctly negative, socially regressive side. If it is true that technological progress enlarges the historical potentiality for freedom, it is also true that the bourgeois control of technology reinforces the established organization of society and everyday life. Technology and the resources of abundance furnish capitalism with the means for assimilating large sections of society to the established system of hierarchy and authority. They provide the system with the weaponry, the detecting devices, and the propaganda media for the threat as well as the reality of massive repression. By their centralistic nature, the resources of abundance reinforce the monopolistic, centralistic, and bureaucratic tendencies in the political apparatus. In short, they furnish the state with historically unprecedented means for manipulating and mobilizing the entire environment of life – and for perpetuating hierarchy, exploitation, and unfreedom. . . .

THE REDEMPTIVE DIALECTIC

Is there a redemptive dialectic that can guide the social development in the direction of an anarchic society where people will attain full control over their daily lives? Or does the social dialectic come to an end with capitalism, its possibilities sealed off by the use of a highly advanced technology for repressive and co-optative purposes?

We must learn here from the limits of Marxism, a project which, understandably in a period of material scarcity, anchored the social dialectic and the contradictions of capitalism in the economic realm. Marx, it has been emphasized, examined the *preconditions for* liberation, not the *conditions of* liberation. The Marxian critique is rooted in the past, in the era of material want and relatively limited technological development. Even its humanistic theory of alienation turns primarily on the issue of work and man's alienation from the product of his labor. Today, however, capitalism is a parasite on the future, a vampire that survives on the technology and resources of freedom. The industrial capitalism of Marx's time organized its commodity relations around a prevailing system of material scarcity; the state capitalism of our time organizes its commodity relations around a prevailing system of material abundance. A century ago scarcity had to be endured; today it has to be enforced – hence the importance of the state in the present era. It is not that modern capitalism has resolved its contradictions and annulled the social dialectic but rather that the social dialectic and the contradictions of capitalism have expanded from the economic to the hierarchical realms of society, from the abstract "historic" domain to the concrete minutiae of everyday experience, from the arena of survival to the arena of life.

The dialectic of bureaucratic state capitalism originates in the contradiction between the repressive character of commodity society and the enormous potential freedom opened by technological advance. This contradiction also opposes the exploitative organization of society to the natural world – a world that includes not only the natural environment but also man's "nature" – his Eros-derived impulses. The contradiction between the exploitative organization of society and the natural environment is beyond co-optation: the atmosphere, the waterways, the soil, and the ecology required for human survival are not redeemable by reforms, concessions, or modifications of strategic policy. There is no technology that can reproduce atmospheric oxygen in sufficient quantities to sustain life on this planet. There is no substitute for the hydrological systems of the earth. There is no technique for removing massive environmental pollution by radioactive isotopes, pesticides, lead, and petroleum wastes. Nor is there the faintest evidence that bourgeois society will relent at any time in the foreseeable future in its disruption of vital ecological processes, in its exploitation of natural resources, in its use of the atmosphere and waterways as dumping areas for wastes, or in its cancerous mode of urbanization and land use.

Even more immediate is the contradiction between the exploitative organization of society and man's Eros-derived impulses – a contradiction that manifests itself as the banalization and impoverishment of experience in a bureaucratically manipulated, impersonal mass society. The Eros-derived impulses in man can be repressed and sublimated, but they can never be eliminated. They are renewed with every birth of a human being and with every generation of youth. It is not surprising today that the young, more than any economic class or stratum, articulate the life-impulses in humanity's nature – the urgings of desire, sensuousness, and the lure of the marvelous. Thus the biological matrix, from which hierarchical society emerged ages ago, reappears at a new level with the era that marks the end of hierarchy, only now this matrix is saturated with social phenomena. Short of manipulating humanity's germ plasm, the life-impulses can be annulled only with the annihilation of man himself.

The contradictions within bureaucratic state capitalism permeate all the hierarchical forms developed and overdeveloped by bourgeois society. The hierarchical forms that nurtured propertied society for ages and promoted its development – the state, city, centralized economy, bureaucracy, patriarchal family, and marketplace – have reached their historic limits. They have exhausted their social functions as modes of stabilization. It is not a question of whether these hierarchical forms were ever "progressive" in the Marxian sense of the term. . . . Today these forms constitute the target of all the revolutionary forces that are generated by modern capitalism, and whether one sees their outcome as nuclear catastrophe or ecological disaster, *they now threaten the very survival of humanity.*

With the development of hierarchical forms into a threat to the very existence of humanity, the social dialectic, far from being annulled, acquires a new dimension. It poses the "social question" in an entirely new way. If man had to acquire the conditions of survival in order to live (as Marx emphasized), now he must acquire the conditions of life in order to survive. By this inversion of the relationship between survival and life, revolution acquires a new sense of urgency. No longer are we faced with Marx's famous choice of socialism or barbarism; we are confronted with the more drastic alternatives of anarchism or annihilation. The problems of necessity and survival have become congruent with the problems of freedom and life.

The Problem of Want and Work
(from "Toward a Liberatory Technology," 1965)

Virtually all the utopias, theories, and revolutionary programs of the early nineteenth century were faced with the problem of *necessity* – of how to allocate labor and material goods at a relatively low level of technological development. These problems permeated revolutionary thought in a way comparable only to the impact of original sin on Christian theology. The fact that men would have to devote a substantial portion of their time to toil, for which they would get scant return, formed a major premise of all socialist ideology – authoritarian and libertarian, utopian and scientific, Marxist and anarchist. Implicit in the Marxist notion of a planned economy was the fact, incontestably clear in Marx's own day, that socialism would still be burdened by relatively scarce resources. Men would have to plan – in effect, to restrict – the distribution of goods and would have to rationalize – in effect, to intensify – the use of labor. Toil, under socialism, would be a duty, a responsibility that every able-bodied individual would have to undertake. Even Proudhon advanced this dour view. "Yes, life is a struggle," he wrote. "But this struggle is not between man and man – it is between man and Nature; and it is each one's duty to share it."[6] This austere, almost biblical emphasis on struggle and duty reflects the harsh quality of socialist thought during the Industrial Revolution.

The problem of want and work – an age-old problem perpetuated by the early Industrial Revolution – produced the great divergence in revolutionary ideas between socialism and anarchism. In the event of a revolution, freedom would still be circumscribed by necessity: How was this world of necessity to be "administered"? How could the allocation of goods and duties be decided? Marx left this decision to a state power – a transitional "proletarian" state power to be sure, but nevertheless a coercive body, established above society. According to Marx, the state would "wither away" as technology developed and enlarged the domain of freedom, granting humanity material plenty and the leisure to control its affairs directly. This strange calculus, in which necessity and freedom were mediated by the state, differed very little politically from the common run of bourgeois–democratic radical opinion in the nineteenth century. The anarchist hope for the abolition of the state, on the other hand, rested largely on a belief in the viability of man's social instincts. Bakunin, for example, thought custom would compel individuals with antisocial proclivities to abide by collectivist values and needs without obliging society to use coercion. Kropotkin, who exercised more influence among anarchists in this area of speculation, invoked man's propensity for mutual aid – essentially a social instinct – as the guarantor of solidarity in an anarchist community (a concept that he derived from his study of natural and social evolution).

The fact remains, however, that both the Marxist and the anarchist answers to the problem of want and work were shot through with ambiguity. The realm of necessity remained brutally present; it could not be conjured away by mere theory and speculation. The Marxists could hope to administer necessity by means of a state, and the anarchists to deal with it through free communities, but given the limited technological development of their time, in the last analysis both schools depended on an act of faith to cope with the problem of want and work. Anarchists could argue against Marxists that any transitional state, however revolutionary its rhetoric and democratic its structure, would be self-perpetuating; it would tend to become an end in itself and to preserve the very material and social conditions it had been created to remove. For such a state to "wither away" (that is, to promote its own dissolution) would require leaders and bureaucrats of superhuman moral qualities. The Marxists, in turn, could invoke history against the anarchists, showing that custom and mutualistic propensities have never been effective barriers to the pressures of material need, or to the onslaught of property, or to the development of exploitation and class domination. Accordingly, they could dismiss anarchism as an ethical doctrine that revived the mystique of "the natural man" and his inborn social virtues.

The problem of want and work – of the realm of necessity – was not satisfactorily resolved by either doctrine in the last century. It is to the lasting credit of anarchism that it uncompromisingly retained its high ideal of freedom – the ideal of spontaneous organization, community and the abolition of all authority – even though this ideal remained only a vision of the future, of the time when technology would eliminate the realm of necessity entirely. Marxism increasingly compromised its ideal of freedom, painfully qualifying it with transitional stages and political expediencies, until today it is an ideology of naked power, pragmatic efficiency, and social centralization almost indistinguishable from the ideologies of modern state capitalism. . . .

In retrospect, it is astonishing how long the problem of want and work cast its shadow over revolutionary theory. In a span of only nine decades – between 1850 and 1940 – Western society created, passed through, and evolved beyond two major epochs of technological history – the paleotechnic age of coal and steel, and the neotechnic age of electric power, synthetic chemicals, electricity, and internal combustion engines. Ironically, both ages of technology seem to have enhanced the importance of toil in society. As the number of industrial workers increased in proportion to other social classes, labor – more precisely toil – acquired an increasingly high status in revolutionary thought. During this period, the propaganda of the socialists often sounded like a paean to toil; not only was toil "ennobling," but the workers were extolled as the only useful individuals in the social fabric. They were endowed with a supposedly superior instinctive ability that made them the arbiters of philosophy, art, and social organization. This puritanical work ethic of the left did not diminish with the passage of time, and in fact it acquired a certain urgency in the 1930s. Mass unemployment made jobs and the social organization of labor the central themes of socialist propaganda in the 1930s. Instead of focusing their message on the emancipation of man from toil, socialists tended to depict socialism as a beehive of industrial activity, humming with work for all. Communists pointed to Russia as the land where every able-bodied individual was employed and where labor was continually in demand. Surprising as it may seem today, little more than a generation ago socialism was equated with a work-oriented society, and liberty with the material security provided by full employment. The world of necessity had subtly invaded and corrupted the ideal of freedom.

That the socialist notions of the last generation now seem anachronistic is not due to any superior insights that prevail today. The last three decades, particularly the late 1950s, mark a turning point in technological development, a technological revolution that has negated all the values, political schemes, and social perspectives held by mankind throughout all previous recorded history. After thousands of years of tortuous development, the countries of the Western world (and potentially all countries) are now confronted by the possibility of a materially abundant, even toilless era in which most of the means of life can be provided by machines. A new technology has developed that could largely replace the realm of necessity with the realm of freedom. So obvious is this fact to millions of people in the United States and Europe that it no longer requires elaborate explanations or theoretical exegeses. This technological revolution and the prospects it holds for society as a whole form the premises of radically new lifestyles among today's young people, a generation that is rapidly divesting itself of the values and age-old work-oriented traditions of its elders. Even recent demands for a guaranteed annual income faintly echo the new reality that currently permeates the thinking of the young. Owing to the development of a cybernetic technology, the notion of a toilless mode of life has become an article of faith to an ever-increasing number of young people.

Cybernation and Automation
(from "Toward a Liberatory Technology," 1965)

For the first time in history, technology has become open-ended. The potential for technological development, for providing machines as substitutes for labor, is virtually unlimited. Technology has finally passed from the realm of *invention* to that of *design* – from fortuitous discoveries to systematic innovations.

The meaning of this qualitative advance was stated in a rather freewheeling way by Vannevar Bush, the wartime director of the Office of Scientific Research and Development, in 1955:

> Suppose, fifty years ago, that someone had proposed making a device which would cause an automobile to follow a white line down the middle of the road, automatically and even if the driver fell asleep. . . . He would have been laughed at, and his idea would have been called preposterous. So it would have been then. But suppose someone called for such a device today, and was willing to pay for it, leaving aside the question of whether it would actually be of any genuine use whatever. Any number of concerns would stand ready to contract and build it. No real invention would be required. There are thousands of young men in the country to whom the design of such a device would be a pleasure. They would simply take off the shelf some photocells, thermionic tubes, servomechanisms, and relays, and if urged, they would build what they call a breadboard model, and it would work. The point is that the presence of a host of versatile, cheap, reliable gadgets, and the presence of men who understand fully all their queer ways, has rendered the building of automatic devices almost straightforward and routine. It is no longer a question of whether they can be built, it is rather a question of whether they are worth building.[7]

. . . Several developments have brought us to this open end, and a number of practical applications have profoundly affected the role of labor in industry and agriculture. Perhaps the most obvious has been the increasing interpenetration of scientific abstraction, mathematics, and analytic methods with the concrete, pragmatic, and rather mundane tasks of industry. This order of relationships is relatively new. Traditionally, speculation, generalization, and rational activity were sharply divorced from technology. This chasm reflected the sharp split between the leisured and the working classes in ancient and medieval society. Aside from the inspired works of a few rare men, applied science did not come into its own until the Renaissance, and it began to flourish only in the eighteenth and nineteenth centuries. The men who personify the application of science to technological innovation are not the inventive tinkerers like Edison but the systematic investigators with catholic interests, like Faraday, who added simultaneously to man's knowledge of scientific principles and to engineering. In our own day this synthesis, once the work of a single inspired genius, is the work of anonymous teams. . . .

[In another remarkable development,] the machine has evolved from an extension of human muscles into an extension of the human nervous system. In the past, tools and machines enhanced man's muscular power over raw materials and natural forces. Not even the mechanical devices and engines developed during the eighteenth and nineteenth centuries replaced human muscles – rather, they enlarged their effectiveness. Although these machines increased output enormously, workers' muscles and brain were still required to operate them, even for fairly routine tasks. Technological advance could be calculated in strict terms of labor productivity: One man using a given machine produced as many commodities as five, ten, fifty, or a hundred had produced without the machine. . . .

The development of fully automatic machines for complex mass-manufacturing operations required that these machines have a built-in ability to correct their own errors; sensory devices for replacing the visual, auditory, and tactile senses of the worker; and finally, devices that replace the worker's judgment, skill, and memory. These three principles presuppose the development of the technological means (the effectors, if you will) for applying the sensory, control, and mindlike devices in everyday industrial operations; further, they presuppose that we can adapt existing machines or develop new ones for handling, shaping, assembling, packaging, and transporting semifinished and finished products. . . .

With the advent of the computer we entered an entirely new dimension of industrial control systems. The computer is capable of performing all the routine tasks that burdened the mind of the worker a generation ago . . . . By virtue of its speed, the computer can perform highly sophisticated mathematical and logical operations . . . It is arguable whether computer "intelligence" is, or ever will be, creative or innovative (although every few years bring sweeping changes in computer technology), but there is no doubt that the digital computer is capable of taking over all the onerous and distinctly uncreative mental tasks of man in industry, science, engineering, information retrieval, and transportation. Modern man, in effect, has produced an electronic "mind" for coordinating, building, and evaluating most of his routine industrial operations. Properly used within the sphere of competence for which they are designed, computers are faster and more efficient than man himself. . . .

Even current systems are now already obsolete. "The next generation of computing machines operates a thousand times as fast – at a pulse rate of one in every three-tenths of a billionth of a second," observes Alice Mary Hilton. "Speeds of millionths and billionths of a second are not really intelligible to our finite minds. But we can certainly understand that the advance has been a thousand-fold within a year or two. A thousand times as much information can be handled or the same amount of information can be handled a thousand times as fast. A job that takes more than sixteen hours can be done in a minute! And without any human intervention! Such a system does not control merely an assembly line but a complete manufacturing and industrial process!"[8]

The basic technological principles involved in cybernating can be applied to virtually every area of mass manufacture – from metallurgy to food processing, from electronics to toy-making, from prefabricated bridges to prefabricated houses. Many phases of steel production, tool and die making, electronic equipment manufacture, and industrial chemical production are now partly or largely automated. . . . To be sure, every industry has its own particular problems, and the application of a toilless technology to a specific plant would doubtless reveal a multitude of kinks that would require painstaking solutions. . . . But there is practically no industry that cannot be fully automated if the product, the plant, the manufacturing procedures, and the handling methods are redesigned. In fact, the difficulty of describing how, where, or when a given industry will be automated arises not from assessing its unique problems but from considering the enormous leaps that occur every few years in modern technology. Almost every account of applied automation today must be regarded as provisional: as soon as one describes a partially automated industry, technological advances make the description obsolete.

There is one area of the economy, however, in which any technological advance is worth describing – the area of work, of toil, that is most brutalizing and degrading for man. If it is true, as Fourier said, that the moral level of a society can be gauged by the way it treats women, its sensitivity to human suffering can be gauged by the working conditions it provides for people in raw materials industries, particularly in mines and quarries. In the ancient world, mining was often a form of penal servitude, reserved primarily for the most hardened criminals, the most intractable slaves, and the most hated prisoners of war. The mine is the day-to-day actualization of man's image of hell; it is a deadening, dismal, inorganic world that demands pure mindless toil.

> Field and forest and stream and ocean are the environment of life; the mine is the environment alone of ores, minerals, metals [writes Lewis Mumford]. . . . In hacking and digging the contents of the earth, the miner has no eye for the forms of things; what he sees is sheer matter and until he gets to his vein it is only an obstacle which he breaks through stubbornly and sends up to the surface. If the miner sees shapes on the walls of his cavern, as the candle flickers, they are only the monstrous distortions of his pick or his arm: shapes of fear. Day has

been abolished and the rhythm of nature broken: continuous day-and-night production first came into existence here. The miner must work by artificial light even though the sun be shining outside; still further down in the seams, he must work by artificial ventilation too: a triumph of the "manufactured environment."[9]

The abolition of mining as a human activity would symbolize, in its own way, the triumph of a liberatory technology. That we can point to this achievement already presages the freedom from toil implicit in the technology of our time. The first major step in this direction was the continuous miner, a giant cutting machine with nine-foot blades that slices up eight tons of coal a minute from the coal face. It was this machine, together with mobile loading machines, power drills, and roof bolting, that reduced mine employment in areas like West Virginia to about a third of 1948 levels, at the same time nearly doubling individual output. Coal mines still require miners to place and operate the machines. The most recent technological advances, however, have replaced operators by radar sensing devices and eliminate the miner completely.

Adding sensing devices to automatic machinery could easily remove the worker from toil not only in mines but in agriculture. The wisdom of industrializing and mechanizing agriculture is highly questionable, but the fact remains that if society were to so choose, it could automate large areas of industrial agriculture, ranging from cotton picking to rice harvesting. Almost any machine, from a giant shovel in an open-strip mine to a grain harvester in the Great Plains, could be operated either by cybernated sensing devices or by remote control with television cameras. The effort needed to operate these devices and machines at a safe distance, in comfortable quarters, would be minimal, assuming that a human operator were required at all.

It is easy to foresee a time, by no means remote, when a rationally organized economy could automatically manufacture small "packaged" factories without human labor, when parts could be produced with so little effort that most maintenance tasks would be simply to remove a defective unit from a machine and replace it with another – a job no more difficult than pulling out and putting in a tray. Machines would make and repair most of the machines required to maintain such a highly industrialized economy. Such a technology, oriented entirely toward human needs and freed from all consideration of profit and loss, would eliminate the pain of want and toil – the penalty, inflicted in the form of denial, suffering, and inhumanity, exacted by a society based on scarcity and labor.

Technology for Life
(from "Toward a Liberatory Technology," 1965)

In a future revolution, the most pressing task of technology will be to produce a surfeit of goods with a minimum of toil. The immediate purpose of this task would be to open the social arena permanently to the revolutionary people, *to keep the revolution in permanence*. Thus far every social revolution has foundered because the peal of the tocsin could not be heard over the din of the workshop. Dreams of freedom and plenty were polluted by the mundane, workaday responsibility for producing the means of survival. In the brute facts of history, as long as revolution meant continual sacrifice and denial for the people, the reins of power fell into the hands of the political "professionals," the mediocrities of Thermidor. How well the liberal Girondins of the French Convention understood this reality can be judged by their effort to reduce the revolutionary fervor of the Parisian popular assemblies – the great sections of 1793 – by decreeing that the meetings should close "at ten in the evening," or as Carlyle tells us, "before the working people come from their jobs."[10] The decree proved ineffective, but it was well aimed. Essentially, the tragedy of past revolutions has been that sooner or later, their doors had to close "at ten in the evening." *The most critical function of modern technology must be to keep the doors of the revolution open forever!* . . .

The future liberated men will choose from a large variety of mutually exclusive or combinable work styles, all of which will be based on unforeseeable technological innovations. Or they may choose to submerge the cybernated machine to a technological world, divorcing it entirely from social life, the community, and creativity. All but hidden from society, machines would work for man. Free communities would stand at the end of a cybernated assembly line with baskets to cart the goods home. Industry, like the autonomic nervous system, would work on its own, subject to the repairs that our own bodies require in occasional bouts of illness. The fracture separating man from machine would not be healed. It would simply be ignored.

Ignoring technology, of course, is no solution. Man would be closing off a vital human experience – the stimulus of productive activity, the stimulus of the machine. Technology can in fact play a vital role in forming the personality of man. Every art, as Lewis Mumford has argued, has its technical side, requiring the self-mobilization of spontaneity into expressed order and providing contact with the objective world during the most ecstatic moments of experience.

A liberated society, I believe, would not want to negate technology, precisely because it is liberated and can strike a balance. It may well want to assimilate the machine to artistic craftsmanship. By this, I mean the machine would remove the toil from the productive process, leaving its artistic completion to man. The machine, in effect, would participate in human creativity. There is no reason that automatic, cybernated machinery cannot be used so that the finishing of products, especially those destined for personal use, is left to the community. The machine could absorb the toil involved in mining, smelting, transporting, and shaping raw materials, leaving the final stages of artistry and craftsmanship to the individual. Most of the stones that make up a medieval cathedral were carefully squared and standardized to facilitate their laying and bonding – a thankless, repetitive, and boring task that modern machines could now do rapidly and effortlessly. Once the stone blocks were set in place, the craftsmen made their appearance; toil was replaced by creative human work. In a liberated community the combination of industrial machines and the craftsman's tools could reach a degree of sophistication and of creative interdependence unparalleled in any period in human history. William Morris's vision of a return to craftsmanship would be freed of its nostalgic nuances. We could truly speak of a qualitatively new advance in technics – a technology for life.

Having acquired a vitalizing respect for the natural environment and its resources, the free decentralized community would give a new interpretation to the word *need*. Marx's "realm of necessity," instead of expanding indefinitely, would tend to contract; needs would be humanized and scaled by a higher valuation of life and creativity. Quality and artistry would supplant the current emphasis on quantity and standardization; durability would replace the current emphasis on expendability; an economy of cherished things, sanctified by a sense of tradition and by a sense of wonder for the personality and artistry of dead generations, would replace the mindless seasonal restyling of commodities; innovations would be made with a sensitivity for the natural inclinations of man as distinguished from the engineered pollution of taste by the mass media. Conservation would replace waste in all things. Freed of bureaucratic manipulation, men would rediscover the beauty of a simpler, uncluttered material life. Clothing, diet, furnishings, and homes would become more artistic, more personalized, and more Spartan. Man would recover a sense of things that are *for* man, as against the things that have been imposed upon man. The repulsive ritual of bargaining and hoarding would be replaced by the sensitive acts of making and giving. Things would cease to be the crutches for impoverished egos and the mediators between aborted personalities; they would become the products of rounded, creative individuals and the gifts of integrated, developing selves.

A technology for life could play the vital role of integrating one community with another. Rescaled to a revival of crafts and a new conception of material needs, technology could also function as the sinews of confederation. A national division of labor and industrial centralization are dangerous because with them technology begins to transcend the human scale; it becomes increasingly incomprehensible and lends itself to bureaucratic manipulation. To the extent that control is shifted away from the community in real terms (technologically and economically), centralized institutions acquire real power over the lives of men and threaten to become sources of coercion. A technology for life must be *based* on the community; it must be tailored to the community and the regional level. On this level, however, the sharing of factories and resources could actually promote solidarity among community groups; it could serve to confederate them on the basis not only of common spiritual and cultural interests but also of common material needs. Depending upon the resources and uniqueness of regions, a rational, humanistic balance could be struck between autarky, industrial confederation, and a national division of labor.

Is society so "complex" that an advanced industrial civilization stands in contradiction to a decentralized technology for life? My answer is a categorical no. Much of the social "complexity" of our time originates in the paperwork, administration, manipulation, and constant wastefulness of capitalist enterprise. The petty bourgeois stands in awe of the bourgeois filing system – the rows of cabinets filled with invoices, accounting books, insurance records, tax forms, and the inevitable dossiers. He is spellbound by the "expertise" of industrial managers, engineers, stylemongers, financial manipulators, and the architects of market consent. He is mystified by the state – the police, courts, jails, federal offices, secretariats, the whole stinking, sick body of coercion, control, and domination. Modern society is indeed incredibly complex, complex even beyond human comprehension, if we grant its premises: property, "production for the sake of production," competition, capital accumulation, exploitation, finance, centralization, coercion, bureaucracy, and the domination of man by man. Linked to each of these premises are the institutions that actualize it – offices, millions of "personnel" forms, immense tons of paper, desks, typewriters, telephones, and of course rows upon rows of filing cabinets. As in Kafka's novels, these things are real but strangely dreamlike, indefinable shadows on the social landscape. The economy has a greater reality to it and is easily mastered by the mind and senses, but it too is highly intricate – if we grant that buttons must be styled in a thousand different forms, textiles varied endlessly in kind and pattern to create the illusion of innovation and novelty, bathroom cabinets filled to overflowing with a dazzling variety of pharmaceuticals and lotions, and kitchens cluttered with endless imbecile appliances. If we singled out from this odious garbage one or two goods of high quality in the more useful categories, and if we eliminated the money economy, the state power, the credit system, the paperwork, and the police work required to hold society in an enforced state of want, insecurity, and domination, society would become not only reasonably human but fairly simple.

Behind a single yard of high-quality electric wiring, to be sure, lies a copper mine, the machinery needed to operate it, a plant for producing insulating material, a copper smelting and shaping complex, and a transportation system for distributing the wiring – and behind each of these complexes are other mines, plants, machine shops, and so forth. Copper mines of a kind that can be exploited by existing machinery are not to be found everywhere, although enough copper and other useful metals can be recovered as scrap from the debris of our present society to provide future generations with all they need. But even if copper can be furnished only by a nationwide system of distribution, in what sense would there still have to be a division of labor in the current sense of the term? There need be none at all. First, copper could be distributed, together with other goods, among free, autonomous communities, between those that mine it and those that require it. This distribution system need not require the mediation for centralized bureaucratic institutions. Second, and perhaps more significant, a community that lives in a region with ample copper resources would not be a mere mining community. Copper mining would be one of many economic activities in which it is engaged – a part of a larger, rounded, organic economic arena. The same would hold for communities whose climate is most suitable for growing specialized foods or whose resources are rare and uniquely valuable to society as a whole. Each community would approximate local or regional autarky. It would seek to achieve wholeness, because wholeness produces complete, rounded men who live in symbiotic relationship with their environment. Even if a substantial portion of the economy fell within the sphere of a national division of labor, the overall economic weight of society would still rest with the community. If there is no distortion of communities, there will be no sacrifice of any portion of humanity to the interests of humanity as a whole.

A basic sense of decency, sympathy, and mutual aid lies at the core of human behavior. Even in this lousy bourgeois society, we do not find it unusual that adults rescue children from danger, even at the risk of imperiling their own lives; we do not find it strange that miners risk death to save their fellow workers in cave-ins, or that soldiers crawl under heavy fire to carry wounded comrades to safety. What shocks us are those occasions when aid is refused – when the cries of a girl being stabbed are ignored in a middle-class neighborhood.

Yet there is nothing in this society that would seem to warrant a molecule of human solidarity. What solidarity we do find exists despite the society, against all its realities, as an unending struggle between the innate decency of man and the innate indecency of society. Can we imagine how men would behave if this decency could find full release, if society earned the respect, even the love, of the individual? We are still the offspring of a violent, blood-soaked, ignoble history – the end products of man's domination of man. We may never end this condition of domination. The future may bring us and our shoddy civilization down in a Wagnerian *Götterdämmerung*. How idiotic it would all be! But we may also end the domination of man by man. We may finally succeed in breaking the chain to the past and gain a humanistic anarchist society. It would be the height of absurdity, indeed of impudence, to gauge the behavior of future generations by the very criteria we despise in our own time. Free men would not be greedy, one liberated community would not try to dominate another because it had a potential monopoly of copper, computer "experts" would not try to enslave grease monkeys, and sentimental novels about pining tubercular virgins would not be written. We can ask only one thing of the free men and women of the future: to forgive us that it took so long to get there and that it was such a hard pull. Like Brecht, we can ask that they try not to think of us too harshly, that they give us their sympathy and understand that we lived in the depths of a social hell.

But then, they will surely know what to think without our telling them.

The Fetishization of Needs
(from *The Ecology of Freedom*, 1982)

Scarcity is not merely a functional phenomenon that can be described primarily in terms of needs or wants. Obviously, without a sufficiency in the means of life, life itself is impossible, and without a certain excess in these means, life is degraded to a cruel struggle for survival, irrespective of the level of needs. Leisure time, under these conditions, is not *free* time that fosters intellectual advances beyond the magical, artistic, and mythopoeic. To a large extent, the "time" of a community on the edge of survival is "suffering time." It is a time when hunger is the all-encompassing fear that persistently lives with the community, a time when the diminution of hunger is the community's constant preoccupation. Clearly, a balance must be struck between a sufficiency of the means of life, a relative freedom of time to fulfill one's abilities on the most advanced levels of human achievement, and ultimately a degree of self-consciousness, complementarity, and reciprocity that can be called truly human in full recognition of humanity's potentialities. Not only the functional dictates of needs and wants but also a concept of human beings as more than "thinking animals" (to use Paul Shepard's expression) must be introduced to define what we mean by scarcity.

These distinctions raise a second and perhaps more complex problem: scarcity can not only impair human survival but impede the actualization of human potentialities. Hence scarcity can be defined in terms of its biological impact and also its *cultural* consequences. There is a point at which society begins to intervene in the formation of needs to produce a very special type of scarcity: a *socially* induced scarcity that expresses social contradictions. Such scarcity may occur even when technical development seems to render material scarcity completely unwarranted. Let me emphasize that I am not referring here to new or more exotic wants that social development may turn into needs. A society that has enlarged the cultural goals of human life may generate material scarcity even when the technical conditions exist for achieving outright superfluity in the means of life.

The issue of scarcity is not merely a matter of quantity or even of kind; it can also be a socially contradictory hypostatization of need as such. Just as capitalism leads to production for the sake of production, so too it leads to consumption for the sake of consumption. The great bourgeois maxim "grow or die" has its counterpart in "buy or die." And just as the production of commodities is no longer related to their function as *use-values,* as objects of real utility, so wants are no longer related to humanity's sense of its real needs. Both commodities and needs acquire a blind life of their own; they assume a fetishized form, an irrational dimension, that seems to determine the destiny of the people who produce and consume them. Marx's famous notion of the "fetishization of commodities" finds its parallel in a "fetishization of needs." Production and consumption, in effect, acquire suprahuman qualities that are no longer related to technical development and the subject's rational control of the conditions of existence. They are governed instead by an ubiquitous market, by a universal competition not only between commodities but also between the creation of needs – a competition that removes commodities and needs from rational cognition and personal control.

Needs, in effect, become a force of production, not a subjective force. They become blind in the same sense that the production of commodities becomes blind. Orchestrated by forces that are external to the subject, they exist beyond its control like the production of the very commodities that are meant to satisfy them. This autonomy of needs is developed at the expense of the autonomy of the subject. It reveals a fatal flaw in subjectivity itself, in the autonomy and spontaneity of the individual to control the conditions of his or her own life.

To break the grip of the "fetishization of needs," to dispel it, is to recover *freedom of choice,* a project that is tied to the freedom of the *self* to choose. The words *freedom* and *choice* must be emphasized: they exist conjointly and are tied to the ideal of the autonomous individual who is possible only in a free society. Although a hunter-gatherer community may be free from the needs that beleaguer us, it must still answer to very strict material imperatives. Such freedom as it has is the product not of choice but of limited means of life. What makes it "free" are the very *limitations* of its tool-kit, not an expansive knowledge of the material world. In a truly *free* society, however, needs would be formed by *consciousness* and by *choice,* not simply by environment and tool-kits. The affluence of a free society would be transformed from a wealth of things into a wealth of culture and individual creativity. Hence want would depend not only on technological development but also on the cultural context in which it is formed. Nature's "stinginess" and technology's level of development would be important, but only as secondary factors in defining scarcity and need.

The problems of needs and scarcity, in short, must be seen as a problem of selectivity – of *choice.* A world in which needs compete with needs just as commodities compete with commodities is the warped realm of a fetishized, limitless world of consumption. This world of limitless needs has been developed by the immense armamentarium of advertising, the mass media, and the grotesque trivialization of daily life, with its steady disengagement of the individual from any authentic contact with history. Although choice presupposes a sufficiency in the means of life, it does not imply the existence of a mindless abundance of goods that smothers the individual's capacity to select use-values rationally, to define his or her needs according to qualitative, ecological, humanistic, indeed, philosophical criteria. Rational choice presupposes not only a sufficiency in the means of life with minimal labor to acquire them; it presupposes above all a *rational society.*

Freedom from scarcity, or *post-scarcity,* must be seen in this light if it is to have any liberatory meaning. The concept presupposes that individuals have the material possibility of choosing what they need – not only a sufficiency of available goods from which to choose but a transformation of work, both qualitatively and quantitatively. *But not one of these achievements is adequate to the idea of post-scarcity if the individual does not have the autonomy, moral insight, and wisdom to choose rationally.* Consumerism and mere abundance are mindless. Choice is vitiated by the association of needs with consumption for the sake of consumption – with the use of advertising and the mass media to render the acquisition of goods an *imperative* – to make "need" into "necessity" devoid of rational judgment. What is ultimately at stake for the individual whose needs are rational is the achievement of an autonomous personality and selfhood. Just as work, to use Marx's concepts, defines the subject's identity and provides it with a sense of the ability to transform or alter reality, so needs too define the subject's rationality and provide it with a capacity to transform and alter the nature of the goods produced by work. In both cases, the subject is obliged to form judgments that reflect the extent to which it is rational or irrational, free and autonomous or under the sway of forces beyond its control. Post-scarcity presupposes the former; consumerism, the latter. *If the object of capitalism or socialism is to increase needs, the object of anarchism is to increase choice.* However much the consumer is deluded into the belief that he or she is choosing freely, the consumer is heteronomous and under the sway of a contrived necessity; the free subject, by contrast, is autonomous and spontaneously fulfills his or her rationally conceived wants.

In summary, it is not in the diminution or expansion of needs that the true history of needs is written. Rather, it is in the *selection* of needs as a function of the free and spontaneous development of the subject that needs become qualitative and rational. Needs are inseparable from the subjectivity of the "needer" and the context in which his or her personality is formed. The autonomy that is given to use-values in the formation of needs leaves out the personal quality, human powers, and intellectual coherence of their user. *It is not industrial productivity that creates mutilated use-values but social irrationality that creates mutilated users.*

Scarcity does not mean the same thing when applied to a "savage," peasant, slave, serf, artisan, or a proletarian, any more than it means the same thing when it is applied to a chieftain, lord, master, noble, guildmaster, or merchant. The *material* needs of a "savage," peasant, slave, serf, artisan, and proletarian are not so decisively different from each other, but the most important differences that do arise derive from the fact that their individual definitions of scarcity have changed significantly as a result of differences between need structures. Often, the needs of these oppressed classes are generated by their ruling-class counterparts. The history of white bread in the anthropology of needs, for example, is a metaphor for the extent to which tastes associated with gentility – not with physical well-being and survival – are turned into the needs of the lowly as compellingly, in the fetishism of needs, as the very means of survival. Similarly, the ascetic rejection by the lowly of their rulers' needs has functioned as a compensating role in imparting to the oppressed a lofty sense of moral and cultural superiority over their betters. In both cases, the fetishism of needs has impeded humanity in using its technics rationally and selecting its needs consciously.

Our own skewed concepts of scarcity and needs are even more compelling evidence of this fetishism. Until comparatively recent times, needs retained some degree of contact with material reality and were tempered by some degree of rationality. For all the cultural differences that surrounded the concept of scarcity and needs in the past, their fetishization was almost minimal in comparison with our own times. But with the emergence of a complete market society, the ideal of both limitless production and limitless needs became thoroughly mystified – no less by socialist ideologues than by their bourgeois counterparts. The restraints that Greek social theorists like Aristotle tried to place on the market, however much they were honored in the breach, were completely removed, and objects or use-values began to infiltrate the lofty human goals that society had elaborated from the days of their conception in the *polis*. The ideals of the past, in effect, had become so thoroughly bewitched by things that they were soon to become things rather than ideals. Honor, today, is more important as a credit rating than as a sense of moral probity; personality is the sum of one's possessions and holdings rather than a sense of self-awareness and self-cultivation. One could continue this list of contrasts indefinitely.

Having demolished all the ethical and moral limits that once kept it in hand, the market society in turn has demolished almost every historic relationship between nature, technics, and material well-being. No longer is nature's "stinginess" a factor in explaining scarcity, nor is scarcity conceived as a function of technical development that explains the creation or satisfaction of needs. Both the culture and the technics of modern capitalism have united to produce crises not of scarcity but of abundance or, at least, the expectation of abundance, all chit-chat about "diminishing resources" aside. Western society may accept the reality of economic crises, inflation, and unemployment, and popular credulity has not rejected the myth of a "stingy" nature that is running out of raw materials and energy resources. Abundance, all the more because it is being denied for structural economic reasons rather than natural ones, still orchestrates the popular culture of present-day society. To mix solid Victorian metaphors with contemporary ones: if "savages" had to perform heroic technical feats to extricate themselves from the "claw and fang" world of the jungle and arrive at a sense of their humanity, then modern consumers in the market society will have to perform equally heroic ethical feats to extricate themselves from the shopping malls and recover their own sense of humanity.

To "disembed" themselves from the shopping mall, they may require more powerful agents than ethics. They may well require a superfluity of goods so immense in quantity that the prevailing fetishism of needs will have to be dispelled on its own terms. Hence the ethical limits that were so redolent with meaning from Hellenic times onward may be inadequate today. We have arrived at a point in history's account of need where the very *capacity* to select needs, which freedom from material scarcity was expected to create, has been subverted by a strictly appetitive sensibility. Society may well have to be overindulged to recover its capacity for selectivity. To lecture society about its "insatiable" appetites, as our resource-conscious environmentalists are wont to do, is precisely what the modern consumer is not prepared to hear. And to impoverish society with contrived shortages, economic dislocations, and material deprivation is certain to shift the mystification of needs over to a more sinister social ethics, the mystification of scarcity. This ethos – already crystallized into the "lifeboat ethic," "triage," and a new bourgeois imagery of claw-and-fang called *survivalism* – marks the first step toward ecofascism.

NOTES

1 Murray Bookchin, introduction to *Post Scarcity Anarchism* (San Francisco: Ramparts Press, 1971; reprinted by Montreal: Black Rose Books, 1977), p. 9.
2 Owen quoted in G.D.H. Cole, *A History of Socialist Thought*, vol. 1, *Socialist Thought: The Forerunners, 1789–1850* (London: Macmillan, 1962), p. 94.
3 Students for a Democratic Society, "America and the New Era" (1963), in Massimo Teodori, ed., *The New Left: A Documentary History* (Indianapolis and New York: Bobbs-Merrill, 1969), p. 174.
4 Mario Savio, "An End to History" (1964), in Teodori, ed., *New Left*, p. 159.
5 Ibid., p. 11.
6 Pierre-Joseph Proudhon, *What Is Property?* (London: Bellamy Library, n.d.), vol. 1, p. 135.
7 Vannevar Bush quoted in US Congress, Joint Committee on the Economic Report, *Automation and Technological Change: Hearings Before the Subcommittee on Economic Stabilization*, 84th cong., 1st sess. (Washington: US Government Printing Office, 1955), p. 81.
8 Alice Mary Hilton, "Cyberculture," Fellowship for Reconciliation paper (Berkeley, CA, 1964), p. 8.
9 Lewis Mumford, *Technics and Civilization* (New York: Harcourt, Brace, and Co., 1934), pp. 69–70.
10 Thomas Carlyle, *The French Revolution* (New York: Modern Library, n.d.), p. 593.

CHAPTER SIX

Marxism

Introduction

Although Marx's writings had a great influence on Bookchin's ideas, it became clear to him early on that a degree of authoritarianism, particularly an acceptance of domination, recurred in the Marxian writings. Even in the 1940s he was cognizant that a centralized state was essential to Marx's views and to the new socialist dispensation that he would create. Moreover, even as Marx and Engels attacked class society, they had taught that hierarchical relationships were indispensable to a socialist society, just as a factory needed hierarchical relationships in order to operate.

In time, Bookchin realized that the ideological rationales for material scarcity that were typical of bourgeois society had been recapitulated in Marxist theory as well. Just as ruling elites had used scarcity to justify their authority, Marxism insisted that the domination of nonhuman nature not only made class society historically inevitable but was a historical precondition for human liberation.

Bookchin's assertion that the idea of dominating nature first arose within society overturned this rationale, common to bourgeois and Marxist ideology alike. Where Marxists argued that an emancipatory society could be created by eliminating class society alone, Bookchin maintained that it was necessary to eliminate hierarchy and domination as well. Where Marxists argued that domination had arisen originally as a mode of organizing human labor, Bookchin argued that domination originated in the rankings of social hierarchy, which often had little to do with material production. The socialist school that followed upon Marx's own death, Bookchin concluded, was thus tainted by the imperative to dominate human beings and first nature alike. As Bookchin summarized it himself, in connection with a criticism of Frankfurt school theorists Theodor Adorno and Max Horkheimer:

However much they opposed domination, neither Adorno nor Horkheimer singled out hierarchy as an underlying problematic in their writings. Indeed, their residual Marxian premises led to a historical fatalism that saw any liberatory enterprise . . . as hopelessly tainted by the need to dominate nature and *consequently* "man." This position stands completely at odds with my own view that the notion – and no more than an *unrealizable* notion – of dominating nature stems from the domination of human by human. This is not a semantic difference in accounting for the origins of domination. Like Marx, the Frankfurt School saw nature as a "domineering" force over humanity that human guile – and class rule – had to exorcise before a classless society was possible. The Frankfurt School, no less than Marxism, placed the onus for domination primarily on the demanding forces of nature.

My own writings radically reverse this very traditional view of the relationship between society and nature. I argue that the idea of dominating nature first arose within *society* as part of its institutionalization into gerontocracies that placed the young in varying degrees of servitude to the old and in patriarchies that placed women in varying degrees of servitude to men – not in any endeavor to "control" nature or natural forces. Various modes of social institutionalization, not modes of organizing human labor (so crucial to Marx), were the first sources of domination, which is not to deny Marx's thesis that class society was economically exploitative. Hence, domination can be definitively removed only by resolving problematics that have their origins in hierarchy and status, not in class and the technological control of nature alone.[1]

It is easy to conclude, from his various critiques, that Bookchin rejected Marxism altogether and sought to annul it. Yet even in his most bitter polemics against 1960s Marxists, he did not abandon Marxism altogether. On the contrary, his lifelong trajectory has been to preserve the dialectical approach of Marx in order to transcend Marxism itself dialectically. Thus, in any study of his work, it is important to identify the aspects of Marxism that he did and did not reject. He rejected, of course, the necessity of hierarchy and domination; the exclusivity of class analysis; the hegemonic role of the proletariat; and the creation of a centralized socialist state. He rejected, too, the repressive regimes that ruled in the name of Marxism.

But he respected many other aspects of Marx's work and incorporated them into social ecology, such as its insights into capitalist development, its theory of the commodity, and the notion that complete freedom has material preconditions. Perhaps most importantly, he respected the dialectical form of reasoning that Marx had inherited from Hegel and that Bookchin himself inherited from Marx. Bookchin considers all of these contributions to be lasting and essential to the revolutionary tradition, regardless of other limitations in the Marxist literature.

Marxism and Domination
(from *The Ecology of Freedom* and "Marxism as Bourgeois Sociology," 1982 and 1979)

The stream of human progress has been a divided one: The development toward material security and social complexity has generated contrapuntal forces that yield material insecurity and social conflict unique to "civilization" as such. On the one side, without the agrarian economy that the early Neolithic introduced, society would have been mired indefinitely in a brute subsistence economy living chronically on the edge of survival. Nature, so the social theorists of the past century held, is normally "stingy," an ungiving and deceptive "mother." She has favored humanity with her bounty only in a few remote areas of the world. Rarely has she been the giving nurturer created in distant times by mythopoeic thought. The "savage" of Victorian ethnography must always struggle (or "wrestle," to use Marx's term) with her to perpetuate life – which is ordinarily miserably and mercifully brief, tolerable at times but never secure, and only marginally plentiful and idyllic. Humanity's emergence from the constrictive world of natural scarcity has thus been perceived as a largely technical problem of placing the ungiving forces of nature under social command, creating and increasing surpluses, dividing labor (notably, separating crafts from agriculture), and sustaining intellectually productive urban elites. Thus, given the leisure time to think and administer society, these elites could create science, enlarge the entire sphere of human knowledge, and sophisticate human culture. As Proudhon plaintively declared, echoing the prevailing spirit of the time: "Yes, life is a struggle. But the struggle is not between man and man – it is between men and Nature; and it is each one's duty to share it."

Marx assumed the same view toward the "burden of nature." But he placed considerable emphasis on human domination as an unavoidable feature of humanity's domination of the natural world. Until the development of modern industry (both Marx and Engels argued), the new surpluses produced by precapitalist technics may vary quantitatively, but rarely are they sufficient to provide abundance and leisure for more than a fortunate minority. Given the relatively low level of preindustrial technics, enough surpluses can be produced to sustain a privileged class of rulers, perhaps even a substantial one under exceptionally favorable geographic and climatic conditions. But these surpluses are not sufficient to free society as a whole from the pressures of want, material insecurity, and toil. If such limited surpluses were equitably divided among the multitudes who produce them, a social condition would emerge in which "*want* is made general," as Marx observed, "and with want the struggle for necessities and all the old shit would necessarily be reproduced." An egalitarian division of the surpluses would merely yield a society based on equality in poverty, an equality that would simply perpetuate the latent conditions for the restoration of class rule. Ultimately, the abolition of classes presupposes the "development of the productive forces," the advance of technology to a point where everyone can be free from the burdens of want, material insecurity, and toil. As long as surpluses are merely marginal, social development occurs in a gray zone between a remote past in which productivity is too low to support classes and a distant future in which it is sufficiently high to abolish class rule.

Hence emerges the other side of humanity's drama: the negative side of its development, which conveys the real meaning of the "social problem" as used by Marxian theorists. Technical progress exacts a penalty for the benefits it ultimately confers on humanity. To resolve the problem of natural scarcity, the development of technics entails the reduction of humanity to a technical force. People become instruments of production, just like the tools and machines they create. They, in turn, are subject to the same forms of coordination, rationalization, and control that society tries to impose on nature and inanimate technical instruments. Labor is both the medium whereby humanity forges its own self-formation and the object of social manipulation. It involves not only the projection of human powers into free expression and selfhood but their repression by the performance principle of toil into obedience and self-renunciation. Self-repression and social repression form the indispensable counterpoint to personal emancipation and social emancipation. . . .

Marxian theory sees "man" as the embodiment of two aspects of material reality: first, as a producer who defines himself by labor; second, as a social being whose functions are primarily economic. When Marx declares that "men may be distinguished from animals by consciousness, by religion or anything else you like [but they] begin to distinguish themselves from animals as soon as they begin to produce their means of subsistence" (*The German Ideology*), he essentially deals with humanity as a force in the productive process that differs from other material forces only to the degree that "man" can conceptualize productive operations that animals perform instinctively. It is difficult to realize how decisively this notion of humanity breaks with the classical concept. To Aristotle, men fulfilled their humanity to the degree that they could live in a *polis* and achieve the "good life." Hellenic thought as a whole distinguished human beings from animals by virtue of their rational capacities. If a "mode of production" is not simply to be regarded as a means of survival but as a "definite *mode of life*," such that "men" are "*what* they produce and *how* they produce" (*German Ideology*), humanity, in effect, can be regarded as an instrument of production. The "domination of man by man" is primarily a *technical* phenomenon rather than an *ethical* one. Within this incredibly reductionist framework, whether it is valid for "man" to dominate "man" is to be judged mainly in terms of technical needs and possibilities, however distasteful such a criterion might have seemed to Marx himself, had he faced it in all its brute clarity. . . .

Society, in turn, becomes a mode of labor that is to be judged by its capacity to meet material needs. Class society remains unavoidable as long as the "mode of production" fails to provide the free time and material abundance for human emancipation. Until the appropriate technical level is achieved, "man's" evolutionary development remains incomplete. Indeed, popular communistic visions of earlier eras are mere ideology because "only *want* is made general" by premature attempts to achieve an egalitarian society, "and with want the struggle for the necessities and all the old shit would necessarily be reproduced" (*The German Ideology*).

Finally, even when technics reaches a relatively high level of development,

> the realm of freedom does not commence until the point is passed where labour under the compulsion of necessity and of external utility is required. In the very nature of things it lies beyond the sphere of material production in the strict meaning of the term. Just as the savage must wrestle with nature, in order to satisfy his wants, in order to maintain his life and reproduce it, so civilized man has to do it, and he must do it in all forms of society and under all possible modes of production. With his development the realm of natural necessity expands, because his wants increase; but at the same time the forces of production increase, by which these wants are satisfied. The freedom in this field cannot consist of anything else but of the fact that socialized man, the associated producers, regulate their interchange with nature rationally, bring it under their common control, instead of being ruled by it as by some blind power; that they accomplish their task with the least expenditure of energy and under conditions most adequate to their human nature and most worthy of it. But it always remains a realm of necessity. Beyond it begins that development of human power, which is its own end, the true realm of freedom, which, however, can flourish

only upon that realm of necessity as its basis. The shortening of the
working day is its fundamental premise. (*Capital,* vol. 3)

The bourgeois conceptual framework reaches its apogee, here in images
of . . . the unlimited expansion of needs that stands opposed to
"ideological" limits to need (that is, the Hellenic concepts of measure,
balance, and self-sufficiency), the rationalization of production and
labor as desiderata in themselves of a strictly technical nature, the sharp
dichotomy between freedom and necessity, and the conflict with nature
as a condition of social life in all its forms – class or classless, propertied
or communistic.

Accordingly, socialism now moves within an orbit in which, to use
Max Horkheimer's formulation, "domination of nature involves
domination of man" – not only "the subjugation of external nature,
human and nonhuman," but human nature (*The Eclipse of Reason*).
Following his split from the natural world, "man" can hope for no
redemption from class society and exploitation until he, as a technical
force among the technics created by his own ingenuity, can transcend
his objectification. The precondition for this transcendence is
quantitatively measurable: the "shortening of the working day is its
fundamental premise." Until these preconditions are achieved, "man"
remains under the tyranny of social law, the compulsion of need and
survival. The proletariat, no less than any other class in history, is
captive to the impersonal processes of history. Indeed, as the class that
is most completely dehumanized by bourgeois conditions, it can
transcend its objectified status only through "urgent, no longer
disguisable, absolutely imperative need." For Marx, "The question is
not what this or that proletarian, or even the whole proletariat at the
moment, *considers* as its aim. The question is *what the proletariat is,*
and what, consequent on that *being,* it will be compelled to do" (*The
Holy Family*). Its "being," here, is that of object, and social law
functions as *compulsion,* not as "destiny." The subjectivity of the
proletariat remains a product of its objectivity – ironically, a notion
that finds a certain degree of truth in the fact that any radical appeal
merely to the objective factors that enter into the forming of a
"proletarian consciousness" or class consciousness strike back like a
whiplash against socialism in the form of a working class that has
bought into capitalism, that seeks to share in the affluence provided
by the system. Thus where reaction is the real basis of action and need
is the basis of motivation, the bourgeois spirit becomes the "world
spirit" of Marxism. . . .

To the degree that the classical view of self-realization through the
polis recedes before the Marxian view of self-preservation through
socialism, the bourgeois spirit acquires a degree of sophistication that
makes its earlier spokesmen (Hobbes, Locke) seem naïve. The incubus

of domination now fully reveals its authoritarian logic. Just as necessity becomes the basis of freedom, authority becomes the basis of rational coordination. This notion, already implicit in Marx's harsh separation of the realms of necessity and freedom – a separation Fourier sharply challenged – is made explicit in Engels's essay "On Authority." To Engels, the factory is a natural fact of technics, not a specifically bourgeois mode of rationalizing labor; hence it will exist under communism as well as capitalism. It will persist "independently of all social organization." To coordinate a factory's operations requires "imperious obedience," in which factory hands lack all "autonomy." Class society or classless, the realm of necessity is also a realm of command and obedience, of ruler and ruled. In a fashion totally congruent with all class ideologists from the inception of class society, Engels weds socialism to command and rule as a natural fact. Domination is reworked from a social attribute into a precondition for self-preservation in a technically advanced society. . . .

To structure a revolutionary project around "social law" that lacks ethical content, order that lacks meaning, a harsh opposition between "man" and nature, compulsion rather than consciousness – all of these, taken together with domination as a precondition for freedom, debase the concept of freedom and assimilate it to its opposite, coercion. Consciousness becomes the recognition of its lack of autonomy, just as freedom becomes the recognition of necessity. A politics of "liberation" emerges that reflects the development of advanced capitalist society into nationalized production, planning, centralization, the rationalized control of nature – and the rationalized control of human beings. If the proletariat cannot comprehend its own "destiny" by itself, a party that speaks in its name becomes justified as the authentic expression of that consciousness, even if it stands opposed to the proletariat itself. If capitalism is the historic means whereby humanity achieves the conquest of nature, the techniques of bourgeois industry need merely be reorganized to serve the goals of socialism. If ethics are merely ideology, socialist goals are the product of history rather than reflection and it is by criteria mandated by history that we are to determine the problems of ends and means, not by reason and disputation.

Marxism and Leninism
(from "Listen, Marxist!" 1969)

THE MYTH OF THE PROLETARIAT

For our age, Marx's greatest contribution to revolutionary thought is his dialectic of social development. Marx laid bare the great movement from primitive communism through private property to communism in its higher form – a communal society resting on a liberatory technology. In this movement, according to Marx, man passes on from the domination of man by nature, to the domination of man by man, and finally to the domination of nature by man and from social domination as such. Within this larger dialectic, Marx examines the dialectic of capitalism itself – a social system that constitutes the last historical "stage" in the domination of man by man. Here Marx not only makes profound contributions to contemporary revolutionary thought (particularly in his brilliant analysis of the commodity relationship) but also exhibits those limitations of time and place that play so confining a role in our own time.

The most serious of these limitations emerges from Marx's attempt to explain the transition from capitalism to socialism, from a class society to a classless society. It is vitally important to emphasize that this explanation was reasoned out almost entirely by analogy with the transition of feudalism to capitalism – that is, *from one class society to another class society,* from one system of property to another. Accordingly, Marx points out that just as the bourgeoisie developed within feudalism as a result of the split between town and country (more precisely, between crafts and agriculture), so the modern proletariat developed within capitalism as a result of the advance of industrial technology. Both classes, we are told, develop social interests of their own – indeed, revolutionary social interests that throw them against the old society in which they were spawned. If the bourgeoisie gained control over economic life long before it overthrew feudal society, the proletariat, in turn, gains its own revolutionary power by the fact that it is "disciplined, united, organized" by the factory system. In both cases, the development of the productive forces becomes incompatible with the traditional system of social relations. "The integument is burst asunder." The old society is replaced by the new.

The critical question we face is this: Can we explain the transition from a class society to a classless society by means of the same dialectic that accounts for the transition from one class society to another? This is not a textbook problem that involves the juggling of logical abstractions, but a very real and concrete issue for our time. There are profound differences between the development of the bourgeoisie under feudalism and the development of the proletariat under capitalism, which Marx either failed to anticipate or never faced clearly. The bourgeoisie controlled economic life long before it took state power; it had become the dominant class materially, culturally, and ideologically before it asserted its dominance politically. The proletariat does not control economic life. Despite its indispensable role in the industrial process, the industrial working class is not even a majority of the population, and its strategic economic position is being eroded by cybernation and other technological advances. Hence it requires an act of high consciousness for the proletariat to use its power to achieve a social revolution. Until now, the achievement of this consciousness has been blocked by the fact that the factory milieu is one of the most well-entrenched arenas of the work ethic, of hierarchical systems of management, of obedience to leaders, and in recent times of production committed to superfluous commodities and armaments. The factory serves not only to "discipline, unite, and organize" the workers but to do so in a thoroughly bourgeois fashion. In the factory, capitalistic production not only renews the social relations of capitalism with each working day, as Marx observed, it also renews the psyche, values, and ideology of capitalism.

Marx sensed this fact sufficiently to look for reasons more compelling than the mere fact of exploitation or conflicts over wages and hours to propel the proletariat into revolutionary action. In his general theory of capitalist accumulation he tried to delineate the harsh, objective laws that force the proletariat to assume a revolutionary role. Accordingly he developed his famous theory of immiseration: Competition between capitalists compels them to undercut each other's prices, which in turn leads to a continual reduction of wages and the absolute impoverishment of the workers. The proletariat is compelled to revolt because with the process of competition and the centralization of capital there "grows the mass of misery, oppression, slavery, degradation."

But capitalism has not stood still since Marx's day. Writing in the middle years of the nineteenth century, Marx could not be expected to have grasped the full consequences of his insights into the centralization of capital and the development of technology. He could not be expected to have foreseen that capitalism would develop not only from mercantilism into the dominant industrial form of his day – from state-aided trading monopolies into highly competitive industrial units – but further, that with the centralization of capital, capitalism would return to its mercantilist origins on a higher level of development and reassume the state-aided monopolistic form. The economy tends to merge with the state and capitalism begins to "plan" its development instead of leaving it exclusively to the interplay of competition and market forces. To be sure, the system does not abolish the traditional class struggle but manages to contain it, using its immense technological resources to assimilate the most strategic sections of the working class.

Thus the full thrust of the immiseration theory is blunted, and in the United States the traditional class struggle fails to develop into the class war. It remains entirely within bourgeois dimensions. Marxism, in fact, becomes ideology. It is assimilated by the most advanced forms of the state capitalist movement – notably Russia. By an incredible irony of history, Marxian "socialism" turns out to be in large part the very state capitalism that Marx failed to anticipate in the dialectic of capitalism. The proletariat, instead of developing into a revolutionary class within the womb of capitalism, turns out to be an organ within the body of bourgeois society. . . .

A qualitatively new situation emerges when man is faced with a transformation from a repressive class society, based on material scarcity, into a liberatory classless society, based on material abundance. From the decomposing traditional class structure a new human type is created in ever-increasing numbers: the *revolutionary*. This revolutionary begins to challenge not only the economic and political premises of hierarchical society but hierarchy as such. He not only raises the need for social revolution but also tries to *live* in a revolutionary manner to the degree that this is possible in the existing society. He not only attacks the forms created by the legacy of domination but also improvises new forms of liberation that take their poetry from the future.

This preparation for the future, this experimentation with liberatory post-scarcity forms of social relations, may be illusory if the future involves a substitution of one class society by another; it is indispensable, however, if the future involves a classless society built on the *ruins* of a class society. What then will be the "agent" of revolutionary change? It will be literally the great majority of society, drawn from all the different traditional classes and fused into a common revolutionary force by the decomposition of the institutions, social forms, values and lifestyles of the prevailing class structure. Typically its most advanced elements are the youth – a generation that has known no chronic economic crisis and that this becoming less and less oriented toward the myth of material security so widespread among the generation of the thirties.

If it is true that a social revolution cannot be achieved without the active or passive support of the workers, it is no less true that it cannot be achieved without the active or passive support of the farmers, technicians and professionals. Above all, a social revolution cannot be achieved without the support of the youth, from which the ruling class recruits its armed forces. If the ruling class retains its armed might, the revolution is lost *no matter how many workers rally to its support.* This has been vividly demonstrated not only by Spain in the thirties but by Hungary in the fifties and Czechoslovakia in the sixties. The revolution of today – by its very nature, indeed, by its *pursuit of wholeness* – wins not only the soldier and the worker *but the very generation from which soldiers, workers, technicians, farmers, scientists, professionals, and even bureaucrats have been recruited.* Discarding the tactical handbooks of the past, the revolution of the future follows the path of least resistance, eating its way into the most susceptible areas of the population irrespective of their "class position." It is nourished by *all* the contradictions in bourgeois society, not simply by the contradictions of the 1860s and 1917. Hence it attracts all those who feel the burdens of exploitation, poverty, racism, imperialism and, yes, those whose lives are frustrated by consumerism, suburbia, the mass media, the family, school, the supermarket, and the prevailing system of repressed sexuality. Here the form of the revolution becomes as total as its content – classless, propertyless, hierarchyless, and *wholly* liberating. . . .

THE MYTH OF THE PARTY

Social revolutions are not made by parties, groups, or cadres. They occur as a result of deep-seated historical forces and contradictions that activate large sections of the population. They occur not merely because the "masses" find the existing society intolerable (as Trotsky argued) but also because of the tension between the actual and the possible, between what-is and what-could-be. Abject misery alone does not produce revolutions; more often than not, it produces an aimless demoralization, or worse, a private, personalized struggle to survive.

The Russian Revolution of 1917 weighs on the brain of the living like a nightmare because it was largely the product of "intolerable conditions," of a devastating imperialistic war. Whatever dreams it had were virtually destroyed by an even bloodier civil war, by famine, and by treachery. What emerged from the revolution were the ruins not of an old society but of whatever hopes existed to achieve a new one. The Russian Revolution failed miserably; it replaced czarism with state capitalism. The Bolsheviks were the tragic victims of their own ideology and paid with their lives in great numbers during the purges of the 1930s. To attempt to acquire any unique wisdom from this scarcity revolution is ridiculous. What we can learn from the revolutions of the past is what all revolutions have in common and their profound limitations compared with the enormous possibilities that are now open to us.

The most striking feature of the past revolutions is that they began spontaneously. Whether it be the French Revolution of 1798, the revolutions of 1848, the Paris Commune, the 1905 revolution in Russia, the overthrow of the czar in 1917, the Hungarian revolution of 1956, or the French general strike of 1968, the opening stages are generally the same: a period of ferment explodes spontaneously into a mass upsurge. Whether the upsurge is successful depends on its resoluteness and on whether the troops go over to the people.

The "glorious party," when there is one, almost invariably lags behind the events. In February 1917 the Petrograd organization of the Bolsheviks opposed the calling of strikes precisely on the eve of the revolution that was destined to overthrow the czar. Fortunately, the workers ignored the Bolshevik "directives" and went on strike anyway. In the events that followed, no one was more surprised by the revolution than the "revolutionary" parties, including the Bolsheviks. As the Bolshevik leader Kayurov recalled: "Absolutely no guiding initiatives from the party were felt . . . the Petrograd committee had been arrested and the representative from the Central Committee, Comrade Shliapnikov, was unable to give any directives for the coming day."[2] Perhaps this was fortunate. Before the Petrograd committee was arrested, its evaluation of the situation and its own role had been so dismal that, had the workers followed its guidance, it is doubtful that the revolution would have occurred when it did.

The same kind of story could be told of the upsurges that preceded 1917 and those that followed – to cite only the most recent, the student uprising and general strike in France during May–June 1968. There is a convenient tendency to forget that close to a dozen "tightly centralized" Bolshevik-type organizations existed in Paris at this time. It is rarely mentioned that virtually every one of these "vanguard" groups disdained the student uprising up to May 7, when the street fighting broke out in earnest. The Trotskyist Jeunesse Communiste Révolutionnaire was a notable exception – and it merely coasted along, essentially following the initiatives of the March 22nd Movement. Up to May 7, all the Maoist groups criticized the student uprising as peripheral and unimportant; the Trotskyist Fédération des Etudiants Révolutionnaires regarded it as "adventuristic" and tried to get the students to leave the barricades on May 10; the Communist Party, of course, played a completely treacherous role. Far from leading the popular movement, the Maoists and Trotskyists were its captives throughout. Ironically, most of these Bolshevik groups used manipulative techniques shamelessly in the Sorbonne student assembly in an effort to "control" it, introducing a disruptive atmosphere that demoralized the entire body. Finally, to complete the irony, all of these Bolshevik groups were to babble about the need for "centralized leadership" when the popular movement collapsed – a movement that occurred despite their "directives" and often in opposition to them.

Revolutions and uprisings worthy of any note not only have an initial phase that is magnificently anarchic *but also tend spontaneously to create their own forms of revolutionary self-management.* The Parisian sections of 1793–4 were the most remarkable forms of self-management to be created by any of the social revolutions in history. More familiar in form were the councils or "soviets" that the Petrograd workers established in 1905. Although less democratic than the sections, the councils were to reappear in a number of later revolutions. Still another form of revolutionary self-management was the factory committees that the anarchists established in the Spanish Revolution of 1936. Finally, the sections reappeared as student assemblies and action committees in the May–June uprising and general strike in Paris in 1968.

At this point we must ask what role the "revolutionary" party plays in all these developments. In the beginning, as we have seen, it tends to have an inhibitory function, not a "vanguard" role. Where it exercises influence, it tends to slow down the flow of events, not "coordinate" the revolutionary forces. This is not accidental. The party is structured along hierarchical lines *that reflect the very society it professes to oppose*. Despite its theoretical pretensions, it is a bourgeois organism, a miniature state, with an apparatus and a cadre whose function it is to *seize* power, not *dissolve* power. Rooted in the prerevolutionary period, it assimilates all the forms, techniques, and mentality of bureaucracy. Its membership is schooled in obedience and in the preconceptions of a rigid dogma and is taught to revere the leadership. The party's leadership, in turn, is schooled in habits born of command, authority, manipulation, and egomania. This situation is worsened when the party participates in parliamentary elections. In election campaigns, the vanguard party models itself completely on existing bourgeois forms and even acquires the paraphernalia of the electoral party. The situation assumes truly critical proportions when the party acquires large presses, costly headquarters, and a large inventory of centrally controlled periodicals and develops a paid apparatus – in short, a bureaucracy with vested material interests.

As the party expands, the distance between the leadership and the ranks invariably increases. Its leaders not only become personages, they lose contact with the living situation below. The local groups, which know their own immediate situation better than any remote leader, are obliged to subordinate their insights to directives from above. The leadership, lacking any direct knowledge of local problems, responds sluggishly and prudently. Although it stakes out a claim to the larger view, to greater theoretical competence, the competence of the leadership tends to diminish as one ascends the hierarchy of command. The more one approaches the level where the real decisions are made, the more conservative is the nature of the decision-making process, the more bureaucratic and extraneous are the factors that come into play, the more considerations of prestige and retrenchment supplant creativity, imagination, and a disinterested dedication to revolutionary goals.

The party becomes less efficient from a revolutionary point of view the more it seeks efficiency by means of hierarchy, cadres, and centralization. Although everyone marches in step, the orders are usually wrong, especially when events move rapidly and take unexpected turns – as they do in all revolutions. The party is efficient in only one respect – in molding society in its own hierarchical image if the revolution is successful. It recreates bureaucracy, centralization, and the state. It fosters the very social conditions that justify this kind of society. Hence, instead of "withering away," the state controlled by the "glorious party" preserves the very conditions that "necessitate" the existence of a state – and a party to guard it.

On the other hand, this kind of party is extremely vulnerable in periods of repression. The bourgeoisie has only to grab its leadership to destroy virtually the entire movement. With its leaders in prison or in hiding, the party becomes paralyzed; obedient membership has no one to obey and tends to flounder. Demoralization sets in rapidly. The party decomposes not only because of the repressive atmosphere but also because of its poverty of inner resources.

The foregoing account is not a series of hypothetical inferences. It is a composite sketch of all the mass Marxian parties of the past century – the Social Democrats, the Communists, and the Trotskyist party of Ceylon (the only mass party of its kind). To claim that these parties failed to take their Marxian principles seriously merely conceals another question: Why did this failure happen in the first place? The fact is, these parties were co-opted into bourgeois society because they were structured along bourgeois lines. The germ of treachery existed in them from birth. . . .

It cannot be stressed too strongly that the Bolsheviks tended to centralize their party to the degree that they became isolated from the working class. This relationship has rarely been investigated in latter-day Leninist circles, although Lenin was honest enough to admit it. The story of the Russian Revolution is not merely the story of the Bolshevik Party and its supporters. Beneath the veneer of official events described by Soviet historians there was another, more basic development – the spontaneous movement of the workers and revolutionary peasants, which later clashed sharply with the bureaucratic policies of the Bolsheviks. With the overthrow of the czar in February 1917, workers in virtually all the factories of Russia spontaneously established factory committees, staking out an increasing claim on industrial operations. In June 1917 an all-Russian conference of factory committees was held in Petrograd that called for the "organization of thorough control by labor over production and distribution." The demands of this conference are rarely mentioned in Leninist accounts of the Russian Revolution, despite the fact that the conference aligned itself with the Bolsheviks. Trotsky, who describes the factory committees as "the most direct and indubitable representation of the proletariat in the whole country," deals with them only peripherally in his massive three-volume history of the revolution. Yet so important were these spontaneous organisms of self-management that Lenin, despairing of winning the soviets in the summer of 1917, was prepared to jettison the slogan "All power to the soviets" for "All power to the factory committees." This demand would have catapulted the Bolsheviks into an anarchosyndicalist position, although it is doubtful that they would have remained there very long.

With the October Revolution, all the factory committees seized control of the plants, ousting the bourgeoisie and completely taking control of industry. In accepting the concept of workers' control, Lenin's famous decree of November 14, 1917, merely acknowledged an accomplished fact: the Bolsheviks dared not oppose the workers at this early date. But they began to whittle down the power of the factory committees. In January 1918, a scant two months after "decreeing" workers' control, Lenin began to advocate that the administration of the factories be placed under trade union control. The story that the Bolsheviks "patiently" experimented with workers' control, only to find it "inefficient" and "chaotic," is a myth. Their "patience" did not last more than a few weeks. Not only did Lenin oppose direct workers' control within a matter of weeks after the November 14 decree, even union control came to an end shortly after it had been established. By the summer of 1918, almost all of Russian industry had been placed under bourgeois forms of management. As Lenin put it, the "revolution demands . . . precisely in the interests of socialism that the masses *unquestionably obey the single will* of the leaders of the labor process."[3] Thereafter, workers' control was denounced not only as "inefficient," "chaotic," and "impractical" but also as "petty bourgeois"!

The Left Communist Osinsky bitterly attacked all of these spurious claims and warned the party, "Socialism and socialist organization must be set up by the proletariat itself, or they will not be set up at all; something else will be set up – state capitalism."[4] In the "interests of socialism" the Bolshevik party elbowed the proletariat out of every domain it had conquered by its own efforts and initiative. The party did not coordinate the revolution or even lead it; it dominated it. First workers' control and later union control were replaced by an elaborate hierarchy as monstrous as any structure that existed in prerevolutionary times. In later years Osinsky's prophecy became reality.

The problem of "who is to prevail" – the Bolsheviks or the Russian "masses" – was by no means limited to the factories. The issue reappeared in the countryside as well as in the cities. A sweeping peasant war had buoyed up the movement of the workers. Contrary to official Leninist accounts, the agrarian upsurge was by no means limited to a redistribution of the land into private plots. In the Ukraine, peasants influenced by the anarchist militias of Nestor Makhno and guided by the communist maxim "From each according to his ability; to each according to his needs," established a multitude of rural communes. Elsewhere, in the north and in Soviet Asia, several thousand of these organisms were established, partly on the initiative of the Left Social Revolutionaries and in large measure as a result of traditional collectivist impulses that stemmed from the Russian village, the *mir*. It matters little whether these communes were numerous or embraced large numbers of peasants; the point is that they were authentic popular organisms, the nuclei of a moral and social spirit that ranged far above the dehumanizing values of bourgeois society.

The Bolsheviks frowned upon these organisms from the very beginning and eventually condemned them. To Lenin, the preferred, the more "socialist" form of agricultural enterprise was the state farm – an agricultural factory in which the state owned the land and farming equipment, appointing managers who hired peasants on a wage basis. One sees in these *attitudes* toward workers' control and agricultural communes the essentially bourgeois spirit and mentality that permeated the Bolshevik Party – a spirit and mentality that emanated not only from its theories but from its corporate mode of organization. In December 1918 Lenin launched an attack on the communes on the pretext that peasants were being forced to enter them. Actually, little if any coercion was used to organize these communistic forms of self-management. As Robert G. Wesson, who studied the Soviet commune in detail, concludes, "Those who went into communes must have done so largely of their own volition."[5] The communes were not suppressed, but their growth was discouraged until Stalin merged the entire development into the forced collectivization drives of the late 1920s and early 1930s.

By 1920, the Bolsheviks had isolated themselves from the Russian working class and peasantry. Taken together, the elimination of workers' control, the suppression of the Makhnovtsy, the restrictive political atmosphere in the country, the inflated bureaucracy, and the crushing material poverty inherited from the civil war years generated a deep hostility toward Bolshevik rule. With the end of hostilities, a movement surged up from the depths of Russian society for a "third revolution" – not to restore the past, as the Bolsheviks claimed, but to realize the very goals of freedom, economic as well as political, that had rallied the masses around the Bolshevik program of 1917. The new movement found its most conscious form in the Petrograd proletariat and among the Kronstadt sailors. It also found expression in the party: the growth of anticentralist and anarchosyndicalist tendencies among the Bolsheviks reached a point where a bloc of oppositional groups, oriented toward these issues, gained 124 seats at a Moscow provincial conference, as against 154 for supporters of the Central Committee.

On March 2, 1921, the "red sailors" of Kronstadt rose in open rebellion, raising the banner of a "Third Revolution of the Toilers." The Kronstadt program centered on demands for free elections to the soviets, freedom of speech and press for the anarchists and the left socialist parties, free trade unions, and the liberation of all prisoners who belonged to socialist parties. The most shameless stories were fabricated by the Bolsheviks to account for this uprising, acknowledged in later years as brazen lies. The revolt was characterized as a "White Guard plot" despite the fact that the great majority of Communist Party members in Kronstadt joined the sailors – *precisely as Communists* – in denouncing the party leaders as betrayers of the October Revolution. As R. V. Daniels observes in his study of Bolshevik oppositional movements, "Ordinary Communists were indeed so unreliable . . . that the government did not depend upon them either in the assault on Kronstadt itself or in keeping order in Petrograd, where Kronstadt's hopes for support chiefly rested. The main body of troops employed were Chekists and officer cadets from Red Army training schools. The final assault on Kronstadt was led by the top officialdom of the Communist Party – a large group of delegates to the Tenth Party Congress was rushed from Moscow for this purpose."[6] So weak was the regime internally that the elite had to do its own dirty work. . . .

We have discussed these events in detail because they lead to a conclusion that the latest crop of Marxist–Leninists tend to avoid: the Bolshevik party reached its maximum degree of centralization in Lenin's day *not to achieve a revolution or suppress a White Guard counter-revolution, but to effect a counterrevolution of its own against the very social forces it professed to represent.* Factions were prohibited and a monolithic party created not to prevent a "capitalist restoration" but to contain a mass movement of workers for soviet democracy and social freedom. The Lenin of 1921 stood opposed to the Lenin of 1917.

Thereafter Lenin simply floundered. This man who above all had sought to anchor the problems of his party in social contradictions found himself literally playing an organizational numbers game in a last-ditch attempt to arrest the very bureaucratization he had himself created. There is nothing more pathetic and tragic than Lenin's last years. Paralyzed by a simplistic body of Marxist formulas, he could think of no better countermeasures than organizational ones. He proposes the formation of the Workers' and Peasants' Inspection to correct bureaucratic deformations in the party and state – and this body falls under Stalin's control and becomes highly bureaucratic in its own right. Lenin then suggests that the size of the Workers' and Peasants' Inspection be reduced and that it be merged with the Control Commission. He advocated enlarging the Central Committee. Thus it rolls along: this body to be enlarged, that one to be merged with another, still a third to be modified or abolished. The strange ballet of organizational forms continues up to his very death, as though the problem could be resolved by organizational means. As Moshe Lewin, an obvious admirer of Lenin, admits, the Bolshevik leader "approached the problem of government more like a chief executive of a strictly 'elitist' turn of mind. He did not apply methods of social analysis to the government and was content to consider it purely in terms of organizational methods."[7]

If it is true that in the bourgeois revolutions the "phrase went beyond the content," in the Bolshevik revolution the forms replaced the content.

The soviets replaced the workers and their factory committees, the party replaced the soviets, the Central Committee replaced the party, and the Political Bureau replaced the Central Committee. In short, means replaced ends. This incredible substitution of form for content is one of the most characteristic traits of Marxism–Leninism. In France during the May–June events, all the Bolshevik organizations were prepared to destroy the Sorbonne student assembly in order to increase their influence and membership. Their principal concern was not the revolution or the authentic social forms created by the students but the growth of their own parties.

Only one force could have arrested the growth of bureaucracy in Russia: a social force. Had the Russian proletariat and peasantry succeeded in increasing the domain of self-management through the development of viable factory committees, rural communes, and free soviets, the history of the country might have taken a dramatically different turn. There can be no question that the failure of socialist revolutions in Europe after the First World War led to the isolation of the revolution in Russia. The material poverty of Russia, coupled with the pressure of the surrounding capitalist world, clearly militated against the development of a socialist or a consistently libertarian society. But by no means was it ordained that Russia had to develop along state capitalist lines; contrary to Lenin's and Trotsky's initial expectations, the revolution was defeated by internal forces, not by invasion of armies from abroad. Had the movement from below restored the initial achievements of the revolution in 1917, a multifaceted social structure might have developed, based on workers' control of industry, on a freely developing peasant economy in agriculture, and on a living interplay of ideas, programs, and political movements. At the very least, Russia would not have been imprisoned in totalitarian chains, and Stalinism would not have poisoned the world revolutionary movement, paving the way for fascism and the Second World War.

The development of the Bolshevik party, however, precluded this development – Lenin's or Trotsky's "good intentions" notwithstanding. By destroying the power of the factory committees in industry and by crushing the Makhnovtsy, the Petrograd workers, and the Kronstadt sailors, the Bolsheviks virtually guaranteed the triumph of the Russian bureaucracy over Russian society. The centralized party – a completely bourgeois institution – became the refuge of counterrevolution in its most sinister form. This was covert counterrevolution that draped itself in the red flag and the terminology of Marx. Ultimately, what the Bolsheviks suppressed in 1921 was not an ideology or a White Guard conspiracy but an *elemental struggle of the Russian people* to free themselves of their shackles and take control of their own destiny. For Russia, this meant the nightmare of Stalinist dictatorship; for the generation of the 1930s, it meant the horror of fascism and the treachery of the Communist parties in Europe and the United States.

THE TWO TRADITIONS

It would be incredibly naïve to suppose that Leninism was the product of a single man. The disease lies much deeper, not only in the limitations of Marxian theory but in the limits of the social era that produced Marxism. If this is not clearly understood, we will remain as blind to the dialectic of events today as Marx, Engels, Lenin, and Trotsky were in their own day. For us this blindness will be all the more reprehensible because behind us lies a wealth of experience that these men lacked in developing their theories.

Karl Marx and Friedrich Engels were centralists – not only politically but socially and economically. They never denied this fact, and their writings are studded with glowing encomiums to political, organizational, and economic centralization. As early as March 1850, in the "Address of the Central Council to the Communist League," they called upon the workers to strive not only for "the single and indivisible German republic, but also strive in it for the most decisive centralization of power in the hands of the state authority." Lest the demand be taken lightly, it was repeated continually in the same paragraph, which concludes: "As in France in 1793, so today in Germany the carrying through of the strictest centralization is the task of the really revolutionary party."

The same theme reappeared continually in later years. With the outbreak of the Franco–Prussian War, for example, Marx wrote to Engels: "The French need a thrashing. If the Prussians win, the centralization of state power will be useful for the centralization of the German working class."[8]

Marx and Engels, however, were not centralists because they believed in the virtues of centralism per se. Quite the contrary: Marxism and anarchism have always agreed that a liberated communist society would entail sweeping decentralization, the dissolution of bureaucracy, the abolition of the state, and the breakup of the large cities. "Abolition of the antithesis between town and country is not merely possible," noted Engels in *Anti-Dühring*. "It has become a direct necessity . . . the present poisoning of the air, water and land can be put to an end only by the fusion of town and country." To Engels this would involve a "uniform distribution of the population over the whole country" – in short, the physical decentralization of the cities.[9]

The origins of Marxian centralism are in problems arising from the formation of the national state. Until well into the latter half of the nineteenth century, Germany and Italy were divided into a multitude of independent duchies, principalities, and kingdoms. The consolidation of these geographical units into unified nations, Marx and Engels believed, was a *sine qua non* for the development of modern industry and capitalism. Their praise of centralism was engendered not by any centralistic mystique but by the events of the period in which they lived – the development of technology, trade, a unified working class, and the national state. Their concern on this score, in short, is with the emergence of capitalism, with the tasks of the bourgeois revolution in an era of unavoidable material scarcity. Marx's approach to a "proletarian revolution," on the other hand, is markedly different. He enthusiastically praised the Paris Commune as a "model to all the industrial centers of France." "This regime," he wrote, "once established in Paris and the secondary centers, the old centralized government would in the provinces, too, have to give way to the *self-government of the producers*" (emphasis added). The unity of the nation, to be sure, would not disappear, and a central government would exist during the transition to communism, but its functions would be limited.

Our object is not to bandy about quotations from Marx and Engels but to emphasize how key tenets of Marxism – which are accepted so uncritically today – were in fact the product of an era that has long been transcended by the development of capitalism in the United States and Western Europe. In his day Marx was occupied not only with problems of the "proletarian revolution" but also with the problems of the bourgeois revolution, particularly in Germany, Spain, Italy, and Eastern Europe. He was dealing with problems of transition from capitalism to socialism in capitalist countries that had not advanced much beyond the coal–steel technology of the Industrial Revolution, and with the problems of transition from feudalism to capitalism in countries that had scarcely advanced much beyond handicrafts and the guild system. To state these concerns broadly, Marx was occupied above all with the *preconditions* of freedom (technological development, national unification, material abundance) rather than with the *conditions* of freedom (decentralization, the formation of communities, the human scale, direct democracy). His theories were still anchored in the realm of *survival,* not the realm of *life.*

Once this is grasped, it is possible to place Marx's theoretical legacy in meaningful perspective – to separate its rich contributions from its historically limited, indeed paralyzing shackles on our own time. The Marxian dialectic, the many seminal insights provided by historical materialism, the superb critique of the commodity relationship, many elements of the economic theories, the theory of alienation, and above all the notion that freedom has material preconditions – these are lasting contributions to revolutionary thought.

By the same token, Marx's emphasis on the industrial proletariat as the "agent" of revolutionary change, his "class analysis" in explaining the transition from a class to a classless society, his concept of the proletarian dictatorship, his emphasis on centralism, his theory of capitalist development (which tends to jumble state capitalism with socialism), his advocacy of political action through electoral parties – these and many related concepts are false in the context of our time and were misleading even in his own day. They emerged from the limitations of his vision – more properly, from the limitations of his time. They make sense only if one remembers that Marx regarded capitalism as historically progressive, as an indispensable stage in the development of socialism, and they have practical applicability only to a time when Germany in particular was confronted by bourgeois-democratic tasks and national unification. We are not trying to say that Marx was correct in holding this approach, merely that the approach makes sense when viewed in its time and place.

NOTES

1 Murray Bookchin, "Thinking Ecologically," in *The Philosophy of Social Ecology*, second ed., rev. (Montreal: Black Rose Books, 1995), p. 142, note 2.
2 Quoted in Leon Trotsky, *The History of the Russian Revolution* (New York: Simon & Schuster, 1932), vol. 1, p. 144.
3 V. I. Lenin, "The Immediate Tasks of the Soviet Government" (April 1918); in *Selected Works*, vol. 7 (New York: International Publishers, 1943), p. 342.
4 V. V. Osinsky, "On the Building of Socialism," *Kommunist*, no. 2 (April 1918), quoted in R. V. Daniels, *The Conscience of the Revolution* (Cambridge, MA: Harvard University Press, 1960), pp. 85–6.
5 Robert G. Wesson, *Soviet Communes* (New Brunswick, NJ: Rutgers University Press, 1963), p. 110.
6 Daniels, *Conscience*, p. 145.
7 Moshe Lewin, *Lenin's Last Struggle* (New York: Pantheon, 1958), p. 122.
8 Karl Marx and Friedrich Engels, *Selected Correspondence* (New York: International Publishers, 1942), p. 292.
9 Friedrich Engels, *Herr Eugen Dühring's Revolution in Science (Anti-Dühring)* (New York: International Publishers, 1939), p. 323.

CHAPTER SEVEN

Anarchism

Introduction

In the epilogue to his 1962 history of anarchism, George Woodcock concluded that anarchism as a movement was all but dead. "During the past forty years," he wrote

> the influence [the movement] once established has dwindled, by defeat after defeat and by the slow draining of hope, almost to nothing. Nor is there any reasonable likelihood of a renaissance of anarchism as we have known it. . . . History suggests that movements which fail to take the chances it offers them are never born again.[1]

Within only a few years of Woodcock's interment of anarchism in the cemetery of defunct social theories, Bookchin was breathing life back into it. With the emergence of the ecological issue and the new potentiality for post-scarcity in the postwar period, anarchism ceased to be merely a utopian fantasy and seemed, on the contrary, to be a logical consequence of developments in European and American history.

Releasing anarchism from the grip of traditional but historically superseded notions, Bookchin brought to the surface tendencies in anarchism that had lain dormant or received insufficient attention in previous generations, especially its relevance to ecology and its emphasis on communalism and confederation. Recasting it in terms of an opposition to hierarchy and domination and melding it with the call for an ecological society, Bookchin advanced his new anarchism within the 1960s' counterculture as the only credible alternative to the destruction of the planet.

In reaction to Marxist authoritarianism, Bookchin was looking for revolutionary institutions that would be genuinely emancipatory:

for "forms of freedom" that would be popular, direct–democratic, and decentralized, in contrast to the domineering centralism he despised. The "legacy of freedom" that he traced through Western history was in large part a search for these institutions: the millenarian Christian sects and democratic communes of medieval Europe, the town meetings of colonial New England, the sectional assemblies of revolutionary Paris.

Anarchism's appeal to Bookchin lay not only in its libertarian principles but in the attention it had given to such institutions, particularly the anarcho-syndicalist collectives of revolutionary Spain. Consistently the anarchism to which he adhered was a communalistic social anarchism, an anarcho-communism that sought a condition of positive freedom for society as a whole, and not the individualistic anarchism represented by the tendency of Max Stirner that sought negative liberty for the isolated ego.

Thus Bookchin did not embrace anarchism *in toto*, any more than he had rejected Marxism *in toto*. He had no patience for its sometime glorifications of individual autonomy at the expense of the community; or for its erstwhile distrust of organizations and institutions as such; or for its tendencies to antinomianism, rejecting all socially established morality; or for its propensities toward anti-intellectualism. On the contrary, he argued that it is precisely through community and institutions – democratic and self-managed – that individual freedom is possible; that a generally accepted, even objectively grounded ethics is a necessary component of that community; and that anarchism must become a theoretically coherent body of ideas rather than content itself with anti-intellectual adventurism.

Utopian anarchism appealed widely to alienated youth of the 1960s, leading to the very "renaissance" that Woodcock had thought unlikely, a "renaissance" that continues, however diminished in momentum, to this day. As historian Peter Marshall affirms, "The thinker who has most renewed anarchist thought and action since World War II is undoubtedly Murray Bookchin."[2]

The Two Traditions: Anarchism
(from "Listen, Marxist!" 1969)

Just as the Russian Revolution included a subterranean movement of the "masses" that conflicted with Bolshevism, so there is a subterranean movement in history that conflicts with all systems of authority. This movement has entered into our time under the name of anarchism, although it has never been encompassed by a single ideology or body of sacred texts. Anarchism is a libidinal movement of humanity against coercion in any form, reaching back in time to the very emergence of propertied society, class rule, and the state. From this period onward, the oppressed have resisted all forms that sought to imprison the spontaneous development of social order. Anarchism has surged to the foreground of the social arena in periods of major transition from one historical era to another. The declining ancient and feudal worlds witnessed the upsurge of mass movements, in some cases wildly Dionysian in character, that demanded an end to all systems of authority, privilege, and coercion.

The anarchic movements of the past failed largely because material scarcity, a function of the low level of technology, vitiated an organic harmonization of human interests. Any society that could promise little more materially than equality of poverty invariably engendered deep-seated tendencies to restore a new system of privilege. In the absence of a technology that could appreciably reduce the working day, the need to work vitiated social institutions based on self-management. The Girondins of the French Revolution shrewdly recognized that they could use the working day against revolutionary Paris. To exclude radical elements from the sections, they tried to enact legislation that would end all assembly meetings before ten p.m., the hour when Parisian workers returned from their jobs. Indeed, it was not only the manipulative techniques and the treachery of the "vanguard" organizations that brought the anarchic phases of past revolutions to an end, it was also the material limits of past eras. The "masses" were always compelled to return to a lifetime of toil and were rarely free to establish organs of self-management that could last beyond the revolution.

Anarchists such as Bakunin and Kropotkin, however, were by no means wrong in criticizing Marx for his emphasis on centralism and his elitist notions of organization. Was centralism absolutely necessary for technological advances in the past? Was the nation-state indispensable to the expansion of commerce? Did the workers' movement benefit from the emergence of highly centralized economic enterprises and the "indivisible" state? We tend to accept these tenets of Marxism too uncritically, largely because capitalism developed within a centralized political arena. The anarchists of the last century warned that Marx's centralistic approach, insofar as it affected the events of the time, would so strengthen the bourgeoisie and the state apparatus that the overthrow of capitalism would be extremely difficult. The revolutionary party, by duplicating these centralistic, hierarchical features, would reproduce hierarchy and centralism in the postrevolutionary society.

Bakunin, Kropotkin, and Malatesta were not so naïve as to believe that anarchism could be established overnight. In imputing this notion to Bakunin, Marx and Engels willfully distorted the Russian anarchist's views. Nor did the anarchists of the last century believe that the abolition of the state involved "laying down arms" immediately after the revolution, to use Marx's obscurantist words, thoughtlessly repeated by Lenin in *State and Revolution*. Indeed, much that passes for "Marxism" in *State and Revolution* is pure anarchism – for example, the substitution of revolutionary militias for professional armed bodies and the substitution of organs of self-management for parliamentary bodies. What is authentically Marxist in Lenin's pamphlet is the demand for "strict centralism," the acceptance of a "new" bureaucracy, and the identification of soviets with a state.

The anarchists of the last century were deeply preoccupied with the question of achieving industrialization without crushing the revolutionary spirit of the "masses" and rearing new obstacles to emancipation. They feared that centralization would reinforce the ability of the bourgeoisie to resist the revolution and instill in the workers a sense of obedience. They tried to rescue all those precapitalist communal forms (such as the Russian *mir* and the Spanish *pueblo*) that might provide a springboard to a free society, in not only a structural sense but also a spiritual one. Hence they emphasized the need for decentralization even under capitalism. In contrast to the Marxian parties, their organizations gave considerable attention to what they called integral education – the development of the *whole* man – to counteract the debasing and banalizing influence of bourgeois society. The anarchists tried to live by the values of the future to the extent that this was possible under capitalism. They believed in direct action to foster the initiative of the "masses," to preserve the spirit of revolt, to encourage spontaneity. They tried to develop organizations based on mutual aid and brotherhood, in which control would be exercised from below upward, not downward from above.

We must pause here to examine the nature of anarchist organizational forms in some detail, if only because the subject has been obscured by an appalling amount of rubbish. Anarchists, or at least anarcho-communists, accept the need for organization. It should be as absurd to have to repeat this point as to argue over whether Marx accepted the need for social revolution.

The real question is not organization versus nonorganization but rather what *kind* of organization the anarcho-communists try to establish. What the different kinds of anarcho-communist organizations have in common is organic developments from below, not bodies engineered into existence from above. They are social movements, combining a creative revolutionary lifestyle with a creative revolutionary theory, not political parties whose mode of life is indistinguishable from the surrounding bourgeois environment and whose ideology is reduced to rigid "tried and tested programs." As much as is humanly possible, they try to reflect the liberated society they seek to achieve, not slavishly duplicate the prevailing system of hierarchy, class, and authority. They are built around intimate groups of brothers and sisters – affinity groups – whose ability to act in common is based on initiative, on convictions freely arrived at, and on a deep personal involvement, not on a bureaucratic apparatus fleshed out by a docile membership and manipulated from above by a handful of all-knowing leaders.

The anarcho-communists do not deny the need for coordination between groups, for discipline, for meticulous planning, and for unity in action. But they believe that coordination, discipline, planning, and unity in action must be achieved *voluntarily,* by means of a self-discipline nourished by conviction and understanding, not by coercion and a mindless, unquestioning obedience to orders from above. They seek to achieve the effectiveness imputed to centralism by means of voluntarism and insight, not by establishing a hierarchical, decentralized structure. Depending upon needs or circumstances, affinity groups can achieve this effectiveness through assemblies, action committees, and local, regional, or national conferences. But they vigorously oppose the establishment of an organizational structure that becomes an end in itself, of committees that linger on after their practical tasks have been completed, of a "leadership" that reduces the "revolutionary" to a mindless robot.

These conclusions are not the result of flighty individualist impulses; quite to the contrary, they emerge from an exacting study of past revolutions, of the impact centralized parties have had on the revolutionary process, and of the nature of social change in an era of potential material abundance. Anarcho-communists *seek to preserve and extend the anarchic phase that opens all the great social revolutions.* Even more than Marxists, they recognize that revolutions are produced by deep historical processes. No central committee "makes" a social revolution; at best it can stage a coup d'état, replacing one hierarchy with another – or worse, arrest a revolutionary process if it exercises any widespread influence. A central committee is an organ for acquiring power, for *recreating* power, for gathering to itself what the "masses" have achieved by their own revolutionary efforts. One must be blind to all that has happened over the past two centuries not to recognize these essential facts.

In the past, Marxists could make an intelligible (although invalid) claim for the need for a centralized party, because the anarchic phase of the revolution was nullified by material scarcity. Economically, the "masses" were always compelled to return to a daily life of toil. The revolution closed at ten o'clock, quite aside from the reactionary intentions of the Girondins of 1793; it was arrested by the low level of technology. Today even this excuse has been removed by the development of a post-scarcity technology, notably in the United States and Western Europe. A point has now been reached where the "masses" can begin, almost overnight, to expand drastically the "realm of freedom" in the Marxian sense – to acquire the leisure time needed to achieve the highest degree of self-management.

What the May–June [1968] events in France demonstrated was the need not for a Bolshevik-type party but for greater consciousness among the "masses." Paris demonstrated that an organization is needed to propagate ideas systematically – and not ideas alone, but *ideas that promote the concept of self-management*. What the French "masses" lacked was not a central committee or a Lenin to "organize" or "command" them, but the conviction that they could have *operated* the factories instead of merely occupying them. It is noteworthy that *not a single Bolshevik-type party in France raised the demand for self-management*. That demand was raised only by the anarchists and Situationists.

There is a need for revolutionary organization – but its function must always be kept clearly in mind. Its first task is propaganda, to "patiently explain," as Lenin put it. In a revolutionary situation, the revolutionary organization presents the most advanced demands: it is prepared at every turn of events to formulate – in the most concrete fashion – the immediate task that should be performed to advance the revolutionary process. It provides the boldest elements in action and in the decision-making organs of the revolution.

In what way, then, do anarcho-communist groups differ from the Bolshevik type of party? Certainly not on such issues as the need for organization, planning, coordination, or propaganda in all its forms or on the need for a social program. Fundamentally, they differ from the Bolshevik type of party in their belief that genuine revolutionaries must function *within the framework of the forms created by the revolution,* not within the forms created by the party. What this means is that their commitment is to the revolutionary organs of self-management, not to the revolutionary organization; to the *social* forms, not the *political* forms. Anarcho-communists seek to persuade the factory committees, assemblies, or soviets to make themselves into *genuine organs of popular self-management,* not to dominate them, manipulate them, or hitch them to an all-knowing political party. Anarcho-communists seek not to rear a state structure over these popular revolutionary organs but, on the contrary, to dissolve all the organizational forms developed in the prerevolutionary period (including their own) into these genuine revolutionary organs.

These differences are decisive. Despite their rhetoric and slogans, the Russian Bolsheviks never believed in the soviets; they regarded them as instruments of the Bolshevik party. . . By 1921, the soviets were virtually dead, and all decisions were made by the Bolshevik Central Committee and Political Bureau. Not only do anarcho-communists seek to prevent Marxist parties from repeating this; they also wish to prevent their own organization from playing a similar role. Accordingly, they try to prevent bureaucracy, hierarchy, and elites from emerging in their midst. No less important, they attempt to *remake themselves;* to root out from their own personalities those authoritarian traits and elitist propensities that are assimilated in hierarchical society almost from birth. The concern of the anarchist movement with lifestyle is a preoccupation not merely with its own integrity but with that of the revolution itself.

In the midst of all the confusing ideological cross-currents of our time, one question must always remain in the foreground: What the hell are we trying to make a revolution for? To recreate hierarchy, dangling a shadowy dream of future freedom before the eyes of humanity? To promote further technological advance, to create an even greater abundance of goods than exists today? To "get even" with the bourgeoisie? . . . To bring the Communist Party to power? Or the Socialist Workers Party? To emancipate such abstractions as "the proletariat," "the people," "history," "society"?

Or is it finally to dissolve hierarchy, class rule, and coercion – *to make it possible for each individual to gain control of his everyday life?* Is it to make each moment as marvelous as it could be and the life-span of each individual an utterly fulfilling experience? . . . We need hardly argue the inane question of whether individual development can be severed from social and communal development; obviously the two go together. The basis for a whole human being is a rounded society; the basis for a free human being is a free society.

These issues aside, we are still faced with the question that Marx raised in 1850: when will we begin to take our poetry from the future instead of the past? The dead must be permitted to bury the dead. Marxism is dead because it was rooted in an era of material scarcity, limited in its possibilities by material want. The most important social message of Marxism is that freedom has material preconditions – we must survive in order to live. With the development of a technology that could not have been conceived by the wildest science fiction of Marx's day, the possibility of a post-scarcity society now lies before us. All the institutions of propertied society – class rule, hierarchy, the patriarchal family, bureaucracy, the city, the state – have been exhausted. Today, decentralization is not only desirable as a means of restoring the human scale, it is necessary to recreate a viable ecology, to preserve life on this planet from destructive pollutants and soil erosion, to preserve a breathable atmosphere and the balance of nature.

Anarchy and Libertarian Utopias
(from *Remaking Society*, 1990)

The radical theorists and utopists following upon the French Revolution exhibited more expansive ideals of freedom than their predecessors in the Enlightenment – and they were to sum up a sweeping body of alternatives to the course followed by history; alternatives that were naïvely ignored by their socialist successors.

Both of these legacies are of immense importance for modern radicalism – the expansiveness of their ideals and the alternatives that confronted humanity. The anarchist thinkers and libertarian utopists were deeply sensitive to *choices* that could have been made in redirecting human society along rational and liberatory lines. They raised the far-reaching questions of whether community and individuality could be brought into harmony with each other; whether the nation was the necessary, indeed the ethical successor to the community or *commune;* whether the State was the unavoidable successor to city and regional confederations; whether the communal use of resources had to be supplanted by private ownership; whether the artisanal production of goods and small, humanly scaled agricultural operations were destined by "historical necessity" to be abandoned for giant assembly lines and mechanized systems of agribusiness. Finally, they raised the question of whether ethics had to give way to statecraft and what would be the destiny of politics if it tried to adapt itself to centralized states.

They saw no contradictions between material well-being and a well-ordered society, between substantive equality and freedom, or between sensuousness, play, and work. They envisioned a society where abundance would be possible and a gender-blind political culture would emerge as the work week, superfluous production, and excessive consumption diminished. These questions, anticipated nearly two centuries ago and infused with the moral fervor of more than two thousand years of heretical movements like the Joachimites, have surfaced in the late twentieth century with a vengeance. Words like *precursors* have become simply meaningless from the standpoint of our crisis-ridden society, which must reevaluate the *entire* history of ideas and the alternatives opened by social history. What is immediately striking about their work is their acute sense of the alternatives to abuses.

We cannot ignore the differences that distinguish the anarchist theorists and the libertarian utopists of the last century from those of a more distant past. Anarchic tendencies such as the primitive Christians, the radical Gnostics, the medieval Brotherhood of the Free Spirit, the Joachimites, and the Anabaptists viewed freedom more as a result of a supernaturalistic visitation than as the product of human activity. This basically passive–receptive mentality, based on mystical underpinnings, is crucial. That certain premodern tendencies in the anarchic tradition *did* act to change the world does not alter the fact that even their very actions were seen as the expression of a theistic preordination. In their eyes, action stemmed from the transmutation of the deity's will into human will. It was the product of a social alchemy that was possible because of a supernatural decision, not because of human autonomy. The "philosopher's stone" of change in this early approach reposed in heaven, not on earth. Freedom had to "come," as it were, from agents that were suprahuman, be they Christ in the "second coming" or a new messiah. Generally, in accord with Gnostic thinking there were always elites like "psychics" who were free of evil or leaders blessed with moral perfection. History, in effect, was as much of a clock as it was a Joachimite chronicle, ticking away metaphysical time until the sins of the world became so intolerable that they activated the deity, who no longer forswore his creation as well as the suffering of the poor, deprived, and oppressed.

The Renaissance, the Enlightenment, and above all the nineteenth century radically altered this naïve social dispensation. The Age of Revolutions, as we may properly characterize the period from the late 1770s to the mid-twentieth century, banished supernatural visitations and a passive–receptive stance by the oppressed from its historical agenda. The oppressed had to *act* if they wished to free themselves. They had to make their own history willfully, an incisive concept that Jean-Jacques Rousseau, for all his failings, added to the history of radical ideas and for which he deserves immortality. The oppressed had to *reason*. There was no appeal to powers other than their own minds. The combination of reason and will, of thought and action, of reflection and intervention, changed the whole landscape of radicalism, divesting it of its mythic, mystical, religious, and intuitive qualities (which, regrettably, are beginning to return today in a disempowered and psychotherapized world).

The radicalism of the Age of Revolutions, however, went further. The Joachimite treatment of history moves, not unlike the Marxist, to the drumbeat of an inexorable "final days," an end, even a Hegelian absolute, where all that was had to be, in some sense, all that unfolded and followed the guidance of a "hidden hand," be it of God, Spirit, and the "cunning of reason" (to use Hegel's language) or of economic interest, however concealed that interest may have been from those who were influenced by it. There were no real alternatives to what was, is, or even would be – as absurd debates about the "inevitability of socialism" revealed a generation or two ago.

The emphasis of anarchist and libertarian utopists on *choice* in history created a radical new point of departure from the increasingly teleological visions of religious and later "scientific" socialisms. In great part, this emphasis explains the attention the nineteenth-century anarchists and libertarian utopists placed on individual autonomy, the individual's capacity to make choices based on rational and ethical judgments. This view is markedly different from the liberal tradition, with which anarchist views of individuality have been associated by their opponents, particularly by Marxists. Liberalism offered the individual a modicum of "freedom," to be sure, but one that was constructed by the "invisible hand" of the competitive marketplace, not by the capacity of free individuals to act according to ethical considerations. The "free entrepreneur" on whom liberalism modeled its image of individual autonomy was in fact completely trapped in a market collectivity, however "emancipated" he seemed from the overtly medieval world of guilds and religious obligations. He was the plaything of a "higher law" of market interactions based on competing egos, each of whom canceled out his egoistic interests in the formation of a general social interest.

Anarchism and the libertarian utopists never cast the free individual in this light. The individual had to be free to function as an *ethical* being, according to anarchist theorists – not as a narrow egoist – in making rational, hopefully disinterested choices between rational and irrational alternatives in history. The Marxist canard that anarchism is a product of liberal or bourgeois individualism has its roots in ideologies that are bourgeois to their very core, such as those based on myths of an "invisible hand" (liberalism), Spirit (Hegelianism), and economic determinism (Marxism). The anarchist and libertarian utopist emphasis on individual freedom meant the emancipation of history itself from an ahistorical preordination and stressed the importance of ethics in influencing choice. The individual is, indeed, truly free and attains true individuality when he or she is guided by a rational, humane, and high-minded notion of the social and communal good.

Finally, anarchist visions of a new world, particularly libertarian utopias, imply that society can always be remade. Indeed, utopia is, by definition, the world as it *should be* according to the canons of reason, in contrast to the world as it is, according to the blind, unthinking interaction of uncomprehending forces. The nineteenth-century anarchist tradition, less graphic and pictorial than the utopists who painted canvases of new and detailed images, reasoned out its theories in accordance with human history, not theological, mystical, or metaphysical history. The world had always made itself through the agency of real flesh-and-blood human beings, facing real choices at turning points of history. And it could remake itself along proven alternative lines that confronted people in the past.

Indeed, much of the anarchist tradition is not a "primitivistic" yearning for the past, as Marxist historians like Hobsbawm would have us believe, but a recognition of past possibilities that remain unfulfilled, such as the far-reaching importance of community, confederation, self-management of the economy, and a new balance between humanity and nature. Marx's famous injunction that the dead should bury the dead is meaningless, however well-intended it may be, when the present tries to parody the past. Only the *living* can bury the dead, and only if they understand what is dead and what is still living – indeed, what is intensely vital in the body-strewn battlefields of history.

Herein lies the power of William Godwin's concern for individual autonomy, for the ethical person whose mind is unfettered by the social burdens of suprahuman forces and all forms of domination, including deities as well as statesmen, the authority of custom as well as the authority of the State. Herein, too, lies the power of Proudhon's concern for municipalism and confederalism as principles of association, indeed, as ways of life whose freedom is unfettered by the nation-state as well as the pernicious role of property. Herein lies Bakunin's hypostatization of popular spontaneity and the transformative role of the revolutionary act, of the deed as an expression of will that is unfettered by constraints of compromise and parliamentary cretinism. Herein finally lies the power of Kropotkin's ecological visions and his practical concern with human scale, decentralization, and the harmonization of humanity with nature as distinguished from the explosive growth of urbanization and centralization. . . .

Let me pause to examine the issue of emancipation of another kind – the emancipation of the body in the form of a new sensuousness and of the human spirit in the form of an ecological sensibility. These issues rarely figure in discussions of social renovation, although they have a prominent place in utopian thinking.

A sense of sheer *joie de vivre* is closely wedded to the anarchic tradition, despite the arid patches of asceticism that surface in its midst. Emma Goldman's admonition – "If I can't dance in your revolution, I don't want it!" – is typically anarchic in its disposition. A colorful tradition exists that dates back centuries to artisan and even certain peasant anarchists who demanded as much for the emancipation of the senses as they did for their communities. The Ophites, in the backwash of antiquity, reread the biblical scriptures to make knowledge the key to salvation; the snake and Eve, the agents of freedom; the ecstatic release of the flesh, the medium for the full expression of the soul. The Brethren of the Free Spirit, an abiding movement over many different names in medieval Europe, rejected the ecclesiastical reverence for self-denial and celebrated their version of Christianity as a message of sheer libertinism as well as social liberation. In Rabelais's "Abbey of Thélème" narrative, the maxim "Do as thou wilt!" removed all restraint from the members of its playful order, who were free to rise, dine, love, and cultivate all the pleasures of the flesh and the mind as they chose.

The technical limits of past eras, the fact that pleasure could rarely be separated from parasitism in a demanding world of toil, made all of these movements and utopias elitist. What the Brethren of the Free Spirit stole from the rich, the rich in turn took from the poor. What the members of the Abbey of Thélème enjoyed as a matter of right was expropriated from the labor of builders, foods cultivators, cooks, and the grooms who served them. Nature was not bountiful, it was assumed, except in a few usually favored areas of the world. Emancipation of the senses was often assumed by the poor and their revolutionary prophets to be a ruling class privilege, although it was more widespread in villages and towns than we have been led to believe. And even the oppressed had their dreams of utopistic pleasures, of visions where nature was indeed bountiful and rivers flowed with milk and honey. But always this marvelous dispensation was the product of a being other than themselves who bestowed the gift of plenty upon them in the form of a "promised land" – be it a deity or an irascible demon – rather than technology and new, more equitable arrangements of work and distribution. . . .

Between the closing years of the French Revolution and the mid-nineteenth century, the ideals of freedom had acquired a solidly naturalistic, technologically viable, and solidly material base. Here was a remarkable turning point in history when humanity, by whatever action, might well have swerved from a path of market-oriented and profit-oriented expansion to one of community-oriented and ecology-oriented harmony – a harmony between human and human that could have been projected by virtue of a new sensibility into a harmony between humanity and nature. If the latter half of the century engulfed society in a degree of industrial development that would remake the natural world into a synthetic one, the first half was filled with the promise of a new integration between society and nature and a cooperative commonwealth that would have satisfied the most generous impulses toward freedom. That this did not occur was due in no small measure to the bourgeois spirit that enfolded Euro-American society – and no less significantly, to the revolutionary project of remaking society that had found such rich expression in the utopians, visionary socialists, and anarchists who followed in the wake of the French Revolution.

The revolutionary project had acquired a richly ethical heritage, a commitment to reconciling the dualities of mind, body, and society that pitted reason against sensuality, work against play, town against country, and humanity against nature. Utopian and anarchist thought at their best saw these contradictions clearly and tried to overcome them with an ideal of freedom based on complementarity, the irreducible minimum, and the equality of unequals. The contradictions were seen as evidence of a society mired in "evil," indeed as a "civilization," to use Fourier's word, that was turned against humanity and culture by the irrational direction it had followed up to that time. Reason, in its power to be employed speculatively beyond the existing state of affairs, was becoming a crude rationalism, based on the efficient exploitation of labor and natural resources. Science, in its searching probe of reality and its underlying order, was turning into a cult of scientism, little more than the instrumental engineering of control over people and nature. Technology, with its promise of ameliorating labor, was turning into a technocratic ensemble of means for exploiting the human and nonhuman world.

The anarchist theorists and the libertarian utopists, despite their understandable belief that reason, science, and technics could be creative forces for remaking society, voiced a collective protest against the reduction of these forces to purely instrumental ends. They were acutely aware, as we can now see retrospectively from the vantage point of our own historical malaise, of the rapid transitions through which the century was going. Their fiery demands for immediate change along liberatory lines was permeated by a sense of anxiety that society as a whole was faced with "embourgeoisement," to use Bakunin's word expressing the remarkably anticipatory fears and the fatalism that gripped him in the last years of his life.

Contrary to the philistine judgments of Gerald Brenan and Eric Hobsbawm, anarchist emphases on "propaganda of the deed" were not primitive acts of violence or mere catharsis in the face of public passivity to the horrors of industrial capitalism. They were, in great part, the product of a desperate insight into the fact that a historic moment in social development was being lost, a loss that would produce immense obstacles in the future to the realization of the revolutionary project. Imbued with ethical and visionary concepts, they rightly saw their time as one that demanded immediate human emancipation, not as one "stage" in the long history of humanity's evolution toward freedom with its endless "preconditions" and technological "substructures."

What the anarchist theorists and libertarian utopists did not see is that ideals of freedom were themselves faced with embourgeoisement. No one, perhaps not even Marx himself, who played so important a role in this infection, could have anticipated that the attempt to make the emancipatory project into a science under the rubric of "scientific socialism" would make it even more of a "dismal science" than economics; indeed, that it would divest it of its ethical heart, its visionary spirit, and its ecological substance. No less compelling, Marx's "scientific socialism" developed in tandem with the bourgeoisie's sinister undoing of the objective as well as the ideological premises of the revolutionary project by justifying the absorption of decentralized units into the centralized state, confederalist visions into chauvinistic nations, and humanly scaled technologies into all-devouring systems of mass production.

Cultures of Revolt
(from *From Urbanization to Cities*, 1987)

Growing industry, commerce, and "commodification" did not seep completely into the neighborhood life of the new cities, nor did it totally destroy the conditions for the regeneration of domestic life. The buffeting that towns and cities of the nineteenth century took from industrialization, however disastrous its initial effects on traditional lifeways, did not destroy the inherently village-like subcultures of workers and middle-class people who were only a generation or two removed from a more rural culture. Like the ethnic groups that entered the New World through New York City throughout much of the nineteenth and early twentieth centuries, displacement was followed by resettlement and recommunalization, even in the most desperately poor slums of the overpopulated cities of Europe and America. The pub in the industrial cities of England, the café in France, and the beer hall in Germany, no less than the various community centers around which ethnic ghettos formed in New York and other American cities, provided foci for a distinctly working-class culture, largely artisan in its outlook, class-oriented in its politics, and knit together by mutual self-help groups.

This recolonization of community life was greatly abetted by the organized labor movement in all its different forms. Socialist clubs, trade union centers, local cooperatives, mutual aid societies, and educational groups created a public space that included classes in reading, writing, literature, and history. The socialist clubs and union centers provided libraries, periodicals, lectures, and discussion groups to "elevate" worker consciousness as well as mobilize them for political and economic ends. Picnics, athletic activities, and outdoor forays into the countryside served to add a very intimate dimension to purely educational projects. The *casas del pueblo* established by Spanish socialists and the *centros obreros* established by the Spanish anarchists, which existed up to the late 1930s, are reminders of the vigorous development of community life even in the most depressed areas of Europe – indeed of an "underground" culture that always paralleled the received culture of the elite orders and classes.

There was always a plebeian cultural domain at the base of society, even in the most dismal and squalid parts of ancient, medieval, and modern cities, that was beyond the reach of the conventional culture and the state apparatus. No economy or state had the technical means, until very recently, to freely infiltrate this domain and dissolve it for a lasting period of time. Left to itself, the "underground" world of the oppressed remained a breeding ground for rebels and conspirators against the prevailing authority. No less urban in character than agrarian, it also remained a school for a grassroots politics that, by definition, involved groups of ordinary people, even in sizable communities, in a plebeian political sphere and often brought them into outright rebellion. This "underground" school created new political forms and new citizens to deal with changing social conditions. Even after the great boulevards of Baron Haussmann ripped into the plebeian *quartiers* of Paris, opening the city to artillery fire and cavalry charges against barricades, the sizable neighborhood pockets left behind retained an imperturbably rebellious vitality that finally culminated in the Paris Commune. Few of Europe's major cities were spared crowd actions and uprisings in the nineteenth century, indeed well into the first half of the twentieth. As industrial capitalism spread out from England into western Europe and America, the initial destabilization it produced as a result of urbanization and mechanization was followed by a regeneration of popular culture along new patterns that also included the integration of old ones. Just as the French village was reproduced as *quartiers* in French cities, and the Spanish *pueblo* as *barrios* in Spanish cities, so the Jewish *shtetl,* the "Little Italys," and "Little Irelands" were reproduced in altered form but with much of their cultural flavor, personal intimacies, and traditional values in world cities such as New York. Even the industrial cities replicated on a local basis the specific cultural origins of their variegated populations and regions. . . .

Every class culture was always a community culture, indeed a civic culture – a fact that links the period of the Industrial Revolution and its urban forms with precapitalist cultures of the past. This continuity has been largely overlooked by contemporary socialists and sociologists. While the factory and mill formed the first line of the class struggle in the last century, a struggle that in no way should be confused with the class war that is supposed to yield working-class insurrections, its lines of supply reached back into the neighborhoods and towns where workers lived and often mingled with middle-class people, farmers, and intellectuals. Wage earners had human faces, not merely mystified "proletarian" faces, and functioned no less as human beings than as class beings. Accordingly, they were fathers and mothers, brothers and sisters, sons and daughters, citizens and neighbors, not only factory hands. Their concerns included issues such as war and peace, environmental dislocations, educational opportunities, the beauty of their surroundings as well as its ugliness, and in times of international conflict, a heavy dose of jingoism and nationalism – indeed, a vast host of problems and concerns that were broadly human, not only class-oriented and rooted in wages and working conditions.

This communal dimension of the industrial era is of tremendous importance in understanding how class conflicts often spilled over beyond economic issues into broadly social, even utopian concerns. Indeed as long as the market did not dissolve the communal dimension of industrialism, there was a richly fecund, highly diversified, cooperative, and innovative domain of social and political life to which the proletariat could retreat after working hours, a domain that retained a vital continuity with precapitalist lifeways and values. This partly municipal, partly domestic terrain formed a strong countervailing force to the impact of an industrial economy and the nation-state. Here workers mingled with a great variety of individuals, particularly artisans, intellectuals, and farmers who brought their produce into the towns. In a purely human fashion that revealed all the facets of their personalities, they developed a sense of shared, active citizenship. This communal or municipal citizenship kept political life alive even in highly centralized and bureaucratized nation-states. It would be difficult to understand not only the radical uprisings of the nineteenth century but those of the twentieth – particularly the series of urban and agrarian uprisings that culminated in the Spanish Civil War – without keeping this communal dimension of the "class struggle" clearly in mind. Every class movement from the late eighteenth to the early twentieth centuries was also a civic movement, a product of neighborhood, town, and village consociation, not only of the factory, farm, and office. It was not until a technology developed that could make deep, perhaps decisive inroads into this "underground" municipal domain that politics and citizenship were faced with the total "commodification" of society, the supremacy of statecraft, and the subversion of the city's ecological diversity and creativity.

Spanish Anarchism: The Collectives
(from "Overview of the Spanish Libertarian Movement" and "After Fifty Years," 1974 and 1985)

However much the fortunes of Spanish anarchism varied from region to region and from period to period, whatever revolutionary movement existed in Spain during this sixty-year period [1875–1935] was essentially anarchist. Even after the First World War, as anarchism began to ebb before Marxian social-democratic and later Bolshevik organizations, Spanish anarchism retained its enormous influence and its revolutionary élan. Viewed from a radical standpoint, the history of the Spanish labor movement remained libertarian and often served to define the contours of the Marxist movements in Spain. "Generally speaking, a small but well-organized group of Anarchists in a Socialist area drove the Socialists to the Left," observes Gerald Brenan, "whereas in predominantly Anarchist areas, Socialists were outstandingly reformist."³ It was not socialism but anarchism that determined the metabolism of the Spanish labor movement – the great general strikes that swept repeatedly over Spain, the recurring insurrections in Barcelona and in the towns and villages of Andalusia, and the gun battles between labor militants and employer-hired thugs in the Mediterranean coastal cities.

It is essential to emphasize that Spanish anarchism was not merely a program embedded in a dense theoretical matrix. It was a way of life: partly the life of the Spanish people as it was lived in the closely knit villages of the countryside and the intense neighborhood life of the working-class barrios; partly, too, the theoretical articulation of that life as projected by Bakunin's concepts of decentralization, mutual aid, and popular organs of self-management. [Inasmuch as Spain's] long tradition of agrarian collectivism . . . was distinctly precapitalist, Spanish Marxism regarded it as anachronistic, in fact as "historically reactionary." Spanish socialism built its agrarian program around the Marxist tenet that the peasantry and its social forms could have no lasting revolutionary value until they were "proletarianized" and "industrialized." Indeed, the sooner the village decayed, the better, and the more rapidly the peasantry became a hereditary proletariat, "disciplined, united, organized by the very mechanism of the process of capitalist production itself" (Marx) – a distinctly hierarchical and authoritarian "mechanism" – the more rapidly Spain would advance to the tasks of socialism.

Spanish anarchism, by contrast, followed a decisively different approach. It sought out the precapitalist collectivist traditions of the village, nourished what was living and vital in them, evoked their revolutionary potentialities as liberatory modes of mutual aid and self-management, and deployed them to vitiate the obedience, hierarchical mentality, and authoritarian outlook fostered by the factory system. Ever mindful of the embourgeoisement of the proletariat . . . , the Spanish anarchists tried to use the precapitalist traditions of the peasantry and working class against the assimilation of the workers' outlook to an authoritarian industrial rationality. In this respect their efforts were favored by the continuous fertilization of the Spanish proletariat by rural workers, who renewed these traditions daily as they migrated to the cities. The revolutionary élan of the Barcelona proletariat – like that of the Petrograd and Parisian proletariats – was due in no small measure to the fact that these workers never solidly sedimented into a hereditary working class, totally removed from precapitalist traditions, whether of the peasant or the craftsman. Along the Mediterranean coastal cities of Spain, many workers retained a living memory of a noncapitalist culture – one in which each moment of life was not strictly regulated by the punch clock, the factory whistle, the foreman, the machine, the highly regulated work day, or the atomizing world of the large city. Spanish anarchism flourished within a tension created by these antagonistic traditions and sensibilities. Indeed, where a "Germanic proletariat" (to use another of Bakunin's cutting phrases) emerged in Spain, it drifted either toward the UGT or toward the Catholic unions. Its political outlook, reformist when not overtly conservative, often clashed with the more *déclassé* working class of Catalonia and the Mediterranean coast, leading to conflicting tendencies within the Spanish proletariat as a whole.

Ultimately, in my view, the destiny of Spanish anarchism depended upon its ability to create libertarian organizational forms that could synthesize the precapitalist collectivist traditions of the village with an industrial economy and a highly urbanized society. I speak here of no mere programmatic "alliance" between the Spanish peasantry and proletariat but, more organically, of new organizational forms and sensibilities that imparted a revolutionary libertarian character to two social classes that lived in conflicting cultures. That Spain required a well-organized libertarian movement was hardly a matter of doubt among the majority of Spanish anarchists. But would this movement reflect a village society or a factory society? Where a conflict existed, could the two be melded in the same movement without violating the libertarian tenets of decentralization, mutual aid, and self-administration? In the classical era of proletarian socialism, between 1848 and 1939, an era that stressed the hegemony of the industrial proletariat in all social struggles, Spanish anarchism followed a historic trajectory that revealed at once the limitations of the era itself and the creative possibilities of anarchic forms of organization.

By comparison with the cities, the Spanish villages that were committed to anarchism raised very few organizational problems. Brenan's emphasis on the *braceros* notwithstanding, the strength of agrarian anarchism in the south and in the Levant lay in the mountain villages, not among the rural proletariat that worked the great plantations of Andalusia. In these relatively isolated villages, a fierce sense of independence and personal dignity whetted the bitter social hatreds engendered by poverty, creating the rural "patriarchs" of anarchism whose entire families were devoted almost apostolically to "the Idea." For these sharply etched and rigorously ascetic individuals, defiance of the State, the Church, and conventional authority in general was almost a way of life. Knit together by the local press – and at various times there were hundreds of anarchist periodicals in Spain – they formed the sinews of agrarian anarchism from the 1870s onward and, to a large extent, the conscience of Spanish anarchism throughout its history.

Their agrarian collectives reflected to a remarkable extent the organizational forms that the anarchists fostered among all the villages under their influence before the 1936 revolution. The revolution in rural communities essentially enlarged the old IWMA [International Working Men's Association] and later CNT [National Confederation of Labor] nuclei, membership groups, or quite simply clans of closely knit anarchist families into popular assemblies. These usually met weekly and formulated the policy decisions of the community as a whole. The assembly form comprised the organizational ideal of village anarchism from the days of the first truly Bakuninist congress of the Spanish IWMA in Córdoba in 1872, stressing the libertarian traditions of Spanish village life. Where such popular assemblies were possible, their decisions were executed by a committee elected from the assembly. Apparently the right to recall committee members was taken for granted, and they certainly enjoyed no privileges, emoluments, or institutional power. Their influence was a function of their obvious dedication and capabilities. It remained a cardinal principle of Spanish anarchists never to pay their delegates, even when the CNT numbered a million members.

Normally, the responsibilities of elected delegates had to be discharged after working hours. Almost all the evenings of anarchist militants were occupied with meetings of one sort or another. Whether at assemblies or committees, they argued, debated, voted, and administered, and when time afforded, they read and passionately discussed "the Idea" to which they dedicated not only their leisure hours but their very lives. For the greater part of the day, they were working men and women, *obrera consciente*, who abjured smoking and drinking, avoided brothels and the bloody bullring, purged their talk of "foul" language, and by their probity, dignity, respect for knowledge, and militancy tried to set a moral example for their entire class. They never used the word *god* in daily conversation (*salud* was preferred over *adios*) and avoided all official contact with clerical and state authorities, indeed, to the point where they refused to legally validate their lifelong "free unions" with marital documents and never baptized or confirmed their children. One must know Catholic Spain to realize how far-reaching were these self-imposed mores – and how quixotically consistent some of them were with the puritanical traditions of the country. . . .

The prospect for libertarian organization in the cities and factories could not depend upon the long tradition of village collectivism – the strong sense of community – that existed in rural anarchist areas. For within the factory itself – the realm of toil, hierarchy, industrial discipline, and brute material necessity – "community" was more a function of the bourgeois division of labor, with its exploitative, even competitive connotations, than of humanistic cooperation, playfully creative work, and mutual aid. Working-class solidarity depended less upon a shared meaningful life nourished by self-fulfilling work than on the common enemy – the boss – who exploded any illusion that under capitalism the worker was more than an industrial resource, an object to be coldly manipulated and ruthlessly exploited. If anarchism can be partly regarded as a revolt of the individual against the industrial system, the profound truth that lies at the heart of that revolt is that the factory routine not only blunts the sensibility of the worker to the rich feast of life; it degrades the worker's image of his or her human potentialities, of his or her capacities to take direct control of the means for administering social life. . . .

It is not surprising that the most communistic collectives in the Spanish Revolution appeared in the countryside rather than in the cities, among villagers who were still influenced by archaic collectivistic traditions and were less ensnared in a market economy than their urban cousins. The ascetic values that so greatly influenced these highly communistic collectives often reflected the extreme poverty of the areas in which they were rooted. Cooperation and mutual aid in such cases formed the preconditions for survival of the community. Elsewhere, in the more arid areas of Spain, the need for sharing water and maintaining irrigation works was an added inducement to collective farming. Here collectivization was also a technological necessity, but one that even the republic did not interfere with. What makes these rural collectives important is not only that many of them practiced communism but that they functioned so effectively under a system of popular self-management. This belies the notion held by so many authoritarian Marxists that economic life must be scrupulously "planned" by a highly centralized state power and the odious canard that popular collectivization, as distinguished from statist national-ization, necessarily pits collectivized enterprises against each other in competition for profits and resources.

In the cities, however, collectivization of the factories, communica-tions systems, and transport facilities took a very different form. Initially [at the beginning of the Spanish Revolution in July 1936] nearly the entire economy in areas controlled by the CNT–FAI [the Iberian Anarchist Federation] had been taken over by committees elected from among the workers and were loosely coordinated by higher union committees. As time went on, this system was increasingly tightened. The higher committee began to preempt the initiative from the lower, although their decisions still had to be ratified by the workers of the facilities involved. The effect of this process was to tend to centralize the economy of CNT–FAI areas in the hands of the union. The extent to which this process unfolded varied greatly from industry to industry and area to area, and with the limited knowledge we have at hand, generalizations are very difficult to formulate. With the entry of the CNT–FAI into the Catalan government in [the late summer of] 1936, the process of centralization continued, and the union-controlled facilities became wedded to the state. By early 1938 a political bureaucracy had largely supplanted the authority of the workers' committees in all Republican-held cities. Although workers' control existed in theory, it had virtually disappeared in fact. . . .

The wave of collectivizations that swept over Spain in the summer and autumn of 1936 has been described as "the greatest experiment in workers' self-management Western Europe has ever seen," a revolution more far-reaching than any that occurred in Russia during 1917–21 and the years before and after it.[4] In anarchist industrial areas like Catalonia, an estimated three-quarters of the economy was placed under workers' control, as it was in anarchist rural areas like Aragon. The figure tapers downward where the UGT shared power with the CNT or else predominated: 50 percent in anarchist and socialist Valencia, and 30 percent in socialist and liberal Madrid. In the more thoroughly anarchist areas, particularly among the agrarian collectives, money was eliminated and the material means of life were allocated strictly according to need rather than work, following the traditional precepts of a libertarian communist society. As a recent BBC–Granada television documentary puts it: "The ancient dream of a collective society without profit or property was made reality in the villages of Aragon. . . . All forms of production were owned by the community, run by their workers."[5]

The administrative apparatus of Republican Spain belonged almost entirely to the unions and their political organizations. Police in many cities were replaced with armed workers' patrols. Militia units were formed everywhere – in factories, on farms, and in socialist and anarchist community centers and union halls, initially including women as well as men. A vast network of local revolutionary committees coordinated the feeding of the cities, the operations of the economy, and the meting out of justice, indeed, almost every facet of Spanish life from production to culture, bringing the whole of Spanish society in the Republican zone into a well-organized and coherent whole. This historically unprecedented appropriation of society by its most oppressed sectors – including women, who were liberated from all the constraints of a highly traditional Catholic country, be it the prohibition of abortion and divorce or a degraded status in the economy – was the work of the Spanish proletariat and peasantry. It was a movement from below that overwhelmed even the revolutionary organizations of the oppressed, including the CNT–FAI.

Critique of Lifestyle Anarchism
(from "Social Anarchism or Lifestyle Anarchism," 1995)

Today's reactionary social context greatly explains the emergence of a phenomenon in Euro-American anarchism that cannot be ignored: the spread of individualist anarchism. In a time when even respectable forms of socialism are in pell-mell retreat from principles that might in any way be construed as radical, issues of lifestyle are once again supplanting social action and revolutionary politics in anarchism. In the traditionally individualist–liberal United States and Britain, the 1990s are awash in self-styled anarchists who – their flamboyant radical rhetoric aside – are cultivating a latter-day anarcho-individualism that I will call *lifestyle anarchism*. Its preoccupations with the ego and its uniqueness and its polymorphous concepts of resistance are steadily eroding the socialistic character of the libertarian tradition. No less than Marxism and other socialisms, anarchism can be profoundly influenced by the bourgeois environment it professes to oppose, with the result that the growing "inwardness" and narcissism of the yuppie generation have left their mark upon many avowed radicals. Ad hoc adventurism, personal bravura, an aversion to theory oddly akin to the antirational biases of postmodernism, celebrations of theoretical incoherence (pluralism), a basically apolitical and anti-organizational commitment to imagination, desire, and ecstasy, and an intensely self-oriented enchantment of everyday life, reflect the toll that social reaction has taken on Euro-American anarchism over the past two decades. . . .

What stands out most compellingly in today's lifestyle anarchism is its appetite for *immediacy* rather than reflection, for a naïve one-to-one relationship between mind and reality. Not only does this immediacy immunize libertarian thinking from demands for nuanced and mediated reflection; it precludes rational analysis and, for that matter, rationality itself. Consigning humanity to the nontemporal, nonspatial, and nonhistorical – a "primal" notion of temporality based on the "eternal" cycles of "Nature" – it thereby divests mind of its creative uniqueness and its freedom to intervene into the natural world. . . .

In the end, the individual ego becomes the supreme temple of reality, excluding history and becoming, democracy and responsibility. Indeed, lived contact with society as such is rendered tenuous by a narcissism so all-embracing that it shrivels consociation to an infantilized ego that is little more than a bundle of shrieking demands and claims for its own satisfactions. Civilization merely obstructs the ecstatic self-realization of this ego's desires, reified as the ultimate fulfillment of emancipation, as though ecstasy and desire were not products of cultivation and historical development but merely innate impulses that appear ab novo in a desocialized world.

Like the petty-bourgeois Stirnerite ego, primitivist lifestyle anarchism allows no room for social institutions, political organizations, and radical programs, still less a public sphere, which [they] automatically identify with statecraft. The sporadic, the unsystematic, the incoherent, the discontinuous, and the intuitive supplant the consistent, purposive, organized, and rational, indeed any sustained and focused activity apart from publishing a "zine" or pamphlet – or burning a garbage can. Imagination is counterposed to reason and desire to theoretical coherence, as though the two were in radical contradiction to each other. Goya's admonition that imagination without reason produces monsters is altered to leave the impression that imagination flourishes on an unmediated experience with an unnuanced "oneness." Thus is social nature essentially dissolved into biological nature; innovative humanity into adaptive animality; temporality into precivilizatory eternality; history into an archaic cyclicity.

A bourgeois reality whose economic harshness grows starker and crasser with every passing day is shrewdly mutated by lifestyle anarchism into constellations of self-indulgence, inchoateness, indiscipline, and incoherence. In the 1960s the Situationists, in the name of a "theory of the spectacle," in fact produced a reified spectacle of the theory, but they at least offered organizational correctives, such as workers' councils, that gave their aestheticism some ballast. Lifestyle anarchism, by assailing organization, programmatic commitment, and serious social analysis, apes the worst aspects of Situationist aestheticism without adhering to the project of building a movement. As the detritus of the 1960s, it wanders aimlessly within the bounds of the ego (renamed by John Zerzan the "bounds of nature") and makes a virtue of bohemian incoherence.

What is most troubling is that the self-indulgent aesthetic vagaries of lifestyle anarchism significantly erode the socialist core of a left-libertarian ideology that once could claim social relevance and weight precisely for its uncompromising commitment to emancipation – not *outside* of history, in the realm of the subjective, but *within* history, in the realm of the objective. The great cry of the First International – which anarcho-syndicalism and anarcho-communism retained after Marx and his supporters abandoned it – was the demand: "No rights without duties, no duties without rights." For generations, this slogan adorned the mastheads of what we must now retrospectively call *social anarchist* periodicals. Today, it stands radically at odds with the basically egocentric demand for "desire armed," and with Taoist contemplation and Buddhist nirvanas. Where social anarchism called upon people to rise in revolution and seek the reconstruction of society, the irate petty bourgeois who populate the subcultural world of lifestyle anarchism call for episodic rebellion and the satisfaction of their "desiring machines," to use the phraseology of Deleuze and Guattari.

The steady retreat from the historic commitment of classical anarchism to social struggle (without which self-realization and the fulfillment of desire in all its dimensions, not merely the instinctive, cannot be achieved) is inevitably accompanied by a disastrous mystification of experience and reality. The ego, identified almost fetishistically as the locus of emancipation, turns out to be identical to the "sovereign individual" of laissez-faire individualism. Detached from its social moorings, it achieves not autonomy but the heteronomous "selfhood" of petty-bourgeois enterprise.

Indeed, far from being free, the ego in its sovereign selfhood is bound hand and foot to the seemingly anonymous laws of the marketplace – the laws of competition and exploitation – which render the myth of individual freedom into another fetish concealing the implacable laws of capital accumulation. Lifestyle anarchism, in effect, turns out to be an additional mystifying bourgeois deception. Its acolytes are no more "autonomous" than the movements of the stock market, than price fluctuations and the mundane facts of bourgeois commerce. All claims to autonomy notwithstanding, this middle-class "rebel," with or without a brick in hand, *is entirely captive to the subterranean market forces that occupy all the allegedly "free" terrains of modern social life,* from food cooperatives to rural communes. Capitalism swirls around us – not only materially but culturally. As Zerzan so memorably put it to a puzzled interviewer who asked about the television set in the home of this foe of technology: "Like all other people, I have to be narcotized."[6]

That lifestyle anarchism itself is a "narcotizing" self-deception can best be seen in Max Stirner's *The Ego and His Own,* where the ego's claim to "uniqueness" in the temple of the sacrosanct "self" far outranks John Stuart Mill's liberal pieties. Indeed, with Stirner, egoism becomes a matter of epistemology. Cutting through the maze of contradictions and woefully incomplete statements that fill *The Ego and His Own,* one finds Stirner's "unique" ego to be a myth because its roots lie in its seeming "other" – society itself. Indeed: "Truth cannot step forward as you do," Stirner addresses the egoist, "cannot move, change, develop; truth awaits and recruits everything from *you,* and itself is only through you; for it exists only – *in your head.*"[7] The Stirnerite egoist, in effect, bids farewell to objective reality, to the facticity of the social, and thereby to fundamental social change and all ethical criteria and ideals beyond personal satisfaction amidst the hidden demons of the bourgeois marketplace. This absence of mediation subverts the very existence of the concrete, not to speak of the authority of the Stirnerite ego itself – a claim so all-encompassing as to exclude the social roots of the self and its formation in history.

Nietzsche, quite independently of Stirner, carried this view of truth to its logical conclusion by erasing the facticity and reality of truth as such: "What, then, is truth?" he asked. "A mobile army of metaphors, metonyms, and anthropomorphisms – in short, a sum of human relations, which have been enhanced, transposed, and embellished poetically and rhetorically."[8] With more forthrightness than Stirner, Nietzsche contended that facts are simply interpretations; indeed, he asked, "is it necessary to posit an interpreter behind the interpretations?" Apparently not, for "even this is invention, hypothesis."[9] Following Nietzsche's unrelenting logic, we are left with a self that not only essentially creates its own reality but also must justify its *own* existence as more than a mere interpretation. Such egoism thus annihilates the ego itself, which vanishes into the mist of Stirner's own unstated premises.

Similarly divested of history, society, and facticity beyond its own metaphors, lifestyle anarchism lives in an asocial domain in which the ego, with its cryptic desires, must evaporate into logical abstractions. But reducing the ego to intuitive immediacy – anchoring it in mere animality, in the "bounds of nature," or in "natural law" – would amount to ignoring the fact that the ego is the product of an *ever-formative* history, indeed, a history that, if it is to consist of more than mere episodes, must avail itself of reason as a guide to standards of progress and regress, necessity and freedom, good and evil, and – yes! – civilization and barbarism. Indeed, an anarchism that seeks to avoid the shoals of sheer solipsism on the one hand and the loss of the "self" as a mere "interpretation" on the other must become explicitly socialist or collectivist. That is to say, it must be a *social* anarchism that seeks freedom through structure and mutual responsibility, not through a vaporous, nomadic ego that eschews the preconditions for social life.

Stated bluntly: Between the socialist pedigree of anarcho-syndicalism and anarcho-communism (which have never denied the importance of self-realization and the fulfillment of desire), and the basically liberal, individualistic pedigree of lifestyle anarchism (which fosters social ineffectuality, if not outright social negation), there exists a divide that cannot be bridged unless we completely disregard the profoundly different goals, methods, and underlying philosophy that distinguish them. Stirner's own project, in fact, emerged in a debate with the socialism of Wilhelm Weitling and Moses Hess, where he invoked egoism precisely to counterpose to socialism. "Personal insurrection rather than general revolution was [Stirner's] message," James J. Martin admiringly observes[10] – a counterposition that lives on today in lifestyle anarchism and its yuppie filiations, as distinguished from social anarchism with its roots in historicism, the social matrix of individuality, and its commitment to a rational society.

The very incongruity of these essentially mixed messages, which coexist on every page of the lifestyle "zines," reflects the feverish voice of the squirming petty bourgeois. If anarchism loses its socialist core and collectivist goal, if it drifts off into aestheticism, ecstasy, and desire, and, incongruously, into Taoist quietism and Buddhist self-effacement as a substitute for a libertarian program, politics, and organization, it will come to represent not social regeneration and a revolutionary vision but social decay and a petulant egoistic rebellion. Worse, it will feed the wave of mysticism that is already sweeping affluent members of the generation now in their teens and twenties. Lifestyle anarchism's exaltation of ecstasy, *certainly laudable in a radical social matrix* but here unabashedly intermingled with "sorcery," is producing a dreamlike absorption with spirits, ghosts, and Jungian archetypes rather than a rational and dialectical awareness of the world. . . .

A return to mere animality – or shall we call it "decivilization"? – *is a return not to freedom but to instinct,* to the domain of "authenticity" that is guided more by genes than by brains. Nothing could be further from the ideals of freedom spelled out in ever-expansive forms by the great revolutions of the past. And nothing could be more unrelenting in its sheer obedience to biochemical imperatives such as DNA or more in contrast to the creativity, ethics, and mutuality opened by culture and struggles for a rational civilization. There is no freedom in "wildness" if, by sheer ferality, we mean the dictates of inborn behavioral patterns that shape mere animality. To malign civilization without due recognition of its enormous potentialities for *self-conscious* freedom – a freedom conferred by reason as well as emotion, by insight as well as desire, by prose as well as poetry – is to retreat back into the shadowy world of brutishness, when thought was dim and intellection was only an evolutionary promise.

TOWARD A DEMOCRATIC COMMUNALISM

My picture of lifestyle anarchism is far from complete; the personalistic thrust of this ideological clay allows it to be molded in many forms provided that words like *imagination, sacred, intuitive, ecstasy,* and *primal* embellish its surface.

Social anarchism, in my view, is made of fundamentally different stuff, heir to the Enlightenment tradition, with due regard to that tradition's limits and incompleteness. Depending upon how it defines reason, social anarchism celebrates the thinking human mind without in any way denying passion, ecstasy, imagination, play, and art. Yet rather than reify them into hazy categories, it tries to incorporate them into everyday life. It is committed to rationality while opposing the rationalization of experience; to technology, while opposing the "megamachine"; to social institutionalization, while opposing class rule and hierarchy; to a genuine politics based on the confederal coordination of municipalities or communes by the people in direct face-to-face democracy, while opposing parliamentarism and the state.

This "Commune of communes," to use a traditional slogan of earlier revolutions, can be appropriately designated as Communalism. Opponents of democracy as "rule" to the contrary notwithstanding, it describes the *democratic* dimension of anarchism as a majoritarian administration of the public sphere. Accordingly, Communalism seeks freedom rather than autonomy in the sense that I have counterposed them. It sharply breaks with the psycho-personal Stirnerite, liberal, and bohemian ego as a self-contained sovereign by asserting that individuality does not emerge ab novo, dressed at birth in "natural rights," but sees individuality in great part as the ever-changing work of historical and social development, a process of self-formation that can be neither petrified by biologism nor arrested by temporally limited dogmas.

The sovereign, self-sufficient "individual" has always been a precarious basis upon which to anchor a left-libertarian outlook. As Max Horkheimer once observed, "individuality is impaired when each man decides to fend for himself. . . . The absolutely isolated individual has always been an illusion. The most esteemed personal qualities, such as independence, will to freedom, sympathy, and the sense of justice, are social as well as individual virtues. The fully developed individual is the consummation of a fully developed society."[11]

If a left-libertarian vision of a future society is not to disappear in a bohemian and lumpen demimonde, it must offer a resolution to social problems, not flit arrogantly from slogan to slogan, shielding itself from rationality with bad poetry and vulgar graphics. Democracy is not antithetical to anarchism; nor are majority rule and nonconsensual decisions incommensurable with a libertarian society.

That no society can exist without institutional structures is transparently clear to anyone who has not been stupefied by Stirner and his kind. By denying institutions and democracy, lifestyle anarchism insulates itself from social reality, so that it can fume all the more with futile rage, thereby remaining a subcultural caper for gullible youth and bored consumers of black garments and ecstasy posters. To argue that democracy and anarchism are incompatible because any impediment to the wishes of even "a minority of one" constitutes a violation of personal autonomy is to advocate not a free society but L. Susan Brown's "collection of individuals" – in short, a herd. No longer would "imagination" come to "power." Power, *which always exists,* will belong either to the collective in a face-to-face and clearly institutionalized democracy, or to the egos of a few oligarchs who will produce a "tyranny of structurelessness." . . .

In the United States and much of Europe, precisely at a time when mass disillusionment with the state has reached unprecedented proportions, anarchism is in retreat. Dissatisfaction with government as such runs high on both sides of the Atlantic – and seldom in recent memory has there been a more compelling popular sentiment for a new politics, even a new social dispensation that can give to people a sense of direction that allows for security and ethical meaning. If the failure of anarchism to address this situation can be attributed to any single source, the insularity of lifestyle anarchism and its individualistic underpinnings must be singled out for aborting the entry of a potential left-libertarian movement into an ever-contracting public sphere.

To its credit, anarcho-syndicalism in its heyday tried to engage in a living practice and create an organized movement – so alien to lifestyle anarchism – within the working class. Its major problems lay not in its desire for structure and involvement, for program and social mobilization, but in the waning of the working class as a revolutionary subject, particularly after the Spanish Revolution. To say that anarchism lacked a politics, however, conceived in its original Greek meaning as the self-management of the community – the historic "Commune of communes" – is to repudiate a historic and *transformative* practice that seeks to radicalize the democracy inherent in any republic and to create a municipalist confederal power to countervail the state.

The most creative feature of traditional anarchism is its commitment to four basic tenets: a confederation of decentralized municipalities; an unwavering opposition to statism; a belief in direct democracy; and a vision of a libertarian communist society. The most important issue that left-libertarianism – libertarian socialism no less than anarchism – faces today is: What will it *do* with these four powerful tenets? How will we give them social form and content? In what ways and by what means will we render them relevant to our time and bring them to the service of an organized popular movement for empowerment and freedom?

Anarchism must not be dissipated in self-indulgent behavior like that of the primitivistic Adamites of the sixteenth century, who "wandered through the woods naked, singing and dancing," as Kenneth Rexroth contemptuously observed, spending "their time in a continuous sexual orgy" until they were hunted down and exterminated – much to the relief of a disgusted peasantry, whose lands they had plundered. It must not retreat into the primitivistic demimonde of the John Zerzans and George Bradfords. I would be the last to contend that anarchists should not live their anarchism as much as possible on a day-to-day basis – personally as well as socially, aesthetically as well as pragmatically. But they should not live an anarchism that diminishes, indeed effaces the most important features that have distinguished anarchism, as a movement, practice, and program, from statist socialism. Anarchism today must resolutely retain its character as a *social* movement – a *programmatic* as well as activist social movement – a movement that melds its embattled vision of a libertarian communist society with its forthright critique of capitalism, unobscured by names like "industrial society."

In short, social anarchism must resolutely affirm its differences with lifestyle anarchism. If a social anarchist movement cannot translate its fourfold tenets – municipal confederalism, opposition to statism, direct democracy, and ultimately libertarian communism – into a lived practice in a new public sphere; if these tenets languish like its memories of past struggles in ceremonial pronouncements and meetings; worse still, if they are subverted by the "libertarian" Ecstasy Industry and by quietistic Asian theisms, then its revolutionary socialistic core will have to be restored under a new name.

Certainly, it is already no longer possible, in my view, to call oneself an anarchist without adding a qualifying adjective to distinguish oneself from lifestyle anarchists. Minimally, social anarchism is radically at odds with anarchism focused on lifestyle, neo-Situationist paeans to ecstasy, and the sovereignty of the ever-shriveling petty-bourgeois ego. The two diverge completely in their defining principles – socialism or individualism. Between a committed revolutionary body of ideas and practice, on the one hand, and a vagrant yearning for privatistic ecstasy and self-realization on the other, there can be no commonality. Mere opposition to the state may well unite fascistic lumpens with Stirnerite lumpens, a phenomenon that is not without its historical precedents.

1 George Woodcock, *Anarchism: A History of Libertarian Ideas and Movements* (Cleveland and New York: World Publishing Co., 1962), p. 468.
2 Peter Marshall, *Demanding the Impossible: A History of Anarchism* (San Francisco: HarperCollins, 1992), p. 602.
3 Gerald Brenan, *The Spanish Labyrinth* (Cambridge: Cambridge University Press, 1967), p. 273.
4 BBC–Granada Ltd., *The Spanish Civil War*, a six-part documentary, especially part 5, "Inside the Revolution."
5 Ibid.
6 Quoted in *The New York Times*, May 7, 1995.
7 Max Stirner, *The Ego and His Own*, ed. James J. Martin, trans. Steven T. Byington (New York: Libertarian Book Club, 1963), part 2, chap. 4, sec. C, "My Self-Engagement," p. 352, emphasis added.
8 Friedrich Nietzsche, "On Truth and Lie in an Extra-Moral Sense" (1873; fragment), in *The Portable Nietzsche*, edited and translated by Walter Kaufmann (New York: Viking Portable Library, 1959), pp. 46–7.
9 Friedrich Nietzsche, fragment 481 (1883–8), *The Will to Power*, trans. Walter Kaufmann and R. J. Hollingdale (New York: Random House, 1967), p. 267.
10 James J. Martin, editor's introduction to Stirner, *Ego and His Own*, p. xviii.
11 Max Horkheimer, *The Eclipse of Reason* (New York: Oxford University Press, 1947), p. 135.

CHAPTER EIGHT

Libertarian Municipalism

Introduction

Bookchin's anarchism shares with traditional anarchism an opposition to the nation-state and a search for libertarian alternatives, but it differs with traditional anarchism on the tangible nature of the alternatives it embraces. Anarchism, in the main, looks to nonpolitical arenas of society as the sites for constructing its alternatives – variously the factory, the cooperative, even the individual lifestyle. The typical ambition of anarchism is to create not libertarian politics but libertarian social institutions; or as Martin Buber once put it, "to substitute society for State to the greatest degree possible, moreover a society that is 'genuine' and not a State in disguise."[1]

Such anarchism has traditionally rejected politics, considering politics synonymous with the nation-state itself. Much of traditional anarchism even rejects grassroots–democratic politics. George Woodcock may be overstating the case when he writes:

> No conception of anarchism is further from the truth than that which regards it as an extreme form of democracy. Democracy advocates the sovereignty of the people. Anarchism advocates the sovereignty of the person.[2]

Still, his characterization is valid for wide sectors of anarchist thought. By contrast, Bookchin looks precisely to politics as the necessary realm for the creation of libertarian alternatives. But politics, for him, is not the professional activity of those who hold office in the nation-state. Rather, politics is direct democracy, the popular self-management of the community by free citizens – a politics he calls "the democratic dimension of anarchism." It seeks to create or recreate a vital public sphere based on cooperation and community. Politics in this sense has flourished at earlier periods of history – especially in ancient Athens, the medieval communes, colonial New England, and revolutionary Paris. But in modern times it has been eroded or even crushed by the nation-state in the service of ruling elites.

Bookchin names this politics libertarian municipalism. Arguing that the most immediate sphere for community self-management is the urban neighborhood (or in rural areas, the town), he advocates that those who would create revolutionary institutions today should form popular assemblies in their municipalities. This small, intimate scale of political life would allow people to become active citizens and recreate the public sphere, democratically making decisions on matters that affect their common life. They would "municipalize" the economy, managing their community's economic life through their popular assemblies. Private property would be abolished and goods would be distributed according to need; post-scarcity technologies would minimize the time consumed by labor, making possible broad political participation.

To address large-scale problems that affect an entire region, and as an antidote to the problem of local parochialism, the democratized popular assemblies of neighboring municipalities would confederate themselves into larger networks. These confederations would ultimately constitute a counterpower to the state, the corporations, and the market, and they could expand at the expense of those forces, ultimately mobilizing a confrontation with them.

Bookchin has been outlining this political program in various works since 1972. In the years that have passed since then, the need for an emancipatory Left that can combat a globalizing capitalism and looming ecological destruction has become ever-more urgent. Libertarian municipalism may well represent the sought-after alternative: a concrete revolutionary path to an ecological, rational society. While efforts have been made in disparate locales to put this political program into practice, it as yet lacks a movement committed wholeheartedly to carrying it out. Whether that movement will emerge remains to be seen.

The New Municipal Agenda
(from *From Urbanization to Cities*, 1987, revised 1995; with interpolations from various essays)

Any agenda that tries to restore and amplify the classical meaning of politics and citizenship must clearly indicate what they are *not*, if only because of the confusion that surrounds the two words. . . . Politics is *not* statecraft, and citizens are *not* "constituents" or "taxpayers." Statecraft consists of operations that engage the state: the exercise of its monopoly of violence, its control of the entire regulative apparatus of society in the form of legal and ordinance-making bodies, and its governance of society by means of professional legislators, armies, police forces, and bureaucracies. Statecraft takes on a political patina when so-called "political parties" attempt, in various power plays, to occupy the offices that make state policy and execute it. This kind of "politics" has an almost tedious typicality. A "political party" is normally a structured hierarchy, fleshed out by a membership that functions in a top-down manner. It is a miniature state, and in some countries, such as the former Soviet Union and Nazi Germany, a party actually constituted the state itself.

The Soviet and Nazi examples of the party *qua* state were the logical extension of the party into the state. Indeed, every party has its roots in the state, not in the citizenry. The conventional party is hitched to the state like a garment to a mannikin. However varied the garment and its design may be, it is not part of the body politic; it merely drapes it. There is nothing authentically political about this phenomenon: it is meant precisely to contain the body politic, to control it and to manipulate it, not to express its will – or even permit it to develop a will. In no sense is a conventional "political" party derivative of the body politic or constituted by it. Leaving metaphors aside, "political" parties are replications of the state when they are out of power and are often synonymous with the state when they are in power. They are formed to mobilize, to command, to acquire power, and to rule. Thus they are as inorganic as the state itself – an excrescence of society that has no real roots in it, no responsiveness to it beyond the needs of faction, power, and mobilization.

Politics, by contrast, is an organic phenomenon. It is organic in the very real sense that it is the activity of a public body – a community, if you will – just as the process of flowering is an organic activity of a plant. Politics, conceived as an activity, involves rational discourse, public empowerment, the exercise of practical reason, and its realization in a shared, indeed participatory, activity. It is the sphere of societal life beyond the family and the personal needs of the individual that still retains the intimacy, involvement, and sense of responsibility enjoyed in private arenas of life. Groups may form to advance specific political views and programs, but these views and programs are no better than their capacity to answer to the needs of an active public body. . . .

By contrast, political movements, in their authentic sense, emerge out of the body politic itself, and although their programs are formulated by theorists, they also emerge from the lived experiences and traditions of the public itself. The populist movements that swept out of agrarian America and tsarist Russia or the anarcho-syndicalist and peasant movements of Spain and Mexico articulated deeply felt, albeit often unconscious, public desires and needs. At their best, genuine political movements bring to consciousness the subterranean aspirations of discontented people and eventually turn this consciousness into political cultures that give coherence to inchoate and formless public desires. . . .

The immediate goal of a libertarian municipalist agenda is not to exercise sudden and massive control by representatives and their bureaucratic agents over the existing economy; its immediate goal is to reopen a public sphere in flat opposition to statism, one that allows for maximum democracy in the literal sense of the term, and to create in embryonic form the institutions that can give power to a people generally. If this perspective can be initially achieved only by morally empowered assemblies on a limited scale, at least it will be a form of popular power that can, in time, expand locally and grow over wide regions. That its future is unforeseeable does not alter the fact that its development depends upon the growing consciousness of the people, not upon the growing power of the state – and how that consciousness, concretized in high democratic institutions, will develop may be an open issue but it will surely be a political adventure.

. . . The recovery and development of politics must, I submit, take its point of departure from the citizen and his or her immediate environment beyond the familial and private arenas of life. There can be no politics without community. And by community I mean a municipal association of people reinforced by its own economic power, its own institutionalization of the grass roots, and the confederal support of nearby communities organized into a territorial network on a local and regional scale. Parties that do not intertwine with these grassroots forms of popular organization are not political in the classical sense of the term. In fact, they are bureaucratic and antithetical to the development of a participatory politics and participating citizens. The authentic unit of political life, in effect, is the municipality, whether as a whole, if it is humanly scaled, or in its various subdivisions, notably the neighborhood. . . .

A new political agenda can be a municipal agenda only if we are to take our commitments to democracy seriously. Otherwise we will be entangled with one or another variant of statecraft, a bureaucratic structure that is demonstrably inimicable to a vibrant public life. The living cell that forms the basic unit of political life is the municipality, from which everything – such as citizenship, interdependence, confederation, and freedom – emerges. There is no way to piece together any politics unless we begin with its most elementary forms: the villages, towns, neighborhoods, and cities in which people live on the most intimate level of political interdependence beyond private life. It is on this level that they can begin to gain a familiarity with the political process, a process that involves a good deal more than voting and information. It is on this level, too, that they can go beyond the private insularity of family life – a life that is currently celebrated for its inwardness and seclusion – and improvise those public institutions that make for broad community participation and consociation.

In short, it is through the municipality that people can reconstitute themselves from isolated monads into an innovative body politic and create an existentially vital, indeed protoplasmic civic life that has continuity and institutional form as well as civic content. I refer here to the block organizations, neighborhood assemblies, town meetings, civic confederations, and the public arenas for discourse that go beyond such episodic, single-issue demonstrations and campaigns, valuable as they may be to redress social injustices. But protest alone is not enough; indeed, it is usually defined by what protestors oppose, not by the social changes they may wish to institute. To ignore the irreducible civic unit of politics and democracy is to play chess without a chessboard, for it is on this civic plane that the long-range endeavor of social renewal must eventually be played out. . . .

All statist objections aside, the problem of restoring municipal assemblies seems formidable if it is cast in strictly structural and spatial terms. New York City and London have no way of "assembling" if they try to emulate ancient Athens, with its comparatively small citizen body. Both cities, in fact, are no longer cities in the classical sense of the term and hardly rate as municipalities even by nineteenth-century standards of urbanism. Viewed in strictly macroscopic terms, they are sprawling urban belts that suck up millions of people daily from communities at a substantial distance from their commercial centers.

But they are also made up of neighborhoods – that is to say, of smaller communities that have a certain measure of identity, whether defined by a shared cultural heritage, economic interests, a commonality of social views, or even an aesthetic tradition such as Greenwich Village in New York or Camden Town in London. However much their administration as logistical, sanitary, and commercial artifacts requires a high degree of coordination by experts and their aides, they are potentially open to political and, in time, physical decentralization. Popular, even block assemblies can be formed irrespective of the size of a city, provided its cultural components are identified and their uniqueness fostered.

At the same time I should emphasize that the libertarian municipalist (or equivalently, communalist) views I propound here are meant to be a *changing and formative perspective* – a concept of politics and citizenship to ultimately transform cities and urban megalopolises ethically as well as spatially, and politically as well as economically. Insofar as these views gain public acceptance, they can be expected not only to enlarge their vision and embrace confederations of neighborhoods but also to advance a goal of *physically* decentralizing urban centers. To the extent that mere electoral "constituents" are transformed by education and experience into active citizens, the issue of humanly scaled communities can hardly be avoided as the "next step" toward a stable and viable form of city life. It would be foolhardy to try to predict in any detail a series of such "next steps" or the pace at which they will occur. Suffice it to say that as a perspective, libertarian municipalism is meant to be an ever-developing, creative, and reconstructive agenda as well as an alternative to the centralized nation-state and to an economy based on profit, competition, and mindless growth.

Minimally then, attempts to initiate assemblies can begin with populations that range anywhere from a modest residential neighborhood to a dozen neighborhoods or more. They can be coordinated by strictly mandated delegates who are rotatable, recallable, and above all, rigorously instructed in written form to either support or oppose whatever issue that appears on the agenda of local confederal councils composed of delegates from several neighborhood assemblies.

There is no mystery involved in this form of organization. The historical evidence for their efficacy and their continual reappearance in times of rapid social change is considerable and persuasive. The Parisian sections of 1793, despite the size of Paris (between 700,000 and a million) and the logistical difficulties of the era (a time when nothing moved faster than a horse) functioned with a great deal of success on their own, coordinated by sectional delegates in the Paris Commune. They were notable not only for their effectiveness in dealing with political issues based on a face-to-face democratic structure; they also played a major role in provisioning the city, in preventing the hoarding of food, and in suppressing speculation, supervising the maximum for fixed prices, and carrying out many other complex administrative tasks. Thus, from a minimal standpoint, no city need be considered so large that popular assemblies cannot *start*, least of all one that has definable neighborhoods that might interlink with each other on ever-broader confederations.

The real difficulty is largely administrative: how to provide for the material amenities of city life, support complex logistical and traffic burdens, or maintain a sanitary environment. This issue is often obscured by a serious confusion between the formulation of policy and its administration. For a community to decide in a participatory manner what specific course of action it should take in dealing with a technical problem does not oblige all its citizens to execute that policy. The decision to build a road, for example, does not mean that everyone must know how to design and construct one. That is a job for engineers, who can offer alternative designs – a very important political function of experts, to be sure, but one whose soundness the people in assembly can be free to decide. To design and construct a road is strictly an administrative responsibility, albeit one that is always open to public scrutiny.

If the distinction between policy making and administration is kept clearly in mind, the role of popular assemblies and the people who administer their decisions easily distinguishes logistical problems from political ones, which are ordinarily entangled with each other in discussions on decentralistic politics. Superficially, the assembly system is "referendum" politics: it is based on a "social contract" to share decision making with the population at large, and abide by the rule of the majority in dealing with problems that confront a municipality, a regional confederation of municipalities, or for that matter, a national entity. . . .

That a municipality can be as parochial as a tribe is fairly obvious – and is no less true today than it has been in the past. Hence any municipal movement that is not confederal – that is to say, that does not enter into a network of mutual obligations to towns and cities in its own region – can no more be regarded as a truly political entity in any traditional sense than a neighborhood that does not work with other neighborhoods in the city in which it is located. Confederation – based on shared responsibilities, full accountability of confederal delegates to their communities, the right to recall, and firmly mandated representatives – forms an indispensable part of a new politics. To demand that existing towns and cities replicate the nation-state on a local level is to surrender any commitment to social change as such. . . .

What is confederalism as conceived in the libertarian municipalist framework, and as it would function in a free ecological society? It would above all be a network of councils whose members or delegates are elected from popular face-to-face democratic assemblies, in the various villages, towns, and even neighborhoods of large cities. These confederal councils would become the means for interlinking villages, towns, neighborhoods, and cities into confederal networks. Power thus would flow from the bottom up instead of from the top down, and in confederations the flow of power from the bottom up would diminish with the scope of the federal council, ranging territorially from localities to regions and from regions to ever-broader territorial areas.

The members of these confederal councils would be strictly mandated, recallable, and responsible to the assemblies that choose them for the purpose of coordinating and administering the policies formulated by the assemblies themselves. The functions of the councils would be purely administrative and practical, unlike representatives in republican systems of government, who have policy-making powers. Indeed, the confederation would make the same distinction that is made on the municipal level, between policy-making and administration. Policy-making would remain exclusively the right of the popular community assemblies based on the practices of participatory democracy. Administration – the coordination and execution of adopted policies – would be the responsibility of the confederal councils. Wherever policy-making slips from the hands of the people, it is devoured by its delegates, who quickly become bureaucrats.

A crucial element in giving reality to confederalism is the interdependence of communities for an authentic mutualism based on shared resources, produce, and policy-making. While a reasonable measure of self-sufficiency is desirable for each locality and region, confederalism is a means for avoiding local parochialism on the one hand and an extravagant national and global division of labor on the other. Unless a community is obliged to count on others generally to satisfy important material needs and realize common political goals, interlinking it to a greater whole, exclusivity and parochialism become genuine possibilities. Only insofar as confederation is an extension of participatory administration – by means of confederal networks – can decentralization and localism prevent the communities that compose larger bodies of association from parochially withdrawing into themselves at the expense of wider areas of human consociation.

Confederalism is thus a way of perpetuating interdependence among communities and regions – indeed, it is a way of democratizing that interdependence without surrendering the principle of local control. Through confederation, a community can retain its identity and roundedness while participating in a sharing way with the larger whole that makes up a balanced ecological society. . . .

Thus libertarian municipalism is not an effort simply to "take over" city councils to construct a more "environmentally friendly" city government. These adherents – or opponents – of libertarian municipalism, in effect, look at the civic structures that exist before their eyes now and essentially (all rhetoric to the contrary notwithstanding) take them as they *exist*. Libertarian municipalism, by contrast, is an effort to *transform* and *democratize* city governments, to root them in popular assemblies, to knit them together along confederal lines, to appropriate a regional economy along confederal and municipal lines.

In fact, libertarian municipalism gains its life and its integrity *precisely* from the dialectical tension it proposes between the nation-state and the municipal confederation. Its "law of life," to use an old Marxian term, consists precisely in its struggle with the State. Then *tension* between municipal confederations and the State must be *clear and uncompromising*. Since these confederations would exist primarily in *opposition* to statecraft, they cannot be compromised by state, provincial or national elections, much less achieved by these means. Libertarian municipalism is *formed* by its struggle with the State, *strengthened* by this struggle, indeed, *defined* by this struggle. Divested of this dialectical tension with the State, of this duality of power that must ultimately be actualized in a free "Commune of communes," libertarian municipalism becomes little more than sewer socialism.

Why is the assembly crucial to self-governance? Is it not enough to use the referendum, as the Swiss do today, and resolve the problem of democratic procedure in a simple and seemingly uncomplicated way? Why can't policy decisions be made electronically at home – as "Third Wave" enthusiasts have suggested – by "autonomous" individuals, each listening to debates and voting in the privacy of his or her home?

A number of vital issues, involving the nature of citizenship and the recovery of an enhanced classical vision of politics, must be considered in answering these questions. The "autonomous" individual *qua* "voter" who, in liberal theory, forms the irreducible unit of the referendum process is a fiction. Left to his or her own private destiny in the name of "autonomy" and "independence," the individual becomes an isolated being whose very freedom is denuded of the living social and political matrix from which his or her individuality acquires its flesh and blood. . . . The notion of independence, which is often confused with independent thinking and freedom, has been so marbled by pure bourgeois egoism that we tend to forget that our individuality depends heavily on community support systems and solidarity. It is not by childishly subordinating ourselves to the community on the one hand or by detaching ourselves from it on the other that we become mature human beings. What distinguishes us as social beings, hopefully with rational institutions, from solitary beings who lack any serious affiliations, is our capacities for solidarity with one another, for mutually enhancing our self-development and creativity and attaining freedom within a socially creative and institutionally rich collectivity.

"Citizenship" apart from community can be as debasing to our political selfhood as "citizenship" in a totalitarian state. In both cases, we are thrust back to the condition of dependence that characterizes infancy and childhood. We are rendered dangerously vulnerable to manipulation, whether by powerful personalities in private life or by the state and by corporations in economic life. In neither case do we attain individuality *or* community. Both, in fact, are dissolved by removing the communal ground on which genuine individuality depends. Rather, it is interdependence within an institutionally rich and rounded community – which no electronic media can produce – that fleshes out the individual with the rationality, solidarity, sense of justice, and ultimately the reality of freedom that makes for a creative and concerned citizen.

Paradoxical as it may seem, the authentic elements of a rational and free society are communal, not individual. Conceived in more institutional terms, the municipality is not only the basis for a free society; it is the irreducible ground for genuine individuality as well.

The significance of the municipality is all the greater because it constitutes the discursive arena in which people can intellectually and emotionally confront one another, indeed, experience one another through dialogue, body language, personal intimacy, and face-to-face modes of expression in the course of making collective decisions. I speak, here, of the all-important process of *communizing,* of the ongoing intercourse of many levels of life, that makes for *solidarity,* not only the "neighborliness" so indispensable for truly organic interpersonal relationships.

The referendum, conducted in the privacy of one's voting booth or, as some "Third Wave" enthusiasts would have it, in the electronic isolation of one's home, *privatizes* democracy and thereby subverts it. Voting, like registering one's preferences for a particular soap or detergent in an opinion poll, is the total quantification of citizenship, politics, individuality, and the very formation of ideas as a mutually informative process. The mere vote reflects a preformulated "percentage" of our perceptions and values, not their full expression. It is the technical debasing of views into mere preferences, of ideals into mere taste, of overall comprehension into quantification such that human aspirations and beliefs can be reduced to numerical digits.

Finally, the "autonomous individual," lacking any community context, support systems, and organic intercourse, is disengaged from the character-building process – the *paideia* – that the ancient Athenians assigned to politics as one of its most important educational functions. True citizenship and politics entail the ongoing formation of personality, education, and a growing sense of public responsibility and commitment that render communizing and an active body politic meaningful, indeed that give it existential substance. It is not in the privacy of the school, any more than in the privacy of the voting booth, that these vital personal and political attributes are formed. They require a public presence, embodied by vocal and thinking individuals, a responsive and discursive public sphere, to achieve reality. "Patriotism," as the etymology of the word indicates, is the nation-state's conception of the citizen as a child, the obedient creature of the nation-state conceived as a paterfamilias or stern father, who orchestrates belief and commands devotion. To the extent that we are the "sons" and "daughters" of a "fatherland," we place ourselves in an infantile relationship to the state.

Solidarity or *philia,* by contrast, implies a sense of commitment. It is created by knowledge, training, experience, and reason – in short, by a political education developed during the course of political participation. *Philia* is the result of the educational and self-formative process that *paideia* is meant to achieve. In the absence of a humanly scaled, comprehensible, and institutionally accessible municipality, this all-important function of politics and its embodiment in citizenship is simply impossible to achieve. In the absence of *philia* or the means to create it, we gauge "political involvement" by the "percentage" of "voters" who "participate" in the "political process" – a degradation of words that totally denatures their authentic meaning and eviscerates their ethical content. . . .

Be they large or small, the initial assemblies and the movement that seeks to foster them in civic elections remain the only real school for citizenship we have. There is no civic "curriculum" other than a living and creative political realm that can give rise to people who take management of public affairs seriously. What we must clearly do in an era of commodification, rivalry, anomie, and egoism is to consciously create a public sphere that will inculcate the values of humanism, cooperation, community, and public service in the everyday practice of civic life. Grassroots citizenship goes hand in hand with grassroots politics.

The Athenian *polis*, for all its many shortcomings, offers us remarkable examples of how a high sense of citizenship can be reinforced not only by systematic education but by an etiquette of civic behavior and an artistic culture that adorns ideals of civic service with the realities of civic practice. Deference to opponents in debates, the use of language to achieve consensus, ongoing public discussion in the *agora* in which even the most prominent of the *polis*'s figures were expected to debate public issues with the least known, the use of wealth not only to meet personal needs but to adorn the *polis* itself (thus placing a high premium on the disaccumulation rather than the accumulation of wealth), a multitude of public festivals, dramas, and satires largely centered on civic affairs and the need to foster civic solidarity – all of these and many other aspects of Athens's political culture created the civic solidarity and responsibility that made for actively involved citizens with a deep sense of civic mission.

For our part, we can do no less – and hopefully, in time, considerably more. The development of citizenship must become an art, not merely an education – and a creative art in the aesthetic sense that appeals to the deeply human desire for self-expression in a meaningful political community. It must be a personal art in which every citizen is fully aware of the fact that his or her community entrusts its destiny to his or her moral probity and rationality. If the ideological authority of state power and statecraft today rests on the assumption that the "citizen" is an incompetent being, the municipalist conception of citizenship rests on precisely the opposite. Every citizen would be regarded as competent to participate directly in the "affairs of state" – indeed, what is more important, he or she would be *encouraged* to do so.

Every means would be provided, whether aesthetic or institutional, to foster participation in full as an educative and ethical process that turns the citizen's latent competence into an actual reality. Social and political life would be consciously orchestrated to foster a profound sensitivity, indeed an active sense of concern for the adjudication of differences without denying the need for vigorous dispute when it is needed. Public service would be seen as a uniquely human attribute, not a "gift" that a citizen confers on the community or an onerous task that he or she must fulfill. Cooperation and civic responsibility would become expressions of acts of sociability and *philia,* not ordinances that the citizen is expected to honor in the breach and evade where he or she can do so.

Put bluntly and clearly, the municipality would become a theater in which life in its most meaningful public form is the plot, a political drama whose grandeur imparts nobility and grandeur to the citizenry that forms the cast. By contrast, our modern cities have become in large part agglomerations of bedroom apartments in which men and women spiritually wither away and their personalities become trivialized by the petty concerns of amusement, consumption, and small talk.

The last and one of the most intractable problems we face is economic. Today, economic issues tend to center on "who owns what," "who owns more than whom," and, above all, how disparities in wealth are to be reconciled with a sense of civic commonality. Nearly all municipalities have been fragmented by differences in economic status, pitting poor, middle, and wealthy classes against each other often to the ruin of municipal freedom itself, as the bloody history of Italy's medieval and Renaissance cities so clearly demonstrates.

These problems have not disappeared in recent times. Indeed, in many cases they are as severe as they have ever been. But what is unique about our own time – a fact so little understood by many liberals and radicals in North America and Europe – is that entirely new *transclass* issues have emerged that concern environment, growth, transportation, cultural degradation, and the quality of urban life generally – issues that have been produced by urbanization, not by citification. Cutting across conflicting class interests are such transclass issues as the massive dangers of thermonuclear war, growing state authoritarianism, and ultimately global ecological breakdown. To an extent unparalleled in American history, an enormous variety of citizens' groups have brought people of all class backgrounds into common projects around problems, often very local in character, that concern the destiny and welfare of their community as a whole.

Issues such as the siting of nuclear reactors or nuclear waste dumps, the dangers of acid rain, and the presence of toxic dumps, to cite only a few of the many problems that beleaguer innumerable American and British municipalities, have united an astonishing variety of people into movements with shared concerns that render a ritualistic class analysis of their motives a matter of secondary importance. Carried still further, the absorption of small communities by larger ones, of cities by urban belts, and urban belts by "standard metropolitan statistical areas" or conurbations has given rise to militant demands for communal integrity and self-government, an issue that surmounts strictly class and economic interests. The literature on the emergence of these transclass movements, so secondary to internecine struggles within cities of earlier times, is so immense that to merely list the sources would require a sizable volume.

I have given this brief overview of an emerging *general social interest* over old particularistic interests to demonstrate that a new politics could easily come into being – indeed one that would be concerned not only with restructuring the political landscape on a municipal level but the economic landscape as well. The old debates between "private property" and "nationalized property," are becoming threadbare. Not that these different kinds of ownership and the forms of exploitation they imply have disappeared; rather, they are being increasingly overshadowed by new realities and concerns. Private property, in the traditional sense, with its case for perpetuating the citizen as an economically self-sufficient and politically self-empowered individual, is fading away. It is disappearing not because "creeping socialism" is devouring "free enterprise" but because "creeping corporatism" is devouring everyone – ironically, in the name of "free enterprise." The Greek ideal of the politically sovereign citizen who can make a rational judgment in public affairs because he is free from material need or clientage has been reduced to a mockery. The oligarchical character of economic life threatens democracy, such as it is, not only on a national level but also on a municipal level, where it still preserves a certain degree of intimacy and leeway.

We come here to a breakthrough approach to a municipalist economics that innovatively dissolves the mystical aura surrounding corporatized property and nationalized property, indeed workplace elitism and "workplace democracy." I refer to the *municipalization of property*, as opposed to its corporatization or its nationalization. . . . Libertarian municipalism proposes that land and enterprises be placed increasingly in the custody of the community – more precisely, the custody of citizens in free assemblies and their deputies in confederal councils. . . . In such a municipal economy – confederal, interdependent, and rational by ecological, not simply technological, standards – we would expect that the special interests that divide people today into workers, professionals, managers, and the like would be melded into a general interest in which people see themselves as citizens guided strictly by the needs of their community and region rather than by personal proclivities and vocational concerns. Here, citizenship would come into its own, and rational as well as ecological interpretations of the public good would supplant class and hierarchical interests.

As for the workplace, public democracy would be substituted for the traditional images of productive management and operation, "economic democracy," and "economic collectivization." Significantly, "economic democracy" in the workplace is no longer incompatible with a corporatized or nationalized economy. Quite to the contrary: the effective use of "workers' participation" in production, even the outright handing over of industrial operations to the workers who perform them, has become another form of time-studied, assembly-line rationalization, another systematic abuse of labor, by bringing labor itself into complicity with its own exploitation.

Many workers, in fact, would like to get away from their workplaces and find more creative types of work, not simply participate in planning their own misery. What "economic democracy" meant in its profoundest sense was free, democratic access to the means of life, the guarantee of freedom from material want – not simply the involvement of workers in onerous productive activities that could better be turned over to machines. It is a blatant bourgeois trick, in which many radicals unknowingly participate, that "economic democracy" has been reinterpreted to mean "employee ownership" or that "workplace democracy" has come to mean workers' "participation" in industrial management rather than freedom from the tyranny of the factory, rationalized labor, and planned production.

A municipal politics, based on communalist principles, scores a significant advance over all of these conceptions by calling for the municipalization of the economy – and its management by the community as part of a politics of self-management. Syndicalist demands for the "collectivization" of industry and "workers' control" of individual industrial units are based on contractual and exchange relationships between all collectivized enterprises, thereby indirectly reprivatizing the economy and opening it to traditional forms of private property – even if each enterprise is collectively owned. By contrast, libertarian municipalism literally *politicizes the economy* by dissolving economic decision-making into the civic domain. Neither factory nor land becomes a separate or potentially competitive unit within a seemingly communal collective.

Nor do workers, farmers, technicians, engineers, professionals, and the like perpetuate their vocational identities as separate interests that exist apart from the citizen body in face-to-face assemblies. "Property" is integrated into the municipality as the material component of a civic framework, indeed as part of a larger whole that is controlled by the citizen body in assembly as citizens – not as workers, farmers, professionals, or any other vocationally oriented special-interest groups.

What is equally important, the famous "contradiction" or "antagonism" between town and country, so crucial in social theory and history, is transcended by the township, the traditional New

England jurisdiction, in which an urban entity is the nucleus of its agricultural and village environs – not a domineering urban entity that stands opposed to them. A township, in effect, is a small region within still larger ones, such as the county and larger political jurisdictions.

So conceived, the municipalization of the economy should be distinguished not only from corporatization but also from seemingly more "radical" demands such as nationalization and collectivization. Nationalization of the economy invariably has led to bureaucratic and top-down economic control; collectivization, in turn, could easily lead to a privatized economy in a collectivized form with the perpetuation of class or caste identities. By contrast, municipalization would bring the economy as a whole into the orbit of the public sphere, where economic policy could be formulated by the *entire* community – notably its citizens in face-to-face relationships working to achieve a general interest that surmounts separate, vocationally defined specific interests. The economy would cease to be merely an economy in the conventional sense of the term, composed of capitalistic, nationalized, or "worker-controlled" enterprises. It would become the economy of the *polis* or the municipality. The municipality, more precisely, the citizen body in face-to-face assembly, would absorb the economy into its public business, divesting it of a separate identity that can become privatized into a self-serving enterprise.

. . . The municipalization of the economy would not only absorb the vocational differences that could militate against a publicly controlled economy; it would also absorb the material means of life into communal forms of distribution. "From each according to his ability and to each according to his needs" – the famous demand of various nineteenth-century socialisms – would be institutionalized as part of the public sphere. This traditional maxim, which is meant to assure that people will have access to the means of life irrespective of the work they are capable of performing, would cease to be merely a precarious credo: it would become a practice, a way of functioning politically – one that is structurally built into the community as a way of existing as a political entity.

Moreover, the enormous growth of the productive forces, rationally and ecologically employed for social rather than private ends, has rendered the age-old problem of material scarcity a moot issue. Potentially, all the basic means for living in comfort and security are available to the populations of the world, notwithstanding the dire – and often fallacious – claims of present-day misanthropes and antihumanists such as Garrett Hardin, Paul Ehrlich, and regrettably, advocates of "simple living," who can barely be parted from their computers even as they deride technological developments of almost any kind. It is easily forgotten that only a few generations ago, famine was no less a plague than deadly infectious diseases like the Black Death, and that the life-span of most people at the turn of the last century in the United States and Europe seldom reached fifty years of age.

No community can hope to achieve economic autarky, nor should it try to do so. Economically, the wide range of resources that are needed to make many of our widely used goods preclude self-enclosed insularity and parochialism. Far from being a liability, this inter-dependence among communities and regions can well be regarded as an asset – culturally as well as politically. Interdependence among com-munities is no less important than interdependence among individuals. Divested of the cultural cross-fertilization that is often a product of economic intercourse, the municipality tends to shrink into itself and disappear into its own civic privatism. Shared needs and resources imply the existence of sharing and, with sharing, communication, rejuvenation by new ideas, and a wider social horizon that yields a wider sensibility to new experiences.

The recent emphasis in environmental theory on "self-sufficiency," if it does not mean a greater degree of prudence in dealing with material resources, is regressive. Localism should never be interpreted to mean parochialism; nor should decentralism ever be interpreted to mean that smallness is a virtue in itself. Small is not necessarily beautiful. The concept of human scale, by far the more preferable expression for a truly ecological policy, is meant to make it possible for people to completely grasp their political environment, not to parochially bury themselves in it to the exclusion of cultural stimuli from outside their community's boundaries.

Given these coordinates, it is possible to envision a new political culture with a new revival of citizenship, popular civic institutions, a new kind of economy, and a countervailing dual power, confederally networked, that could arrest and hopefully reverse the growing centralization of the state and corporate enterprises. Moreover, it is also possible to envision an eminently practical point of departure for going beyond the town and city as we have known them up to now and for developing future forms of habitation as communities that seek to achieve a new harmonization between people and between humanity and the natural world. I have emphasized its practicality because it is now clear that any attempt to tailor a human community to a natural "ecosystem" in which it is located cuts completely against the grain of centralized power, be it state or corporate. Centralized power invariably reproduces itself in centralized forms at all levels of social, political, and economic life. It not only is big; it thinks big. Indeed, this way of being and thinking is a condition for its survival, not only its growth.

As for the technological bases for decentralized communities, we are now witnessing a revolution that would have seemed hopelessly utopian only a few decades ago. Until recently, smaller-scale ecotechnologies were used mainly by individuals, and their efficiency barely compared with that of conventional energy sources, such as fossil fuels and nuclear power plants. This situation has changed dramatically in the past fifteen to twenty years. In the United States, wind turbines have been developed and are currently in use that generate electric power at a cost of 7 to 9 cents per kilowatt-hour, compared with 20 cents only a decade earlier. This figure is very close to the 4- to-6-cent cost of power plants fueled by natural gas or coal. These comparisons, which can be expected to improve in favor of wind power in the years to come, have fostered the expansion of this nonfossil-fuel source throughout the entire world, particularly in India, where there has been "a major wind boom" in 1994, according to the Worldwatch Institute.[3]

A similar "boom" seems to be in the making in a variety of solar power devices. New solar collectors have been designed that increasingly approximate the costs of conventional energy sources, particularly in heating water for domestic uses. Photovoltaic cells, in which silicon is used to convert solar energy into electrons, have been developed to a point where "thousands of villagers in the developing world [are] using photovoltaic cells to power lights, televisions, and water pumps, needs that are otherwise met with kerosene lamps, lead-acid batteries, or diesel engines." In fact, more than 200,000 homes in Mexico, Indonesia, South Africa, and some 2,000 in the Dominican Republic have been "solarized," probably with a good many more to come.[4] It can be said with reasonable confidence that this increasingly sophisticated technology will become one of the most important – if not the most important – sources of electrical energy in the years to come, yet one that is eminently suitable for humanly scaled communities.

To view technological advances as intrinsically harmful, particularly nonpolluting sources of energy and automated machinery that can free human beings of mindless toil in a rational society, is as shortsighted as it is arrogant. Understandably, people today will not accept a diet of pious moral platitudes that call for "simple means" that presumably will give them "rich ends," whatever these may be, especially if these platitudes are delivered by well-paid academics and privileged Euro-Americans who have no serious quarrel with the present social order apart from whether it affords them access to "wilderness" theme parks.

For the majority of humanity, toil and needless shortages of food are an everyday reality. To expect them to become active citizens in a vital political, ecologically-oriented community while engaging in arduous work for most of their lives, often on empty bellies, is an unfeeling middle-class presumption. Unless they can enjoy a decent sufficiency in the means of life and freedom from mindless, often involuntary toil, it is the height of arrogance to degrade their humanity by calling them "mouths," as many demographers do, or "consumers," as certain very comfortable environmentalists do.

Indeed, it is the height of elitism and privilege to deny them the opportunity and the means for choosing the kind of lifeways they want to pursue. Nor have the well-to-do strata of Euro-American society deprived themselves of that very freedom of choice – a choice, in fact, that they take for granted as a matter of course. Without fostering promising advances in technology that can free humanity as a whole from its subservience to the present, irrational – and, let me emphasize, anti-ecological – social order, we will almost certainly never achieve the free society whose existence is a precondition for harmony between human and human and between humanity and the natural world.

Which is not to say that we can ignore the need for a visionary ethical ideal. Ironically, it has been the Right's shrewd emphasis on ethics and matters of spirit in an increasingly meaningless world that has given it a considerable edge over the forces of progress. Nazism achieved much of its success among the German people a half century ago not because of any economic panaceas it offered but because of its mythic ideal of nationhood, community, and moral regeneration. In recent times, reactionary movements in America have won millions to their cause on such values as the integrity of the family, religious belief, the renewal of patriotism, and the right to life – a message, I may add, that has been construed not only as a justification for anti-abortion legislation but as a hypostatization of the individual's sacredness, unborn as well as born.

Characteristically, liberal and radical causes are still mired in exclusively economistic and productivistic approaches to political issues. Their moral message, once a heightened plea for social justice, has given way increasingly to strictly material demands. Far more than the Right, which practices egoism and class war against the poor even as it emphasizes community virtues, the political middle ground and the Left take up the eminently practical issue of bread on the table and money in the bank but offer few values that are socially inspirational. Having emphasized the need to resolve the problems of material scarcity, it is equally necessary to emphasize the need to address the moral emptiness that a market society produces among large numbers of people today.

Morality and ethics, let me add, cannot be reduced to mere rhetoric to match the claims of reactionaries but must be the felt spiritual underpinnings of a new social outlook. They must be viewed not as a patronizing sermon but as a living practice that people can incorporate into their personal lives and their communities. The vacuity and triviality of life today must be replaced precisely by radical ideals of solidarity and freedom that sustain the human side of life as well as its material side, or else the ideals by which a rational future should be guided will disappear in the commodity-oriented world we call the "marketplace of ideas."

The most indecent aspect of this "marketplace" is that ideals tend to become artifacts – mere commodities – that lack even the value of the material things we need to sustain us. They become the ideological ornaments to garnish an inherently antihuman and anti-ecological society, one that threatens to undermine moral integrity as such and the simple social amenities that foster human intercourse.

Thus a municipal agenda that is meant to countervail urbanization and the nation-state must be more than a mere electoral platform, such as we expect from conventional parties. It must also be a message, comparable to the great manifestos advanced by various socialist movements in the last century, which called for moral as well as material and institutional reconstruction. Today's electoral platforms, whether "green" or "red," radical or liberal, are generally shopping lists of demands, precisely suited for that "marketplace of ideas" we have misnamed "politics."

Nor can a municipal agenda be a means for effacing serious differences in outlook. The need for thinking out ideas and struggling vigorously to give them coherence, which alone renders an agenda for a new municipal politics intelligible, is often sacrificed to ideological confusion in the name of achieving a specious "unity." A cranky pluralism is replacing an appreciation of focused thinking; a shallow relativism is replacing a sense of continuity and meaningful values; a confused eclecticism is replacing wholeness, clarity, and consistency. Many promising movements for basic social change in the recent past were plagued by a pluralism in which totally contradictory views were never worked out or followed to their logical conclusions, a problem that has grown even worse today due to the cultural illiteracy that plagues contemporary society. . . .

A serious political movement that seeks to advance a libertarian municipalist agenda, in turn, must be patient – just as the Russian populists of the last century (one of whom is cited in the dedication to this book) were. The 1960s upsurge, with all its generous ideals, fell apart because young radicals demanded immediate gratification and sensational successes. The protracted efforts that are so direly needed for building a serious movement – perhaps one whose goals cannot be realized within a single lifetime – were woefully absent. Many of the radicals of thirty years ago, burning with fervor for fundamental change, have since withdrawn into the university system they once denounced, the parliamentary positions they formerly disdained, and the business enterprises they furiously attacked.

A libertarian municipalist movement, in particular, would not – and should not – achieve sudden success and wide public accolades. The present period of political malaise at best and outright reaction at worst renders any sensational successes impossible. If such a libertarian municipalist movement runs candidates for municipal councils with demands for the institution of public assemblies, it will more likely lose electoral races today rather than win even slight successes. Depending upon the political climate at any given time or place, years may pass before it wins even the most modest success.

In any very real sense, however, this protracted development is a desideratum. With rapid success, many naïve members of a municipal electorate expect rapid changes – which no minority, however substantial, can ever hope to achieve at once. For an unpredictable amount of time, electoral activity will primarily be an educational activity, an endeavor to enter the public sphere, however small and contained it may be on the local level, and to educate and interact with ever larger numbers of people.

Even where a measure of electoral success on the local level can be achieved, the prospect of implementing a radically democratic policy is likely to be obstructed by the opposition of the nation-state and the weak position of municipalities in modern "democratic" nation-states. Although it is highly doubtful that even civic authorities would allow a neighborhood assembly to acquire the legal power to make civic policy, still less state and national authorities, let me emphasize that assemblies that have no legal power can exercise enormous moral power. A popular assembly that sternly voices its views on many issues can cause considerable disquiet among local authorities and generate a widespread public reaction in its favor over a large region, indeed even on a national scale.

An interesting case in point is the nuclear freeze resolution that was adopted by more than a hundred town meetings in Vermont a decade ago. Not only did this resolution resonate throughout the entire United States, leading to ad hoc "town meetings" in regions of the country that had never seen them, it affected national policy on this issue and culminated in a demonstration of approximately a million people in New York City. Yet none of the town meetings had the "legal" authority to enforce a nuclear freeze, nor did the issue fall within the purview of a typical New England town meeting's agenda. Historically, in fact, few civic projects that resemble libertarian municipalism began with a view toward establishing a radical democracy of any sort.

The forty-eight Parisian sections of 1793 actually derived from the sixty Parisian electoral districts of 1789. These districts were initially established through a complicated process (deliberately designed to exclude the poorer people of Paris) to choose the Parisian members of the Third Estate when the king convoked the Estates General at

Versailles. Thereafter the districts, having chosen their deputies, were expected to disband. In fact, the sixty districts refused to desist from meeting regularly, despite their lack of legal status, and a year later became an integral part of the city's government. With the radicalization of the French Revolution, the fearful city and national authorities tried to weaken the power of the districts by reducing their number of forty-eight – hence, the mutation of the old districts into sections. Finally, the sections opened their doors to everyone, some including women, without any property or status qualifications. This most radical of civic structures, which produced the most democratic assemblies theretofore seen in history, thus slowly elbowed its way into authority, initially without any legal authority whatever and in flat defiance of the nation-state. For all their limitations, the Parisian sections remain an abiding example of how a seemingly nonlegal assembly system can be transformed into a network of revolutionary popular institutions around which a new society can be structured. . . .

What is of immense practical importance is that prestatist institutions, traditions, and sentiments remain alive in varying degrees throughout most of the world. Resistance to the encroachment of oppressive states has been nourished by village, neighborhood, and town community networks; witness such struggles in South Africa, the Middle East, and Latin America. The tremors that are now shaking Soviet Russia are due not solely to demands for greater freedom but to movements for regional and local autonomy that challenge its very existence as a centralized nation-state. To ignore the communal basis of this movement would be as myopic as to ignore the latent instability of every nation-state; worse would be to take the nation-state as it is for granted and deal with it merely on its own terms. Indeed, whether a state remains "more" of a state or "less" – no trifling matter to radical theorists as disparate as Bakunin and Marx – depends heavily upon the power of local, confederal, and community movements to countervail it and hopefully to establish a dual power that will replace it. The major role that the Madrid Citizens' Movement played nearly three decades ago in weakening the Franco regime would require a major study to do it justice.

The problem of dealing with the growing power of nation-states and of centralized corporations, property ownership, production, and the like is *precisely a question of power* – that is to say, who shall have it or who shall be denied any power at all. Michel Foucault has done our age no service by making power an evil as such. Foucauldian postmodernist views notwithstanding, the broad mass of people in the world today lack what they need most – the power to challenge the nation-state and arrest the centralization of economic resources, lest future generations see all the gains of humanity dissipated and freedom disappear from social discourse.

Minimally, if power is to be socially redistributed so that the ordinary people who do the real work of the world can effectively speak back to those who run social and economic affairs, a movement is vitally needed to educate, mobilize, and, using the wisdom of ordinary and extraordinary people alike, *initiate* local steps to regain power in its most popular and democratic forms. Power of this kind must be collected, if we are to take democracy seriously, in newly developed institutions such as assemblies that allow for the direct participation of citizens in public affairs. Without a movement to work toward such a democratic end, including educators who are prepared, in turn, to be educated, and intellectually sophisticated people who can develop and popularize this project, efforts to challenge power as it is now constituted will simply sputter out in escapades, riots, adventures, and protests. . . .

Power that is not retained by the people is power that is given over to the state. Conversely, whatever power the people gain is power that must be taken away from the state. There can be no institutional vacuum where power exists: it is either invested in the people or it is invested in the state. Where the two "share" power, this condition is extremely precarious and often temporary. Sooner or later, the control of society and its destiny will either shift toward the people and their communities at its base or toward the professional practitioners of statecraft at its summit. Only if the whole existing pyramidal social structure is dismembered and radically democratized will the issue of domination as such disappear and be completely replaced by participation and the principle of complementarity.

Power, however, must be conceived as real, indeed solid and tangible, not only as spiritual and psychological. To ignore the fact that power is a muscular fact of life is to drift from the visionary into the ethereal and mislead the public as to its crucial significance in affecting society's destiny.

What this means is that if power is to be regained by the people from the state, the management of society must be deprofessionalized as much as possible. That is to say, it must be simplified and rendered transparent, indeed, clear, accessible, and manageable such that most of its affairs can be run by ordinary citizens. This emphasis on amateurism as distinguished from professionalism is not new. It formed the basis of Athenian democratic practice for generations. Indeed, it was so ably practiced that sortition rather than election formed the basis of the *polis's* democracy. It resurfaced repeatedly, for example, in early medieval city charters and confederations, and in the great democratic revolutions of the eighteenth century.

Power is also a solid and tangible fact to be reckoned with militarily, notably in the ubiquitous truth that the power of the state or the people eventually reposes in force. Whether the state has power ultimately depends upon whether it exercises a monopoly of violence. By the same token, whether the people have power ultimately depends upon whether they are armed and create their own grassroots militia, to guard not only themselves from criminals or invaders but their own power and freedom from the ever-encroaching power of the state itself. Here, too, the Athenian, British, and American yeomen knew only too well that a professional military was a threat to liberty and the state was a vehicle for disarming the people.

A true civicism that tries to create a genuine politics, an empowered citizenry, and a municipalized economy would be a vulnerable project indeed if it failed to replace the police and the professional army with a popular militia – more specifically, a civic guard, composed of rotating patrols for police purposes and well-trained citizen military contingents for dealing with external dangers to freedom. Greek democracy would never have survived the repeated assaults of the Greek aristocracy without its militia of citizen hoplites, those foot soldiers who could answer the call to arms with their own weapons and elected commanders. The tragic history of the state's ascendancy over free municipalities, even the rise of oligarchy within free cities of the past, is the story of armed professionals who commandeered power from unarmed peoples or disarmed them presumably (as so many liberals would have it today) from the "hazards" of domestic and neighborhood "shootouts." Typically, this is the cowboy or "gunslinger" image of the "American Dream," often cynically imposed on its more traditional yeoman face.

Beyond the municipal agenda that I have presented thus far lies another, more long-range, one: the vision of a political world in which the state as such would finally be replaced completely by a confederal network of municipal assemblies; all socially important forms of property would be absorbed into a truly political economy in which municipalities, interacting with each other economically as well as politically, would resolve their material problems as citizens in open assemblies, not simply as professionals, farmers, and blue- or white-collar workers; and humanly scaled and physically decentralized municipalities.

Not only would people then be able to transform themselves from occupational beings into communally-oriented citizens; they would create a world in which all weapons could indeed be beaten into plowshares. Ultimately, it would be possible for new networks of communities to emerge that would be exquisitely tailored – psychologically and spiritually as well as technologically, architecturally, and structurally – to the natural environments in which they exist.

This agenda for a more distant future embodies the "ultimate" vision I have elaborated in greater detail in my previous writings. Its achievement can no longer be seen as a sudden "revolution" that within a brief span of time will replace the present society with a radically new one. Actually, such revolutions never really happened in history. Even the French Revolution, which radicals have long regarded as a paradigm of sudden social change, was generations in making and did not come to its definitive end until a century later, when the last of the sans culottes were virtually exterminated on the barricades of the Paris Commune of 1871.

Nor can we afford today the myth today that barricades are more than a symbol. What links my minimal agenda to my ultimate one is a *process,* an admittedly long development in which the existing institutions and traditions of freedom are slowly enlarged and expanded. For the present, we must try increasingly to democratize the republic, a call that consists of preserving – and expanding – freedoms we have earned centuries ago, together with the institutions that give them reality. For the future it means that we must radicalize the democracy we create, imparting an even more creative content to the democratic institutions we have rescued and tried to develop.

Admittedly, at that later point we will have moved from a countervailing position that tries to play our democratic institutions against the state into a militant attempt to replace the state with municipally based confederal structures. It is to be devoutly hoped that by that time, too, the state power itself will have been hollowed out institutionally by local or civic structures, indeed that its very legitimacy, not to speak of its authority as a coercive force, will simply lead to its collapse in any period of confrontation. If the great revolutions of the past provide us with examples of how so major a shift is possible, it would be well to remember that seemingly all-powerful monarchies that the republics replaced two centuries ago were so denuded of power that they crumbled rather than "fell," much as a mummified corpse turns to dust after it has been suddenly exposed to air.

Another future prospect also faces us, a chilling one, in which urbanization so completely devours the city and the countryside that community becomes an archaism; in which a market society filters into the most private recesses of our lives as individuals and effaces all sense of personality, let alone individuality; in which a state renders politics and citizenship not only a mockery but a maw that absorbs the very notion of freedom itself.

This prospect is still sufficiently removed from our most immediate experience that its realization can be arrested by those countervailing forces – that dual power – that I have outlined. Given the persistent destructuring of the natural world as well as the social, more than human freedom is in the balance. The rise of reactionary nationalisms and proliferation of nuclear weapons are only two reminders that we may be reaching a point of cosmic finality in our affairs on the planet. Thus the recovery of a classical concept of politics and citizenship is not only a precondition for a free society; it is also a precondition for our survival as a species. Looming before us is the image of a completely destructured and simplified natural world as well as a completely destructured and simplified urban world – a natural and social world so divested of its variety that we, like all other complex life-forms, will be unable to exist as viable beings.

NOTES

1 Martin Buber, *Paths in Utopia* (Boston: Beacon Press, 1958), p. 80.
2 George Woodcock, *Anarchism: A History of Libertarian Ideas and Movements* (Cleveland and New York: World Publishing Co., 1962, 1969), p. 33.
3 Lester Brown *et al.*, *State of the World: 1995* (New York and London: W. W. Norton and Co., 1995), pp. 60–70.
4 Ibid., p. 67.

CHAPTER NINE

Dialectical Naturalism

Introduction

For much of the twentieth century relativism has plagued philosophical thought, casting into ever-greater philosophical doubt all claims to objective knowledge of reality. In the 1980s and 1990s the rise of postmodernism and deconstruction have given academic philosophy a further relativistic charge. Claims to objective knowledge have now become deeply problematic – and the tendency is growing, when competing claims to knowledge are debated, to end merely with an agnostic shrug.

Despite such intellectual fashions, however, it is a staple of political action in any era that it must have a philosophical grounding in objective reality. Political action presupposes that a group of people have a coherent understanding of their social condition, a belief that it is necessary and possible to change those surroundings, and the willingness to make a long-term commitment to change them. A merely existential or personal justification, which is all that relativistic philosophy provides, is inadequate, since it leaves the political actor's choices arbitrary and susceptible to change from day to day; it provides no ethics as a foundation for political action, since it finds the very concept of objective ethics even more abhorrent than the concept of objective knowledge.

Like any political and social approach, Bookchin's social ecology requires a philosophical grounding. Having absorbed, via the Marxist tradition, the humanism and rationalism of the Enlightenment, Bookchin retains an active commitment to these foundation stones of Western thought to construct not only his political approach but his nature philosophy. His dialectical naturalism, as he calls it, draws specifically on the dialectical tradition in Western philosophy, whose most important sources are Aristotle's *Metaphysics,* Hegel's science of logic, and Marx's *Capital.*

As an adherent of the humanistic and rationalistic tradition, Bookchin holds that it is indeed possible to gain objective knowledge of first nature. As a participant in the dialectical tradition, he maintains that first nature is a reality in the process of becoming. Substance not only exists, contrary to today's agnostics; it is developing, indeed evolving. That first nature is evolutionary makes it especially suitable for comprehension by dialectical philosophy, which emphasizes processes of directional change – that is, becoming – as opposed to being.

Aristotle, Hegel, and Marx saw reality as a developmental rather than a static process, with tendencies in the direction of ever-greater differentiation, complexity, subjectivity, and wholeness. Bookchin, in keeping with his own ecological approach, melded evolutionary theory into their account, giving dialectical philosophy a naturalistic dimension and rejecting earlier recourses to objective idealism (Hegel) and a crude materialism (Engels) in that tradition. And in keeping with his social anarchistic approach, he explored the libertarian dimensions of the tradition, rejecting the teleology of earlier dialectical thinkers while retaining a concept of tendency or directionality.

Like Hegel, Bookchin considers dialectics not only to give an account of the objective world but to be a mode of understanding that world. Thus, dialectical naturalism is not only an account of causation; it is also a form of reasoning.

Much ecological thinking today, Bookchin maintains, partakes of the relativism so characteristic of the twentieth century. It sees the Western mechanistic worldview as a major cause of the ecological crisis, and it considers reason to be endemic to mechanism. Indeed, such thinkers argue, the Enlightenment humanistic tradition has generally given priority to human interests over those of first nature; its emphasis on reason is merely part and parcel of this ecocidal anthropocentrism. They thus reject reason in favor of intuitionism and mysticism as a mode of apprehending – or obfuscating – reality.

Bookchin, by contrast, sees the Enlightenment itself as ecological in the sense that it refocused human attention away from God and the supernatural precisely onto first nature and naturalistic concerns. To be sure, he admits, a type of reason – the instrumental and analytical kind – has been a factor in ecological destruction as well as promoting human misery, when it has been applied inappropriately. This "conventional" reason – his shorthand name for it – focuses on mechanical causality, the separation of fact and value, and crude empiricism; it is best suited for apprehending nonprocessual phenomena. But it has been applied outside its province, to organic life-forms and especially to human society, where it engenders a one-sided and static view of developmental phenomena. Bookchin proposes that dialectical reasoning is a more appropriate mode of engagement with the organic and social worlds, since it emphasizes becoming rather than stasis and regards causes, which may be elicited, or educed, as "emergent."

Dialectical philosophy not only furnishes a form of "ecological thinking"; it allows us to educe an objective ethic that can guide us in the present ecological crisis – one that will provide an objective ground for advancing an ethical socialism against the market economy, and for creating a free society.

In his discussions of ecological ethics, Bookchin has been criticized – by relativists, among others – for succumbing to the "naturalistic fallacy" – that is, for making specious analogies between first nature and second nature. He justifies the appropriateness of diversity, cooperation, and mutuality for human society, they argue, by adducing those very features in first nature. By such reasoning, they argue, we could just as easily claim that first nature is "red in tooth and claw" and use that fact to justify social Darwinism in society.

But Bookchin is not suggesting that society should mimic first nature, however benign certain aspects of it may be. Rather, he is arguing that certain tendencies – an increase in subjectivity and range of choice, for example – are objectively part of evolution and as such should be promoted wherever possible by human beings. He contends that the values that can be educed from what "should be" follow rationally from these objective potentialities in natural and social development, which exist as latent realities, not as speculations or abstract values.

This tendency toward greater consciousness and choice constitutes the potential by which the natural and social worlds may become self-conscious and self-directive – in human reason and rational action. The self-formative biosphere, including both first and second nature, could potentially find its realization in a "free nature." Since this ecological and rational society has not yet been attained, its potentiality exists as an ethical "should be" against which we may judge the failings of present society; its attainment would be the fulfillment of human emancipation.

Objectively Grounded Ethics
(from "Rethinking Ethics, Nature, and Society," 1985)

If we desperately need an ethics that will join the ideal with the real and give words like *realism* a richer, more rational meaning than they have, then we are faced with a traditional dilemma. How can we objectively validate ethical claims in an era of moral relativism, when good and bad, right and wrong, virtue and evil, even the selection of strategies for social change are completely subjectivized into matters of taste or opinion? The overstated claim that what is good for a highly personalized "me" may not be good for an equally personalized "you" speaks to the growing amorality of our time. Accordingly, such a moral relativism . . . has acquired the sanctity of a constitutional precept in our system of government. It has become the standard by which to determine the criminality of behavior and the guiding principles of diplomacy, religion, politics, and education, not to mention business and personal affairs. The subjectivization of behavioral precepts reflects the universal opportunism of the time; its emphasis is on operational ways of life as distinguished from philosophical ones, especially on ways to survive and function rather than on ideas imbued with meaning.

That moral relativism can deliver us to a totally noncritical view of a world in which mere taste and fleeting opinion justify anything, including nuclear immolation, has been stressed enough not to require further elucidation. If mere opinion suffices to validate social behavior, then the social order itself can be validated simply by public opinion polls. Hence, whether capital punishment is "right" or "wrong" ceases to be an ethical question about the sanctity of life. The issue becomes a problem of juggling percentages, which may justify the slaughter of homicidal felons during one year and their right to live during another. Whether the figures of our polls go up or down can decide whether a given number of people will be put to death or not. Carried to its logical conclusion, this personalistic, operational view of morality can justify a totalitarian society, which abolishes the very claims of the individual. It was not from a sense of irony or perversity that visitors to Mussolini's Italy in the 1920s applauded a fascist regime because Italian trains operated on time. The efficiency of a social system and mere matters of personal convenience were identified with its claims to be the embodiment of the public welfare.

To exorcise moral relativism, with its distasteful extensions into a politics of lesser evils and a practice structured around risk-versus-benefit calculations, is a vexing problem indeed. The converse of a radical moral relativism is a radical moral absolutism, which can be as totalitarian in its power to control as its relativistic opposite is democratic in its power to relax. Both live in a curious intellectual symbiosis; the seeming pluralism of a moral democracy has been known to encompass a fascistic ethics as easily as an anarchic one – which raises the question of how to keep a democracy from voting itself out of existence.

Suffice it to say that moral absolutism is neither better nor worse than the *concrete* message it has to offer. An ethics grounded in ecology can yield a salad of "natural laws" that are as tyrannical in their conclusions as the chaos of moral relativism is precariously wayward.

To appeal from ecology to God is to leap from nature to supernature – that is, ironically, from the human subject as it exists in the real world to the way it exists in the imagination. Religious precepts are the products of priests and visionaries, not of an objective world from which we can gain an ethical direction that is the commanding dictum neither of "natural law" on the one hand nor of supernatural "law" on the other. We have learned only too well that Hitler's "blood and soil" naturism, like Stalin's cosmological "dialectics," can be used as viciously as notions of "natural law" (with all their Darwinian connotations of "fitness to survive" and "natural selection") to collect millions of people in concentration camps, where they are worked to death, incinerated, or both.

Indeed, the suspicion surrounding the choice of nature as a *ground* for ethics is justified by a history of nature philosophies that gave validity to oligarchy (Plato), slavery (Aristotle), hierarchy (Aquinas), necessity (Spinoza), and domination (Marx), to single out the better-known thinkers of Western philosophy. Rarely indeed has nature itself been seen as a nascent domain of freedom, selfhood, and consciousness. Almost invariably, Western thinkers have dealt with the natural world as a wilderness that has always been hostile to humanity or controlled by "natural law," a lawfulness unerring in its necessitarian relationships.

It is here that social ecology fills a void in an objective ethics that is neither absolutist nor relativist, authoritarian nor chaotic, necessitarian nor arbitrary – with all the pitfalls for humanity that these paired notions have yielded. Given social ecology's emphasis on nature's fecundity, on its thrust toward increasing variety, on its limitless capacity to differentiate life-forms and its development of richer, more varied evolutionary pathways that steadily involve ever-more complex species, our vision of the natural world begins to change. We no longer need look upon it as a necessitarian, withholding, or stingy redoubt of blind cruelty and harsh determinism. Although never a "realm of freedom," nature is not reducible to an equally fictitious "realm of necessity," as earlier philosophers, social thinkers, and scientists claimed. The possibility of freedom and individuation is opened up by the rudimentary forms of self-selection, perhaps even "choice," if you will, of the most nascent and barely formed kind that emerges from the increasing complexity of species and their alternate pathways of evolution. Here, without doing violence to the facts, we can begin to point to a thrust in evolution that contains the potentialities of freedom and individuation. Here, too, we can see certain premises for social life – conceived, to be sure, as the institutionalization of the animal community into a potentially rational, self-governing form of association – and, owing to the ever-greater complexity of the nervous system and brain, for the emergence of reason itself.

This ensemble of ideas, I submit, provides us with the basis for an ecological ethics that sees selfhood, reason, and freedom as emerging *from* nature – not in sharp opposition to nature. Natural evolution over time gives rise from within itself to a rich wealth of gradations that open the way to social evolution – in short, two evolutionary pathways in which one is parent to the other. The traditional dualism in human thought that pitted humanity against animality, society against nature, freedom against necessity, mind against body, and in its most insidious hierarchical form, man against woman is transcended by due recognition of the continuity between the two, but without a reductionism or "oneness" that yields, in Hegel's words, "a night in which all cows are black."[1] This transcendence is achieved *historically,* not by arguing out the problem from within the trenches of biology and society – as though each could be discussed and explored separately from the other – and then constructing some kind of mechanical apparatus to "bridge" the gap between these dualities. With the use of an evolutionary approach to explain the evolution of humanity out of animality, society out of nature, and mind out of body, we shed sociobiology's tyrannical "morality of the gene." We also free ourselves from antihumanism's reductionist dissolution of human uniqueness into a cosmic "community" in which ants are equatable with people, from the infamous "lifeboat ethic" that denies the need to share the means of life with others who are less privileged, from an overtly National Socialist outlook that validates the authority of self-appointed "supermen" to dominate "subhumans," and from a Stalinist reduction of human beings to the raw material of a "History" governed by the inexorable "laws" of dialectical materialism.

Let me emphasize that social ecology, while viewing nature as a ground for an ethics of freedom and individuation, does not see an inexorable "lawfulness" at work that derives the human from the nonhuman or society from nature. Social ecology is not only a philosophy of process, it is also a philosophy of potentiality. Potentiality involves a sensitivity to the latent possibilities that inhere in a given constellation of phenomena, not a surrender to predetermined inevitability. It is the capability "to be" that is not as yet in being, a process in which the conditions for a specific line of development exist but have yet to achieve fruition as a "whole" with all its wealth of fullness, self-development, and uniqueness. Analogies more often tell us what this approach to reality is than propositional elucidations: the acorn, for example, which has the potentiality to become an oak tree or the human embryo which has the potentiality to become a fully mature and creative adult. This notion, in any case, is a message of freedom, not of necessity; it speaks to an immanent striving for realization, not to a predetermined certainty of completion. What is potential in an acorn that yields an oak tree or in a human embryo that yields a mature, creative adult is equivalent to what is potential in nature that yields society and what is potential in society that yields freedom, selfhood, and consciousness.

A Philosophical Naturalism
(from the introduction to *The Philosophy of Social Ecology*, 1990)

Today, even sensitive people in growing numbers feel betrayed by the centuries-long glorification of reason, with its icy claims to efficiency, objectivity, and freedom from ethical constraint – the form of reason that has nourished particularly destructive technologies like nucleonics and weaponry. This negative popular reaction is understandable. But swerving away from a specific form of reason that is largely instrumental and coldly analytical creates problems that are no less disturbing than those questions from which we are seeking to escape.

In our aversion to an insensitive and unfeeling form of reason, we may easily opt for a cloudy intuitionism and mysticism as an alternative. Unlike instrumental and analytical reason, after all, a surrender to emotion and mythic beliefs yields cooperative feelings of "interconnectedness" with the natural world and perhaps even a caring attitude toward it. But precisely because intuition and mystical beliefs are so cloudy and arbitrary – which is to say, so *un*-reasoned – they may also "connect" us with things we really shouldn't be connected with at all – namely, racism, sexism, and an abject subservience to charismatic leaders.

Indeed, following this intuitional alternative could potentially render our ecological outlook very dangerous. Vital as the idea of "interconnectedness" may be to our views, it has historically often been the basis of myths and supernatural beliefs that became means for social control and political manipulation. The first half of the twentieth century is in great part the story of brutal movements like National Socialism that fed on a popular antirationalism and anti-intellectualism, and a personal sense of alienation, among other things. This movement mobilized and homogenized millions of people with an antisocial, perverted "ecologistic" ideology based on intuition, with an "interconnectedness" of earth, folk, and "blood and soil" that was militaristic and murderous rather than freely communitarian. Insulated from the challenge of rational critique by its anti-intellectualism and mythic nationalism, the National Socialist movement eventually turned much of Europe into a cemetery. Yet ideologically, this fascist totalitarianism had gained sustenance from the intuitional and mystical credo of the Romantic movement of the century before – something no one could have foreseen at the time.

Feeling, sentiment, and a moral outlook we surely need if instrumental and analytical reason are not to divest us of our *passion* for truth. But myths, mind-numbing rituals, and charismatic personalities can also rob us of the critical faculties that thought provides. Recently, a Green organization in Canada flippantly proclaimed that it seeks "cooperation" as part of its "new paradigm" rather than "confrontation," which it considers part of the rejected "old paradigm." In a more radical era, confrontation was the stated purpose of radical movements! The mythic and uncritical aspect of "interconnectedness" that rejects confrontation seems to have reduced this organization to the level of outright accommodation with the status quo. Here, the need not only to confront the evils of our time but to uncompromisingly oppose them has disappeared into a New Age quagmire of unthinking "good vibes." The "loving" path of compromises along which such "good vibes" lead us can easily end in sheer opportunism.

If our contemporary revolt against reason rests on the misguided belief that the only alternative to our present reality is mysticism, it also rests on the equally misguided belief that only one kind of reason exists. In reacting against instrumental and analytical forms of reason, which are usually identified with reason as such, we may well overlook *other forms of reason* that are organic and yet retain critical qualities; that are developmental and yet retain analytical insights; that are ethical and yet retain contact with reality. The "value-free" rationalism that we normally identify with the physical sciences and technology is in fact not the only form of reason that Western philosophy has developed over the centuries – I refer specifically to the great tradition of dialectical reason that originated in Greece some twenty-five centuries ago and reached its high point, but by no means its completion, in the logical works of Hegel.

What dialectical thinkers from Heraclitus onward have had in common, in varying degrees, is a view of reality as developmental – of *Being* as an ever-unfolding *Becoming*. Ever since Plato created a dualism between a supranatural world of ideal forms and a transient world of imperfect sensible copies, the perplexing question of identity amid change and change amid identity has haunted Western philosophy. Instrumental and analytical forms of reason – what I will here generically call *conventional reason* – rest on a fundamental principle, the famous "principle of identity," or *A equals A,* which means that any given phenomenon can be only itself and cannot be other than what it is, or what we immediately perceive it to be, at a given moment in time. Without this principle, logical consistency in conventional reason would be impossible.

Conventional reason is based on an analysis of phenomena as precisely defined, and whose truth depends upon the internal consistency and their practicality. It focuses on a thing or phenomenon as fixed, with clear-cut boundaries that are immutable for analytical purposes. We know an entity, in this widely accepted notion of reason, when we can analyze it into its irreducible components and determine how they work as a functioning whole, so that knowledge of the entity will have operational applicability. When the boundaries that "define" a developing thing change – as, for instance, when sand becomes soil – then conventional reason treats sand as sand and soil as soil, much as if they were independent of each other. The *zone of interest* in this kind of rationality is a thing or phenomenon's fixity, its independence, and its basically mechanical interaction with similar or dissimilar things and phenomena. The causality that conventional reason describes, moreover, is a matter of kinetics: one billiard ball strikes another and causes them both to move from one position to another – that is to say, by means of *efficient cause*. The two billiard balls are not altered by the blow but are merely repositioned on the billiards table.

But conventional reason cannot address the problem of change at all. It views a mammal, for example, as a creature marked by a highly fixed set of traits that distinguish it from everything that is not mammalian. To "know" a mammal is to explore its structure, literally to analyze it by dismembering it, to reduce it to its components, to identify its organs and their functions, and to ascertain the way they operate together to assure the mammal's survival and reproduction. Similarly, conventional reason views a human being in terms of particular stages of the life-cycle: a person is an infant at one time, a child at another, an adolescent at still another, a youth and finally an adult. When we analyze an infant by means of conventional reason, we do not explore what it is *becoming* in the process of developing into an adult. Doubtless, when developmental psychologists and anatomists study an individual life-cycle, few of them – however conventional their rationality may be – ignore the fact that every infant is in the process of becoming an adult and that the two stages in the life-cycle are in various ways related to each other. But the principle of A *equals* A remains a basic premise. Its logical framework is the authority of consistency, and deductions almost mechanically follow from premises. Conventional reason thus serves the practical function of describing a given entity's identity and telling us how that entity is organized to be itself. But it cannot systematically explore processes of becoming, or how a living entity is patterned as a *potentiality* to phase from one stage of its development into another.

Dialectical reason, unlike conventional reason, acknowledges the developmental nature of reality by asserting in one fashion or another that A *equals not only A but also not*-A. The dialectical thinker who examines the human life-cycle sees an infant as a self-maintaining human identity while simultaneously developing into a child, from a child into an adolescent, from an adolescent into a youth, and from a youth into an adult. Dialectical reason grasps not only how an entity is organized at a particular moment but how it is organized to go beyond that level of development and become *other* than what it is, even as it retains its identity. The contradictory nature of identity – notably, that *A equals both A and not-A* – is an intrinsic feature of identity itself. The unity of opposites is, in fact, a unity *qua* the emerging "other," what Hegel called "the identity of identity and nonidentity."

The thinking of conventional reason today is exemplified – and disastrously reinforced – by the "true or false" questions that make up most standardized tests. One must darken a box to indicate that a statement is either "true" or "false" – and do so quickly, with minimal reflection. These tests, so commonplace today, allow for no nuanced thought or awareness of transitions. That a phenomenon or statement may well be *both true and false* – depending on its context and its place in a process of becoming other than what it is – is excluded by the logical premise on which these tests are based. This testing procedure makes for bad mental habits among young people, who are schooled to take such tests successfully, and whose careers and future lifeways depend on their scores. But the process of thinking in the way such tests demand compartmentalizes and essentially computerizes otherwise rich minds, depriving young people of their native ability to think organically and to understand the developmental nature of the real world.

Another major presupposition of conventional reason – one that follows from its concepts of identity and causality – is that history is a layered series of separate phenomena, a mere *succession* of strata, each independent of the ones that preceded and followed it. These strata may be cemented together by phases, but these phases are themselves analyzed into components and explored independently of each other. Thus, Mesozoic rock strata are independent of Cenozoic, and each stratum exists very much on its own, as do the ones that cement them together. In human history, the medieval period is independent of the modern, and the former is connected to the latter by a series of independent segments, each relatively autonomous in relation to the preceding and subsequent ones. From the standpoint of conventional reason, it is not always clear how historical change occurred or what meaning history has. Despite postmodernism and present-day historical relativism, which examine history using conventional reason and thereby ravage it, there was a time in the recent past when most historians, influenced by theories of evolution and by Marxism, regarded history as a developmental phenomenon and subsequent periods as at least depending upon prior ones. It is this tradition that dialectical reason upholds.

The intuitional approach to history is no improvement over that of conventional reason – indeed, it does the opposite: it literally dissolves historical development into an undifferentiated continuum and even into a ubiquitous, all-embracing "One." The mystical counterpart of mechanico-materialistic stratification is the reductionism that says that everything is "One" or "interconnected," that all phenomena originated from a pulse of primal energy, like the Victorian physicist who believed that when he pounded his fist on a table, Sirius trembled, however faintly. That the universe had an origin, whatever it was, does not warrant the naïve belief that the universe still "really" consists of nothing but its originating source, any more than an adult human being can be explained entirely by reference to his or her parents. This way of thinking is not far removed from the kinetic cause–effect approach of conventional reason. Nor does the "interconnectedness" of all life-forms preclude the sharp distinctions between prey and predators, or between instinctively guided life-forms and potentially rational ones. Yet these countless differentiations reflect innumerable innovations in evolutionary pathways, indeed different *kinds* of evolution – be they inorganic, organic, or social. Instead of apprehending things and phenomena as both differentiated and yet cumulatively related, the mystical alternative to conventional reason tends to see them, to use Hegel's famous remark, as "a night in which all cows are black."

Conventional reason, to be sure, has its useful side. Its internal consistency of propositions, irrespective of content, plays an indispensable role in mathematical thinking and mathematical sciences, in engineering, and in the nuts-and-bolts activities of everyday life. It is indispensable when building a bridge or a house; for such purposes, there is no point in thinking along evolutionary or developmental lines. If we used a logic based on anything but the principle of identity to build a bridge or a house, a catastrophe would no doubt occur. The physiological operations of our bodies, not to speak of the flight of birds and the pumplike workings of a mammalian heart, depend in great part upon principles we associate with conventional reason. To understand or design a mechanical entity requires a form of reason that is instrumental and an analysis of reality into its components and their functioning. The truths of conventional reason, based on consistency, are useful in these areas of life. Indeed, conventional reason has contributed immeasurably to our knowledge of the universe.

For several centuries, in fact, conventional reason held out a promise to dispel the dogmatic authority of the church, the arbitrary behavior of absolute monarchs, and the frightening ghosts of superstition – and indeed, it did a great deal to fulfill this promise. But to achieve the consistency that constitutes its fundamental principle, conventional reason removes ethics from its discourse and concerns. And as an instrument for achieving certain ends, the moral character of those ends, the values, ideals, beliefs, and theories people cherish, are irrelevant to it, arbitrary matters of personal mood and taste. With its message of identity and consistency as truth, conventional reason failed us not because it is false as such but because it has staked out too broad a claim for its own validity in explaining reality. It even redefines reality to fit its claim, just as many mathematical physicists redefine reality as that which can be formulated in mathematical terms. It should come as no surprise, then, that in our highly rationalized industrial society, conventional reason has come to seem repellent. Pervasive authority, an impersonal technocracy, an unfeeling science and insensitive, monolithic bureaucracies – the very existence of all these is imputed to reason as such.

... Let us grant that the principles of identity, of efficient causality, and of stratification do apply to a particular commonsensical reality that is rendered intelligible by their use. But when we go beyond that particular reality, we can no longer reduce the rich wealth of differentiation, flux, development, organic causality, and developmental reality to a vague "One" or to an equally vague notion of "interconnectedness." A very considerable literature dating back to the ancient Greeks provides the basis of an *organic* form of reason and a *developmental* interpretation of reality.

With a few notable exceptions, the Platonic dualism of identity and change reverberated in one way or another throughout Western philosophy until the nineteenth century, when Hegel's logical works largely resolved this paradox by systematically showing that identity, or self-persistence, actually expresses itself *through* change as an ever-variegated unfolding of "unity in diversity," to use his own words. The grandeur of Hegel's effort has no equal in the history of Western philosophy. Like Aristotle before him, he had an "emergent" interpretation of causality, of how the implicit becomes explicit through the unfolding of its latent form and possibilities. On a vast scale over the course of two sizable volumes, he assembled nearly all the categories by which reason explains reality, and educed one from the other in an intelligible and meaningful continuum that is graded into a richly differentiated, increasingly comprehensive, or "adequate" whole, to use some of his terms.

We may reject what Hegel called his "absolute idealism," the transition from his logic to his philosophy of nature, his teleological culmination of the subjective and objective in a godlike "Absolute," and his idea of a cosmic Spirit (*Geist*). Hegel rarefied dialectical reason into a cosmological system that verged on the theological by trying to reconcile it with idealism, absolute knowledge, and a mystical unfolding *logos* that he often designated "God." Unfamiliar with ecology, Hegel rejected natural evolution as a viable theory in favor of a static hierarchy of Being. By the same token, Friedrich Engels intermingled dialectical reason with natural "laws" that more closely resemble the premises of nineteenth-century physics than a plastic metaphysics or an organismic outlook, producing a crude dialectical materialism. Indeed, so enamored was Engels of matter and motion as the irreducible "attributes" of Being that a kineticism based on mere motion invaded his dialectic of organic development.

To dismiss dialectical reason because of the failings of Hegel's idealism and Engels's materialism, however, would be to lose sight of the extraordinary coherence that dialectical reason can furnish and its extraordinary applicability to ecology – particularly to an ecology rooted in evolutionary development. Despite Hegel's own prejudices against organic evolution, what stands out amid the metaphysical and often theological archaisms in his work is his overall eduction of logical categories as the subjective anatomy of a developmental reality. What is needed is to free this form of reason from both the quasi-mystical and the narrowly scientistic worldviews that in the past have made it remote from the living world; to separate it from Hegel's empyrean, basically antinaturalistic dialectical idealism and the wooden, often scientistic dialectical materialism of orthodox Marxists. Shorn of both its idealism and its materialism, dialectical reason may be rendered naturalistic and ecological and conceived as a naturalistic form of thinking.

This *dialectical naturalism* offers an alternative to an ecology movement that rightly distrusts conventional reason. It can bring coherence to ecological thinking, and it can dispel arbitrary and anti-intellectual tendencies toward the sentimental, cloudy, and theistic at best and the dangerously antirational, mystical, and potentially reactionary at worst. As a way of reasoning about reality, dialectical naturalism is organic enough to give a more liberatory meaning to vague words like *interconnectedness* and *holism* without sacrificing intellectuality. It can answer the questions I posed at the beginning of this essay: what nature is, humanity's place in nature, the thrust of natural evolution, and society's relationship with the natural world. Equally important, dialectical naturalism adds an evolutionary perspective to ecological thinking – despite Hegel's rejection of natural evolution and Engels's recourse to the mechanistic evolutionary theories of a century ago. Dialectical naturalism discerns evolutionary phenomena fluidly and plastically, yet it does not divest evolution of rational interpretation. Finally, a dialectic that has been "ecologized," or given a naturalistic core, and a truly developmental understanding of reality could provide the basis for a living ecological ethics. . . .

Minimally, we must assume that there is order in the world, an assumption that even ordinary science must make if it is to exist. Minimally, too, we must assume that there are growth and processes that lead to differentiation, not merely the kind of motion that results from push-pull, gravitational, electromagnetic, and similar forces. Finally, minimally, we must assume that there is some kind of directionality toward ever-greater differentiation or wholeness insofar as potentiality is realized in its full actuality. We need not return to medieval teleological notions of an unswerving predetermination in a hierarchy of Being to accept this directionality; rather, we need only point to the fact that there is a generally orderly development in the real world or, to use philosophical terminology, a "logical" development when a development succeeds in becoming what it is *structured* to become.

In Hegel's logical works, as in Aristotle's *Metaphysics*, dialectics is more than a remarkable "method" for dealing with reality. Conceived as the logical expression of a wide-ranging form of developmental causality, logic, in Hegel's work, joins hands with ontology. Dialectic is simultaneously a way of reasoning and an account of the objective world, with an ontological causality. As a form of reasoning, the most basic categories in dialectic – even such vague categories as Being and Nothing – are differentiated by their own inner logic into fuller, more complex categories. Each category, in turn, is a potentiality that by means of eductive thinking, directed toward an exploration of its latent and implicit possibilities, yields logical expression in self-realization, or what Hegel called "actuality" (*Wirklichkeit*).

Precisely because it is also a system of causality, dialectic is ontological, objective, and therefore naturalistic, as well as a form of reason. In ontological terms, dialectical causality is not merely motion, force, or changes of form but things and phenomena in development. Indeed, since all Being is Becoming, dialectical causality is the differentiation of potentiality into actuality, in the course of which each new actuality becomes the potentiality for further differentiation and actualization. Dialectics explicates how processes occur not only in the natural world but in the social.

How the implicit but relatively undifferentiated form latent with possibility becomes a more differentiated form that is true to its potential form is clarified in Hegel's own words. "The plant, for example, does not lose itself in mere indefinite change," he writes. It has a distinct directionality – in the case of conscious beings, purpose as well. "From the germ much is produced when at first nothing was to be seen, but the whole of what is brought forth, if not developed, is yet hidden and ideally contained within itself." It is worth noting, in this passage, that what may be "brought forth" is not necessarily developed: an acorn, for example, may become food for a squirrel or wither on a concrete sidewalk, rather than develop into what it is potentially constituted to become – notably, an oak tree. "The principle of this projection into existence is that the germ cannot remain merely implicit," Hegel goes on to observe, "but is impelled towards development, since it presents the contradiction of being only implicit."[2]

What we vaguely call the "immanent" factors that produce a self-unfolding of a development, the Hegelian dialectic regards as the contradictory nature of a being that is unfulfilled in the sense that it is only implicit or incomplete. As mere potentiality, it has not "come to itself," so to speak. A thing or phenomenon in dialectical causality remains unsettled, unstable, in tension – much as a fetus ripening toward birth strains to be born because of the way it is constituted – until it develops itself into what it "should be" in all its wholeness or fullness. It cannot remain in endless tension or "contradiction" with what it is organized to become without warping or undoing itself. It must ripen into the fullness of its being.

Modern science has tried to describe nearly all phenomena in terms of efficient cause or the kinetic impact of forces on a thing or phenomenon, reacting against medieval conceptions of causality in terms of *final cause* – notably, in terms of the existence of a deity who impels development, if only by virtue of "His" own "perfection." Hegel's notion of "imperfection" – more appropriately, of "inadequacy" or of contradiction – as an impelling factor for development partly went beyond both efficient and final notions of causality. I say "partly" for a specific reason: the philosophical archaisms that run through Hegel's dialectic weaken his position from a naturalistic viewpoint. From Plato's time until the beginning of the modern world, theological notions of perfection, infinity, and eternality permeated philosophical thought. Plato's "ideal forms" were the "perfect" and the "eternal," of which all existential things were copies. Aristotle's God, particularly as it was Christianized by the medieval Scholastics, was the "perfect" One toward which all things strove, given their finite "imperfection" and inherent limitations. In this way a supranatural ideal defined the "imperfection" of natural phenomena and thereby dynamized them in their striving toward "perfection." There is an element of this quasi-theological thinking in Hegel's notion of contradiction: the whole course of the dialectic culminates in the "Absolute," which is "perfect" in its fullness, wholeness, and unity.

Dialectical naturalism, on the contrary, conceives finiteness and contradiction as distinctly *natural* in the sense that things and phenomena are incomplete and unactualized in their development – not "imperfect" in any idealistic or supranatural sense. Until they are what they have been constituted to become, they exist in a dynamic tension. A dialectical naturalist view thus has nothing to do with the supposition that finite things or phenomena fail to approximate a Platonic ideal or a Scholastic God. Rather, they are still in the process of becoming or, more mundanely, *developing*. Dialectical naturalism thus does not terminate in a Hegelian Absolute at the end of a cosmic developmental path, but rather advances the vision of an ever-increasing wholeness, fullness, and richness of differentiation and subjectivity.

Dialectical contradiction exists within the structure of a thing or phenomenon by virtue of a formal arrangement that is incomplete, inadequate, implicit, and unfulfilled in relation to what it "should be." A naturalistic framework does not limit us to efficient causality with a mechanistic tilt. Nor need we have recourse to theistic "perfection" to explain the almost magnetic eliciting of a development. Dialectical causality is uniquely organic because it operates within a development – the degree of form of a thing or phenomenon, the way in which that form is organized, the tensions or "contradictions" to which its formal ensemble gives rise, and its metabolic self-maintenance and self-development. Perhaps the most suitable word for this kind of development is *growth* – growth not by mere accretion but by a truly immanent process of organic self-formation in a graded and increasingly differentiated direction.

A distinctive continuum emerges from dialectical causality. Here cause and effect are not merely coexisting phenomena or "correlations," to use a common positivist term; nor are they clearly distinct from each other, such that a cause externally impacts upon a thing or phenomenon to produce an effect mechanically. Dialectical causality is cumulative: the implicit or "in itself" (*an sich*), to use Hegel's terminology, is not simply replaced or negated by its more developed explicit or "for itself" (*für sich*); rather, it is absorbed into and developed beyond the explicit into a fuller, more differentiated, and more adequate form – the Hegelian "in and for itself" (*an und für sich*). Insofar as the implicit is *fully* actualized by becoming what it is constituted to be, the process is truly rational, that is to say, it is fulfilled by virtue of its *internal logic*. The continuum of a development is cumulative, containing the history of its development.

Reality is not simply what we experience: there is a sense in which the rational has its own reality. Thus, there are existing realities that are irrational and unrealized realities that are rational. A society that fails to actualize its potentialities for human happiness and progress is "real" enough in the sense that it exists, but it is less than truly social. It is incomplete and distorted insofar as it persists, and hence it is irrational. It is less than what it should be socially, just as a generally defective animal is less than what it should be biologically. Although it is "real" in an existential sense, it is unfulfilled and hence "unreal" *in terms of its potentialities*.

Dialectical naturalism asks which is truly real – the incomplete, aborted, irrational "what is," or the complete, fully developed, rational "what should be." Reason, cast as dialectical causality as well as dialectical logic, yields an unconventional understanding of reality. A process that follows its immanent self-development to its logical actuality is more properly "real" than a given "what is" that is aborted or distorted and hence, in Hegelian terms, "untrue" to its possibilities. *Reason* has the obligation to explore the potentialities that are latent in any social development and educe its authentic actualization, its fulfillment and "truth" through a new and more rational social dispensation.

It would be philosophically frivolous to embrace the "what is" of a thing or phenomenon as constituting its "reality" without considering it in the light of the "what should be" that would logically emerge from its potentialities. Nor do we ordinarily do so in practice. We rightly evaluate an individual in terms of his or her known potentialities, and we form understandable judgments about whether the individual has truly "fulfilled" himself or herself. Indeed, in privacy, individuals make such self-evaluations repeatedly, which may have important effects upon their behavior, creativity, and self-esteem.

The "what is," conceived as the strictly existential, is a slippery "reality." Accepted empirically without qualification, it excludes the past because, strictly speaking, the past no longer "is." At the same time, it yields a discontinuity with the future that – again, strictly speaking – has yet to "exist." What is more, the "what is," conceived in strictly empirical terms, excludes subjectivity – certainly conceptual thought – from any role in the world but a spectatorial one, which may or may not be a force in behavior.

In the logic of a strictly empirical philosophy, mind simply registers or coordinates experience. "Reality" is a given temporal moment that exists as an experienced segment of an assumed continuum. The "real" is a frozen "here and now" to which we merely *add* an adventitious past and *presume* a future in order to experience reality intelligibly. The kind of radical empiricism advanced by David Hume replaced the notion of Being as Becoming with the experience of a given moment that renders thinking of the past as "unreal" as making inferences about the future. This kind of "reality," as Hume himself fully sensed, is impossible to live with in everyday life; hence he was obliged to define continuity, although he did so in terms of custom and habit, not in terms of causality. Conceiving immediate empirical reality as the totality of the "real" essentially banishes hindsight and foresight as little more than mere conveniences. Indeed, a strictly empirical approach dissolves the logical tissue that integrates the organic, cumulative continuity of the past with the present and that of both with the future.

By contrast, in a naturalistic dialectic, both past and future are part of a cumulative, logical, and objective continuum that includes the present. Reason is not only a means for analyzing and interpreting reality; it extends the *boundaries* of reality beyond the immediately experienced present. Past, present, and future are a cumulatively graded process that thought can truly interpret and render meaningful. We can legitimately explore such a process in terms of whether its potentialities have been realized, aborted, or warped.

In a naturalistic dialectic, the word *reality* thus acquires two distinctly different meanings. There is the immediately present empirical "reality" – or *Realität*, to use Hegel's language – that need not be the fulfillment of a potentiality, and there is the dialectical "actuality" – *Wirklichkeit* – that constitutes a complete fulfillment of a rational process. Even though *Wirklichkeit* appears as a projection of thought into a future that has yet to be existentially realized, the potentiality from which that *Wirklichkeit* develops is as existential as the world we sense in direct and immediate ordinary experience. For example, an egg patently and empirically exists, even though the bird whose potential it contains has yet to develop and reach maturity. Just so, the given potentiality of any process exists and constitutes the basis for a process that should be realized. Hence, the potentiality *does* exist objectively, even in empirical terms. *Wirklichkeit* is what dialectical naturalism *infers* from an objectively given potentiality; it is present, if only implicitly, as an existential fact, and dialectical reason can analyze and subject it to processual inferences. Even in the seemingly most subjective projections of speculative reason, *Wirklichkeit*, the "what should be," is anchored in a continuum that emerges from an objective potentiality, or "what is."

Dialectical naturalism is thus integrally wedded to the objective world – a world in which Being is Becoming. Let me emphasize that dialectical naturalism not only grasps reality as an existentially unfolding continuum, but it also forms an *objective* framework for making ethical judgments. The "what should be" becomes an ethical criterion for judging the truth or validity of an objective "what is." Thus ethics is not merely a matter of personal taste and values; it is factually anchored in the world itself as an objective standard of self-realization. Whether a society is "good" or "bad," moral or immoral, for example, can be *objectively* determined by whether it has fulfilled its potentialities for rationality and morality. Potentialities that are themselves actualizations of a dialectical continuum present the challenge of ethical self-fulfillment – not simply in the privacy of the mind but in the reality of the processual world. Herein lies the only meaningful basis for a truly ethical socialism or anarchism, one that is more than a body of subjective preferences that rest on opinion and taste. . . .

If dialectical naturalism is to explain things or phenomena properly, its ontology and premises must be understood as more than mere motion and interconnection. A continuum is a more relevant premise for dialectical reason than either motion or the interdependence of phenomena. It was one of the failings of "dialectical materialism" that it premised dialectic on the nineteenth century's physics of matter and motion, from which development somehow managed to emerge. It would be just as limited to replace the entelechial processes involved in differentiation and the realization of potentiality with "interconnectedness." A dialectic based merely on a notion of "interconnectedness" would tend to be more descriptive than eductive; it would not clearly explain how interdependencies lead to a graded entelechial development – that is, to self-formation through the self-realization of potentiality. . . .

The continuum that dialectical reason investigates is a highly graded, richly entelechial, logically eductive, and self-directive process of unfolding toward ever-greater differentiation, wholeness, and adequacy, insofar as each potentiality is fully actualized given a specific range of development. External factors, internal rearrangements, accidents, even gross irrationalities may distort or preclude a potential development. But insofar as order does exist in reality and is not simply imposed upon it by mind, reality has a rational dimension. More colloquially, there is a "logic" in the development of phenomena, a *general* directiveness that accounts for the fact that the inorganic did become organic, as a result of its *implicit capacity* for organicity; and for the fact that the organic did become more differentiated and metabolically self-maintaining and self-aware, as a result of potentialities that made for highly developed hormonal and nervous systems.

Stephen Jay Gould may luxuriate in the randomness – actually, the fecundity – of nature, and poststructuralists may try to dissolve both natural and social evolution into an aggregation of unrelated events, but directiveness of organic evolution unremittingly surfaces in even these rather chaotic collections of "brute facts." Like it or not, human beings, primates, mammals, vertebrates, and so forth back to the most elementary protozoans are a sequential presence in the fossil record itself, each emerging out of preceding life-forms. As Gould asserts, the Burgess Shale of British Columbia attests to a large variety of fossils that cannot be classified into a unilinear "chain of being." But far from challenging the existence of directionality in evolution toward greater subjectivity, the Burgess Shale provides extraordinary evidence of the fecundity of nature. Nature's fecundity rests on the existence of chance, indeed variety, as a *precondition* for complexity in organisms and ecosystems and, by virtue of that fecundity, for the emergence of humanity from potentialities that involve increasing subjectivity.

Our ontological and eductive premise for dialectical naturalism, however, remains the graded continuum I have already described – and the Burgess Shale notwithstanding, human beings are not only patently *here*, but our evolution can be *explained*. Dialectical reason cuts across the grain of conventional ways of thinking about the natural world and mystical interpretations of it. Nature is not simply the landscape we see from behind a picture window, in a moment disconnected from those that preceded and will follow it; nor is it a vista from a lofty mountain peak. . . . Nature is certainly all of these things – but it is significantly more. Biological nature is above all the cumulative evolution of ever-differentiating and increasingly complex life-forms with a vibrant and interactive inorganic world. Following in a tradition that goes back at least to Cicero, we can call this relatively unconscious natural development "first nature." It is first nature in the primal sense of a fossil record that clearly leads to mammalian, primate, and human life – not to mention its extraordinary fecundity of other life-forms – and it is first nature that exhibits a high degree of orderly continuity in the actualization of potentialities that made for more complex and self-aware or subjective life-forms. Insofar as this continuity is intelligible, it has meaning and rationality in terms of its results: the elaboration of life-forms that can conceptualize, understand, and communicate with each other in increasingly symbolic terms.

In their most differentiated and fully developed forms, these self-reflexive and communicative capacities are conceptual thought and language. The human species has these capacities to an extent that is unprecedented in any existing life-form. Humanity's awareness of itself, its ability to generalize this awareness to the level of a highly systematic understanding of its environment in the form of philosophy, science, ethics, and aesthetics, and finally, its capacity to alter itself and its environment systematically by means of knowledge and technology place it beyond the realm of the subjectivity that exists in first nature.

By singling out humanity as a unique life-form that can consciously change the entire realm of first nature, I do not claim that first nature was "made" to be "exploited" by humanity, as those ecologists critical of "anthropocentrism" sometimes charge. The idea of a *made* world has its origin in theology, notably in the belief that a supernatural being created the natural world and that evolution is infused with a theistic principle, both in the service of human needs. By the same token, humans cannot "exploit" nature, owing to a "commanding" place in a supposed "hierarchy" of nature. Words like *commanding, exploitation,* and *hierarchy* are actually *social* terms that describe how people relate to each other; applied to the natural world, they are merely anthropomorphic.

Far more relevant from the standpoint of dialectical naturalism is the fact that humanity's vast capacity to alter first nature is itself a product of natural evolution – not of a deity or the embodiment of a cosmic Spirit. From an evolutionary viewpoint, humanity has been *constituted* to intervene actively, consciously, and purposively into first nature with unparalleled effectiveness and to alter it on a planetary scale. To denigrate this capacity is to deny the thrust of natural evolution itself toward organic complexity and subjectivity – the potentiality of first nature to actualize itself in self-conscious intellectuality. One may choose to argue that this thrust was predetermined with inexorable certainty as a result of a deity, or one may contend that it was strictly fortuitous, or one may claim – as I would – that there is a natural *tendency* toward greater complexity and subjectivity in first nature, arising from the very interactivity of matter, indeed a *nisus* toward self-consciousness. But what is decisive here is the compelling fact that humanity's natural capacity to consciously intervene into and act upon first nature has given rise to a "second nature," a cultural, social, and political "nature" that today has all but absorbed first nature.

There is no part of the world that has not been profoundly affected by human activity – neither the remote fastnesses of Antarctica nor the canyons of the ocean's depths. Even wilderness areas require protection from human intervention; much that is designated as wilderness today has already been profoundly affected by human activity. Indeed, wilderness can be said to exist primarily as a result of a human decision to preserve it. Nearly all the nonhuman life-forms that exist today are, like it or not, to some degree in human custody, and whether they are preserved in their wild lifeways depends largely on human attitudes and behavior.

That second nature is the outcome of evolution in first nature and can thereby be designated as natural does not mean that second nature is necessarily creative or even fully conscious of itself in any evolutionary sense. Second nature is synonymous with society and human internal nature, both of which are undergoing evolution for better or worse. Although social evolution is grounded in, indeed phases out of, organic evolution, it is also profoundly different from organic evolution. Consciousness, will, alterable institutions, and the operation of economic forces and technics may be deployed to enhance the organic world or carry it to the point of destruction. Second nature as it exists today is marked by monstrous attributes, notably hierarchy, class, the state, private property, and a competitive market economy that obliges economic rivals to grow at the expense of each other or perish. This ethical judgement, I may note, has meaning *only* if we assume that there is potentiality and self-directiveness in organic evolution toward greater subjectivity, consciousness, self-reflexivity; by inference, it is the *responsibility* of the most conscious of life-forms – humanity – to be the "voice" of a mute nature and to act to intelligently foster organic evolution.

If this tendency or *nisus* in organic evolution is denied, there is no reason why the human species, like any other species, should not utilize its capacities to serve its own needs or attain its own "self-realization" at the expense of other life-forms that impede its interests and desires. To denounce humanity for "exploiting" organic nature, "degrading" it, "abusing" it, and behaving "anthropocentrically" is simply an oblique way of acknowledging that second nature is the bearer of moral responsibilities that do not exist in the realm of first nature. It is to acknowledge that if all life-forms have an "intrinsic worth" that should be respected, they have it only because human intellectual, moral, and aesthetic abilities have attributed it to them – abilities that no other life-form possesses. It is only human beings that can even *formulate* the concept of "intrinsic worth" and endow it with ethical responsibility. The "intrinsic worth" of human beings is thus patently exceptional, indeed extraordinary.

It is essential to emphasize that second nature is, in fact, an *unfinished,* indeed inadequate, development of nature as a whole. Hegel viewed human history as a slaughterbench. Hierarchy, class, the state, and the like are evidence – and, by no means, purely accidental evidence – of the unfulfilled potentialities of nature to actualize itself as a nature that is self-consciously creative. *Humanity as it now exists is not nature rendered self-conscious.* The future of the biosphere depends overwhelmingly on whether second nature can be *transcended* in a new system of social and organic conciliation, one that I would call "free nature" – a nature that would diminish the pain and suffering that exist in both first and second nature. Free nature, in effect, would be a conscious and ethical nature, an ecological society that I have explored in detail elsewhere.

Ecologizing the Dialectic
(from "Thinking Ecologically: A Dialectical Approach," 1987)

It is eminently *natural* for humanity to create a second nature from its evolution in "first nature." By *second nature,* I mean the development of uniquely human culture, with a wide variety of institutionalized human communities, effective human technics, richly symbolic languages, and carefully managed sources of nutriment. . . . The real question, I submit, is not whether second nature parallels, opposes, or blandly "participates" in an "egalitarian" first nature; rather, it is how second nature is *derived* from first nature. More specifically, in what ways did the highly graded and many-phased evolution from first nature into second give rise to social institutions, forms of interactions between people, and an interaction between first and second nature that, in the best of cases, enriches both and yields a second nature that has an evolutionary development of its own? The ecological crisis we face today is very much a crisis in the emergence of society out of biology, in the problems (the rise of hierarchy, domination, patriarchy, classes, and the state) that unfolded with this development, and in the liberatory pathways that provide an alternative to this warped history.

The fact that first and second nature exist and can never be dualized into "parallels" or simplistically reduced to each other accounts, in great part, for my phrase *social ecology*. Additionally, social ecology has the special meaning that the ecological crisis that beleaguers us stems from a social crisis, a crisis that the crude biologism of deep ecology generally ignores. Still further, that the resolution of this social crisis can only be achieved by reorganizing society along rational lines, imbued with an ecological philosophy and sensibility. . . .

An ecological dialectic would have to address the fact that Aristotle and Hegel did not work with an evolutionary theory of nature but rather saw the natural world more as a scala naturae, a ladder of "being," than as a flowing continuum. An ecological dialectic introduces evolution into this tradition and replaces the notion of a scala naturae with a richly mediated continuum. Both thinkers were more profoundly influenced by Plato than their writings would seem to indicate, with the result that in the case of Hegel, we move within a realm of concepts more than history (however historical Hegel's dialectic invariably was). Hegel was strongly preoccupied with the "idea" of nature rather than with its existential details, although he honored this preoccupation in the breach. Finally, the overarching teleology of the two philosophers tends to subordinate the contingency, spontaneity, and creativity that mark natural phenomena. Hegel, with his strong theological bent, terminated the unfolding of the world in an "Absolute" that encompasses it in an identity of subject and object. In an ecological dialectic, by contrast, there would be no terminality that could culminate in a God or an Absolute. "Actuality," to use Hegel's special term, is the almost momentary culmination of maturity, so that the objectivity of the potential, which is crucial for an objective ethics, is subordinated to its actualization. . . .

Dialectic, let me emphasize, is not merely change, motion, or even process, all banal imputations to the contrary notwithstanding. Nor can it be subsumed under "process philosophy." Dialectic is *development,* not only change; it is *derivation,* not only motion; it is *mediation,* not mere process; and it is *cumulative,* not only continuous. That it is also change, motion, process, and a continuum tells us only part of its true content. But denied its immanent self-directiveness and its entelechial eduction of the potential into the actual, this "process philosophy," indeed this remarkable notion of *causality,* ceases to be dialectic. Instead, it becomes a mere husk that our current flock of "eco"-faddists can reduce to "kinetics," "dynamics," "fluctuations," and "feedback loops" – the same mechanistic verbiage with which systems theory dresses itself up as a developmental philosophy.

As Hegel warned in the course of educing the complexity of the dialectical process: knowledge has "no other object than to draw out what is inward or implicit and thus to become objective." But if that which is implicit comes into existence, it certainly passes into change, yet it *remains one and the same.* . . . The plant, for example, does not lose itself in mere indefinite change. From the germ much is produced when at first nothing was to be seen; but the whole of what is brought forth, if not developed, is yet hidden and ideally contained within itself. The principle of *this projection into existence* is that the germ cannot remain merely implicit, but is impelled toward development, since it presents the contradiction of being only implicitly and yet not desiring to be so.[3]

Thus dialectic is not wayward motion, the mere kinetics of change. There is a rational "end in view" – not one that is preordained, to state this point from an ecological viewpoint rather than a theological one, but one that actualizes what is implicit in the potential. Every "if-then" proposition is premised not on any *if* that springs into one's head like a gambler's hunch; it posits a potentiality that has its ancestry in the dialectical processes that preceded it. . . .

In the organic world, the metabolic activity of the simplest life-forms constitutes the sense of self-identity, however germinal, from which nature acquires a rudimentary subjectivity. Not only does this rudimentary subjectivity (which reductionism necessarily cannot encompass) derive from the metabolic process of self-maintenance, a process that defines any life-form as a unique whole; it extends itself beyond self-maintenance to become a *striving* activity, not unlike the development from the vegetative to the animative, that ultimately yields mind, will, and the potentiality for freedom. Conceived dialectically, organic evolution is, in a broad sense, subjective insofar as life-forms begin to exercise choices in adapting to new environments – a conception that stands much at odds with that clearly definable fixity we blissfully call "clear thinking." Systems theory enters into the reductionist tableau in a sinister way: by dissolving the subjective element in biological phenomena so that they can be treated as mathematical symbols, systems theory permits evolutionary interaction, subjective development, and even process itself, to be taken over by "the system," just as the individual, the family, and the community are destructured into "the System" embodied by the economic corporation and the state. Life ceases to have subjectivity and becomes a mechanism in which the tendency of life-forms toward ever-greater elaboration is replaced with "feedback loops," and their evolutionary antecedents with programmed "information." A "systems view of life" literally conceives of life as a system, not only as "fluctuations" and "cycles" – mechanistic as these concepts are in themselves.

Despite the external selective factors with which Darwinians describe evolution, the tendency of life toward a greater complexity of selfhood – a tendency that yields increasing degrees of subjectivity – constitutes the internal or immanent impulse of evolution toward growing self-awareness. This evolutionary dialectic constitutes the essence of life as a self-maintaining organism that bears the *potential* for the development of self-conscious organisms. Dialectic, in effect, is not merely a "logic" or a "method" that can be bounced around and "applied" promiscuously to a content. It has no "handbook" other than *reason itself* to guide those who seek to develop a dialectical sensibility. Dialectic can no more be applied to problems in engineering than can Einstein's general theory of relativity be applied to plumbing; these problems can best be resolved by conventional forms of logic, common sense, and the pragmatic knowledge acquired through experience. Dialectic can only explicate a rationally developmental phenomenon, just as systems theory can only explicate the workings of a fluctuating and cyclical system. The kind of verification that validates or invalidates the soundness of dialectical reasoning, in turn, must be *developmental,* not relatively static or for that matter "fluctuating" kinds of phenomena. . . .

Freed of its theological trappings, dialectic *explains,* with a power beyond that of any conventional logic, how the organic flow of first into second nature is a reworking of biological into social reality. Each phase or "moment," pressed by its own internal logic into an antithetical and ultimately a more transcendent form, emerges as a more complex unity-in-diversity that encompasses its earlier moments even as it goes beyond them. Despite the imagery of strife that permeates the Hegelian version of this process, the ultimate point in the Hegelian *Aufhebung* is reconciliation, not the nihilism of pure negation. Moreover, norms – the actualization of the potential "is" into the ethical "ought" – are anchored in the objective reality of potentiality itself, not as it always "is," to be sure, but as it "should be," such that speculation becomes a valid account of reality in its truth. Hegel, I would argue, *radically expanded the very concept of Being in philosophy and in the real world to encompass the potential and its actualization into the rational "what should be,"* not only as an existential "what is."

Dialectical speculation, despite Hegel's own view of the retrospective function of philosophy, thus is *projective* in a sharply critical sense (quite unlike "futurology," which dissolves the future by making it a mere extrapolation of the present). In its restless critique of reality we can call dialectic a "negative philosophy" – in contrast, I should add, to Adorno's nihilism or "negative dialectics." By the same token, speculation is creative in that it ceaselessly contrasts the free, rational, and moral actuality of "what could be," which inheres in nature's thrust toward self-reflexivity, with the existential reality of "what is." Speculation can ask why (not only how) the real has become the irrational – indeed, the inhuman and anti-ecological – precisely because dialectic alone is capable of grounding an ecological ethics in the potential, that is, in its objective possibilities for the realization of reason and truth.

This objectivization of possibilities – of potentiality continuous with its yet unrealized actualization – is the ground for a genuinely objective ethics, as distinguished from an ethical relativism subject to the waywardness of the opinion poll. An ecological dialectic, in effect, opens the way to an ethics that is rooted in the objectivity of the potential, not in the commandments of a deity or in the eternality of a supramundane and transcendental "reality." Hence, the "what should be" is not only objective, it forms the objective critique of the given reality. . . .

BEYOND FIRST AND SECOND NATURE

We must try to bring the threads of our discussion together and examine the important implications dialectic has for ecological thinking. A "dialectical view of life" is a special form of process philosophy. Its emphasis is not on change alone but on development. It is eductive rather than merely deductive, mediated rather than merely processual, and cumulative rather than merely continuous. Its objectivity begins with the existence of the potential, not with the mere facticity of the real; hence its ethics seeks the "what should be" as a realm of *objective* possibilities. That "possibilities" are objective, albeit not in the sense of a simplistic materialism, is dialectically justified by the perception that potentiality and its latent possibilities form an existential continuum that constitutes the authentic world of truth – the world of the "what should be," not simply the world of the "what is," with all its incompleteness and falsehood.

From a dialectical viewpoint, a change in a given level of biotic, communal, or, for that matter, social organization consists not simply of the appearance of a new, possibly more complex ensemble of "feedback loops." Rather, it consists of qualitatively new attributes, interrelationships, and degrees of subjectivity that express and radically condition the emergence of a new potentiality, opening a new realm of possibility with its own unique tendency – not a greater or lesser number of "fluctuations" and "rhythms." Moreover, this new potentiality is itself the result of other actualizations of potentialities that, taken together historically and cumulatively, constitute a developmental continuum – not a bullet "shot from a pistol" that explodes into Being without a history of its own or a continuum of which it is part.

Dialectical logic is an immanent logic of process – an *ontological* logic, not only a logic of concepts, categories, and symbols. This logic is emergent, in the sense that one speaks of the "logic of events." Considered in terms of its emphasis on differentiation, this logic is provocatively concrete in its relationship to abstract generalizations – hence Hegel's seemingly paradoxical expression "concrete universal." Dialectic thereby overcomes Plato's dualistic separation of exemplary ideas from the phenomenal world of imperfect "copies" – hence its ethical thrust is literally structured, cumulatively as well as sequentially, in the concrete. Emerging from this superb ensemble is a world that is always ethically problematical but also an ethics that is always objective, a recognition of selfhood and subjectivity that embodies nonhuman and human nature, and a development from metabolic self-maintenance to rational self-direction and innovation that locates the origins of reason *within* nature, not in a supramundane domain *apart* from nature. The social is thus wedded to the natural, and human reason is wedded to nonhuman subjectivity through processes that are richly mediated and graded in a shared continuum of development. This ecological interpretation of dialectic not only overcomes dualism but moves through differentiation away from reductionism.

Ecology cleanses the remarkable heritage of European organismic thought of the hard teleological predeterminations it acquired from Greek theology, the Platonistic denigration of physicality, and the Christian preoccupation with human inwardness as "soul" and a reverence for God. Only ecology can ventilate the dialectic as an orientation toward the objective world by rendering it coextensive with natural evolution, a possibility that arose in the last century with the appearance of evolutionary theory.

As such, an ecological dialectic is not solely a way of thinking organically; it can be a source of *meaning* to natural evolution – of *ethical* meaning, not only rational meaning. To state this idea more provocatively: we cannot hope to find humanity's "place in nature" without knowing how it *emerged* from nature, with all its problems and possibilities. An ecological dialectic produces a creative paradox: second nature in an ecological society would be the actualization of first nature's potentiality to achieve mind and truth. Human intellection in an ecological society would thus "fold back" upon the evolutionary continuum that exists in first nature. In this sense – and in this sense alone – second nature would thus become first nature rendered self-reflexive, a thinking nature that would know itself and could guide its own evolution, not an unthinking nature that "sought its own balance" through the "dynamics" of "fluctuations" and "feedback" that cause needless pain, suffering, and death. Although thought, society, and culture would retain their integrity, they would consciously express the abiding tendency within first nature to press itself toward the level of conscious self-directiveness.

In a very real sense, an ecological society would be *a transcendence of both first nature and second nature* into a new domain of a *free nature,* a nature that in a truly rational humanity reached the level of conceptual thought – in short, a nature that would willfully and thinkingly cope with conflict, contingency, waste, and compulsion. In this new synthesis, where first and second nature are melded into a free, rational, and ethical nature, neither first nor second would lose its specificity and integrity. Humanity, far from diminishing the integrity of nature, would add the dimension of freedom, reason, and ethics to it and raise evolution to a level of self-reflexivity that has always been latent in the emergence of the natural world. . . .

If we understand that human beings are indeed moral agents because natural evolution confers upon them a clear responsibility toward the natural world, we cannot emphasize their unique attributes too strongly. For it is this unique ability to think conceptually and feel a deep empathy for the world of life that makes it possible for humanity to reverse the devastation it has inflicted on the biosphere and create a rational society. This implies not only that humanity, once it came into its own as the actualization of its potentialities, *could* be a rational expression of nature's creativity and fecundity, but that human intervention into natural processes *could* be as creative as natural evolution itself.

This evolutionary and dialectical viewpoint, which derives the human species from nature as the embodiment of nature's own thrust toward self-reflexivity, changes the entire argument around competing "rights" between human and nonhuman life-forms into an exploration of the *ways* in which human beings intervene into the biosphere. Whether humanity recognizes that an ecological society would be the fulfillment of a major tendency in natural evolution, or remains blind to its own humanity as a moral and ecological agent in nature, becomes a *social* problem that requires a *social* ecology. The self-effacing quietism and "spirituality" so rampant today afflict a sizable, highly privileged sector of Euro-American society – human types so consumed by a "love" of nature and life that they may well ignore the needless but very real suffering and pain that exist in nature and society alike.

NOTES

1 G.W.F. Hegel, *The Phenomenology of Mind*, trans. Baillie (New York: Humanities Press, 1910), p. 79.
2 G.W.F. Hegel, *Lectures on the History of Philosophy*, vol. 1, trans. E. S. Haldane and Frances H. Simson (New York: Humanities Press, 1955), p. 22.
3 Ibid. (emphasis added).

CHAPTER TEN

Reason and History

Introduction

The ecological society that Bookchin described in 1964 remains a constant social ideal over three decades of his writing, projecting a clear and steady image of an ecological society, integrating town and country, individual and community, technology and ethics, politics and economy. The communistic principles he attributed to organic society in 1982 remain pillars of the society he has always envisioned: interdependence must replace hierarchy, and freedom must be defined not in opposition to first nature but as latent within it. The "legacy of freedom" is one he cherishes even more fervently, in the face of an ever-more powerful "legacy of domination."

But other aspects of Bookchin's work have undergone notable change over the years, as do those of all thinkers who are engaged in the public realm over a long period of time and who are alert to changes that take place there. Chastened by the emergence of eco-mysticism, primitivism, and biocentrism in the ecology and anarchist movements, Bookchin today is far less lavish in his praise of organic society than he was in 1982. In the face of primitivistic rejections of civilization as such, for example, he no longer puts the word *civilization* in quotation marks; on the contrary, he capitalizes it. In the face of general rejections of progress as such, he is careful to define the kind of progress he endorses – namely, that which is associated with cooperation and community and that represents a heightening of ethical standards. He would no longer associate the Promethean impulse with domination or the "conquest of nature," as he once did; now he regards it as a laudable metaphor for aspirations to advance the human condition.

His view of imagination, too, has undergone a shift: where once he extolled the cry "Imagination to power!" raised by the Parisian students in 1968 as "a glowing vision of the estheticization of personality and society," now he warns that "in the absence of rational objective standards of behavior, imagination may be as demonic as it may be liberatory." Indeed, where he once wrote of an *ecological* society, he now writes more frequently of a *rational* society, which in his view presupposes sound ecological practices, without yielding to mysticism or other forms of supernaturalism.

"History, Civilization, and Progress," written in 1994, is a critique of current philosophical tendencies that condemn history, civilization, and progress as inherently repressive. An ecological humanism, Bookchin says today, would perform the difficult work of disclosing what is rational in what is ordinarily called history, civilization, and progress, and giving this rational core its due, rather than merely repudiating history, civilization, and progress as such.

Moreover, he now gives an enlarged meaning to the "legacy of freedom": it means not only the particular events in the history of libertarian alternatives, but the gradual if uneven unfolding of potentialities for freedom, self-consciousness, and cooperation in human society. In true dialectical fashion this legacy, far from repudiating history, civilization, and progress, actively participates in them. The richness of Bookchin's late work is to create this new synthesis, to show how emancipatory ideas infuse history despite its bleakest and cruelest moments. The creation of an ecological society must itself constitute an advance toward civilization and progress, or it will not have been an endeavor worth making.

History, Civilization, and Progress
(from "History, Civilization, and Progress," 1994)

Rarely have the concepts that literally define the best of Western culture – its notions of a meaningful History, a universal Civilization, and the possibility of Progress – been called so radically into question as they are today. In recent decades, both in the United States and abroad, the academy and a subculture of self-styled postmodernist intellectuals have nourished an entirely new ensemble of cultural conventions that stem from a corrosive social, political, and moral relativism. This ensemble encompasses a crude nominalism, pluralism, and skepticism, an extreme subjectivism, and even outright nihilism and antihumanism in various combinations and permutations, sometimes of a thoroughly misanthropic nature. This relativistic ensemble is pitted against coherent thought as such and against the "principle of hope" (to use Ernst Bloch's expression) that marked radical theory of the recent past. Such notions percolate from so-called radical academics into the general public, where they take the form of personalism, amoralism, and neoprimitivism. . . .

History, I wish to contend, is the *rational* content and continuity of events (with due regard for qualitative "leaps") that are grounded in humanity's potentialities for freedom, self-consciousness, and cooperation, in the self-formative development of increasingly libertarian forms of consociation. It is the rational "infrastructure," so to speak, that coheres human actions and institutions over the past and the present in the direction of an emancipatory society and emancipated individual. That is to say, History is precisely what is rational in human development. It is what is rational, moreover, in the dialectical sense of the implicit that unfolds, expands, and begins in varying degrees through increasing differentiation to actualize humanity's very real potentialities for freedom, self-consciousness, and cooperation.

It will immediately be objected that irrational events, unrelated to this actualization, explode upon us at all times, in all eras and cultures. But insofar as they defy rational interpretation, they remain precisely *events,* not History, however consequential their effects may be on the course of other events. Their impact may be very powerful, to be sure, but they are not dialectically rooted in humanity's potentialities for freedom, self-consciousness, and cooperation. They can be assembled into *Chronicles,* the stuff out of which a Froissart constructed his largely anecdotal "histories," but not History in the sense I am describing. Events may even "overtake History," so to speak, and ultimately submerge it in the irrational and the evil. But without an increasingly self-reflexive History, which present-day relativism threatens to extinguish, we would not even know that it had happened.

If we deny that humanity has these potentialities for freedom, self-consciousness, and cooperation – conceived as one ensemble – then along with many self-styled "socialists" and even former anarchists like Daniel Cohn-Bendit, we may well conclude that "capitalism has won," as one disillusioned friend put it; that history has reached its terminus in "bourgeois democracy" (however tentative this "terminus" may actually be); and that rather than attempt to enlarge the realm of the rational and the free, we would do best to ensconce ourselves in the lap of capitalism and make it as comfortable a resting place as possible for ourselves.

As a mere adaptation to what exists, to the "what is," such behavior is merely animalistic. Sociobiologists may even regard it as genetically unavoidable. But my critics need not be sociobiologists to observe that the historical record exhibits a great deal of adaptation and worse – of irrationality and violence, of pleasure in the destruction of oneself and others – and to question my assertion that History is the unfolding of human potentialities for freedom, self-consciousness, and cooperation. Indeed, humans have engaged in destruction and luxuriated in real and imaginary cruelties toward one another that have produced hells on earth. They have created the monstrosities of Hitler's death camps and

Stalin's gulags, not to speak of the mountains of skulls that Mongol and Tartar invaders of Eurasia left behind in distant centuries. But this record hardly supplants a dialectic of unfolding and maturing of potentialities in social development, nor is the *capacity* of humans to inflict cruelties on each other equivalent to their *potentialities* for freedom, self-consciousness, and cooperation.

Here, capacities and human potentialities must be distinguished from each other. The human capacity for inflicting injury belongs to the realm of natural history, to what humans share with animals in the biological world, or first nature. First nature is the domain of survival, of core feelings of pain and fear, and in that sense our behavior remains animalistic, which is by no means altered with the emergence of social or second nature. *Unknowing* animals merely try to survive and adapt to one degree or another to the world in which they exist. By contrast, humans are animals of a very special kind; they are *knowing* animals, they have the intelligence to calculate and to devise, even in the service of needs that they share with nonhuman life-forms. Human reason and knowledge have commonly served aims of self-preservation and self-maximization by the use of a formal logic of expediency, a logic that rulers have deployed for social control and the manipulation of society. These methods have their roots in the animal realm of simple means–ends choices to survive.

But humans also have the capacity to deliberately inflict pain and fear, to use their reason for perverse passions, in order to coerce others or merely for cruelty for its own sake. Only knowing animals, ironically capable of intelligent innovation, with the *Schadenfreude* to enjoy vicariously the torment of others, can inflict fear and pain in a coldly calculated or even passionate manner. The Foucauldian hypostasization of the body as the "terrain" of sado-masochistic pleasure can be easily elaborated into a metaphysical justification of violence, depending, to be sure, on what "pleases" a particular perpetrating ego.[1] In this sense, human beings are too intelligent *not* to live in a rational society, *not* to live within institutions formed by reason and ethics that restrict their capacity for irrationality and violence.[2] Insofar as they do not, humans remain dangerously wayward and unformed creatures with enormous powers of destruction as well as creation.

Humanity may have a "potentiality for evil," as one colleague has argued. But that over the course of social development people have exhibited an explosive capacity to perpetrate the most appallingly evil acts does not mean that human potentiality is constituted to produce evil and a nihilistic destructiveness. The capacity of certain Germans to establish an Auschwitz, indeed the means and the goal to exterminate a whole people in a terrifyingly industrial manner, was inherent neither in Germany's development nor in the development of industrial rationalization as such. However anti-Semitic many Germans were over the previous two centuries, Eastern Europeans were equally or even more so; ironically, industrial development in Western Europe may have done more to achieve Jewish juridical emancipation in the nineteenth and twentieth centuries than all the Christian pieties that marked preindustrial life during the Middle Ages. Indeed, evil may have a "logic" – that is to say, it may be explained. But most general accounts explain the evolution of evil in terms of adventitious evil acts and events, if this can be regarded as explanation at all. Hitler's takeover of Germany, made possible more by economic and political dislocations than by the racial views he espoused, was precisely a terrible *event* that cannot be explained in terms of any human potentiality for evil. The horror of Auschwitz lies almost as much in its *inexplicability*, in its appallingly extraordinary character, as in the monstrosities that the Nazis generally inflicted on European Jews. It is in this sense that Auschwitz remains hauntingly *inhuman* and that it has tragically produced an abiding mistrust by many people of Civilization and Progress.

When explanations of evil are not merely narrations of events, they explain evil in terms of instrumental or conventional logic. The knowing animal, the human being, who is viciously harmful, does not use the developmental reason of dialectic, the reason of ethical reflection; nor a coherent reflective reason, grounded in a knowledge of History and Civilization; nor even the knowing of an ambiguous, arbitrary, self-generated "imaginary," or a morality of personal taste and pleasure. Rather, the knowing animal uses instrumental calculation to serve evil ends, including the infliction of pain.

The very existence of irrationalism and evil in many social phenomena today compels us to uphold a clear standard of the rational and the good by which to judge the one against the other. A purely personalistic, relativistic, or functional approach will hardly do for establishing ethical standards – as many critiques of subjectivism and subjective reason have shown. The personal tastes from which subjectivism and relativism derive their ethical standards are as transient and fleeting as moods. Nor will a nominalistic approach suffice: to reduce History to an incomprehensible assortment of patterns or to inexplicable products of the imagination is to deny social development all internal *ethical* coherence. Indeed, an unsorted, ungraded, unmediated approach reduces our understanding of History to a crude eclecticism rather than an insightful coherence, to an overemphasis on differentiae (so easy to do, these mindless days!) and on the idiosyncratic rather than on the meaningful and the universal, more often attracting the commonsensical individual to the psychoanalytic couch than helping him or her reconstitute a left–libertarian social movement.

If our views of social development are to be structured around the differences that distinguish one culture or period from another, we will ignore underlying tendencies that, with extraordinary universality, have greatly expanded the material and cultural conditions for freedom on various levels of individual and social self-understanding. By grossly emphasizing disjunctions, social isolates, unique configurations, and chance events, we will reduce shared, clearly common social developments to an archipelago of cultures, each essentially unrelated to those that preceded and followed it. Yet many historical forces have emerged, declined, and emerged again, despite the formidable obstacles that often seemed to stand in their way. One does not have to explain "everything" in "foundational" terms to recognize the existence of abiding problems such as scarcity, exploitation, class rule, domination, and hierarchy that have agonized oppressed peoples for thousands of years. If critics were correct in dubbing dialectic a mystery for claiming to encompass *all* phenomena by a few cosmic formulas, then they would be obliged to regard human social development as a mystery if they claimed that it lacks any continuity and unity – that is, the bases for a philosophy of History. Without a notion of continuity in History, how could we explain the extraordinary efflorescence of culture and technique that Homo sapiens produced during the Magdalenian period, some twenty or thirty thousand years ago? How could we explain the clearly unrelated evolution of complex agricultural systems in at least three separate parts of the world – the Middle East, Southeast Asia, and Mesoamerica – that apparently had no contact with one another and that were based on the cultivation of very different grains, notably wheat, rice, and maize? How could we explain the great gathering of social forces in which, after ten thousand years of arising, stagnating, and disappearing, cities finally gained control over the agrarian world that had impeded their development, yielding the "urban revolution," as V. Gordon Childe called it, in zones of the world that could have had no contact with one another?

Mesoamerica and Mesopotamia, most clearly, could not have had any contact with each other since Paleolithic times, yet their agriculture, towns and cities, literacy, and mathematics developed in ways that are remarkably similar. Initially Paleolithic foragers, both cultures ultimately produced highly urbanized cultures based on grain cultivation, glyphs, accurate calendrics, and very elaborate pottery, to cite only the most striking parallels. The wheel was known to Mesoamericans, although they do not seem to have used it, probably for want of appropriate draft animals, as well as the zero, despite the absence of any communication with Eurasian societies. It requires an astonishing disregard for the unity of Civilization on the part of historical relativists to emphasize often minor differences, such as clothing, some daily customs, and myths, at the expense of a remarkable unity of consciousness and social development that the two cultures exhibited on two separate continents after many millennia of isolation from each other. . . .

Caprice, accident, irrationality, and "imaginaries" certainly enter into social development for better or worse. But they have no meaning if there is no ethical standard by which to define the "other" of what we are presupposing with our standard. Seemingly accidental or eccentric factors must be raised to the level of *social theory* rather than be shriveled to the level of nominalistic minutiae if we are to understand them. Despite the accidents, failures, and other aberrations that can alter the course of *rational* social and individual development, there is a "legacy of freedom," as I named a key chapter in my book *The Ecology of Freedom*, a tradition of increasing approximation of humanity toward freedom and self-consciousness, in ideas and moral values and the overall terrain of social life. Indeed, the existence of History as a coherent unfolding of real emancipatory potentialities is clearly verified by the existence of *Civilization*, the potentialities of History embodied and partially actualized. It consists of the concrete advances, material as well as cultural and psychological, that humanity *has* made toward greater degrees of freedom, self-consciousness, and cooperation, as well as rationality itself. To have transcended the limitations of the kinship tie; to have gone beyond mere foraging into agriculture and industry; to have replaced the parochial band or tribe with the increasingly universal city; to have devised writing, produced literature, and developed richer forms of expression than nonliterate peoples could have ever imagined – all of these and many more advances have provided the conditions for evolving increasingly sophisticated notions of individuality and expanding notions of reason that remain stunning achievements to this very day.

It is dialectical reason rather than conventional reason that apprehends the development of this tradition. Indeed, dialectical logic can hardly be treated coequally with eruptions of brutality, however calculated they may be, since in no sense can *episodic capacities* be equated with an *unfolding potentiality*. A dialectical understanding of History apprehends differentiae in quality, logical continuity, and maturation in historical development, as distinguished from the kinetics of mere change or a simple directivity of "social dynamics." Rarefying projects for human liberation . . . without relevance to the realities of the overall human experience and the insights of speculative reason, can cause us to overlook the existential impact of these developments and the promise they hold for ever-greater freedom, self-consciousness, and cooperation. We take these achievements all too easily for granted without asking what kind of human beings we would be if they had not occurred as a result of historical and cultural movements more fundamental than eccentric factors. These achievements, let us acknowledge quite clearly, *are* Civilization, indeed a civilizing continuum that is nonetheless infused by terribly barbaric, indeed animalistic features. The civilizing process has been ambiguous, as I emphasized in my "Ambiguities of Freedom,"[3] but it has nonetheless historically turned folk into citizens, while the process of environmental adaptation that humans share with animals has been transformed into a wide-ranging, strictly human process of *innovation* in distinctly alterable environments. It is a process that reached its greatest universality primarily in Europe, however much other parts of the world have fed into the experience. Those of us who understandably fear that the barrier between Civilization and chaos is fragile actually presuppose the existence of Civilization, not simply of chaos, and the existence of rational coherence, not simply of irrational incoherence.

Moreover, the dialectic of freedom has emerged again and again in recurring struggles for freedom, ideological as well as physical, that have abidingly expanded overall goals of freedom, self-consciousness, and cooperation – as much in social evolution as a whole as within specific temporal periods. The past is replete with instances in which masses of people, however disparate their cultures, have tried to resolve the same millennia-old problems in remarkably similar ways and with remarkably similar views. The famous cry for equality that the English peasants raised in their 1381 revolt – "When Adam delved and Eve span, who was then the gentleman?" – is as meaningful for contemporary revolts as it was six hundred years ago, in a world that presumably had a far different "imaginary" from our own. The denial of a rational universal History, of Civilization, of Progress, and of social continuity renders any historical perspective impossible and hence any revolutionary praxis meaningless except as a matter of personal, indeed often very personal, taste.

Even as social movements attempt to attain what they might call a rational society, in developing humanity's potentialities for freedom, self-consciousness, and cooperation, History may constitute itself as an ever-developing whole. This whole, I should emphasize, must be distinguished from a terminal Hegelian "Absolute," just as demands for coherence in a body of views must be distinguished from the worship of such an Absolute and just as the capacity of speculative reason to educe in a dialectically logical manner the very real potentialities of humanity for freedom is neither teleological nor absolutist, much less totalitarian. There is nothing teleological, mystical, or absolutist about History. Wholeness is no teleological referent, whose evolving components are merely parts of a predetermined Absolute. Neither the rational unfolding of human potentialities nor their actualization in an eternally given "Totality" is predestined.

Nor is the working out of our potentialities some vague sort of suprahuman activity. Human beings are not the passive tools of a Spirit (*Geist*) that works out its complete and final self-realization and self-consciousness. Rather, they are active agents, the authentic "constituents" of History, who may or may not elaborate their potentialities in social evolution. Aborted the revolutionary tradition has been here, and discontinuous it has been there – and for all we know it may ultimately be aborted for humanity as such. Whether an "ultimate" rational society will even exist as a liberatory "end of history" is beyond anyone's predictive powers. We cannot say what the scope of a rational, free, and cooperative society would be, let alone presume to claim knowledge of its limits. Indeed, insofar as the historical process effected by living human agents is likely to expand our notions of the rational, the democratic, the free, and the cooperative, it is undesirable to dogmatically assert that they have any finality. History forms its own ideal of these notions at various times, which in turn have been expanded and enriched.

Every society has the possibility of attaining a remarkable degree of rationality, given the material, cultural, and intellectual conditions that allow for it or, at least, are available to it. Within the limits of a slave, patriarchal, warrior, and urban world, for example, the ancient Athenian *polis* functioned *more* rationally than Sparta or other Greek *poleis*. It is precisely the task of speculative reason to educe *what should exist* at any given period, based on the very real potentialities for the expansion of these notions. To conclude that "the end of history" has been attained in liberal capitalism would be to jettison the historical legacy of these magnificent efforts to create a free society – efforts that claimed countless lives in the great revolutions of the past. For my part, I and probably many revolutionaries today want no place in such an "end of history"; nor do I want to forget the great emancipatory movements for popular freedom in all their many forms that occurred over the ages.

History, Civilization, and Progress are the dialectically rational social dispensations that form, even with all the impediments they face, a dialectical legacy of freedom. The existence of this legacy of freedom in no way denies the existence of a "legacy of domination," which remains within the realm of the irrational. Indeed, these "legacies" intertwine with and condition each other. Human ideals, struggles, and achievements of various approximations to freedom cannot be separated from the cruelties and barbarities that have marked social development over the centuries, often giving rise to new social configurations whose development is highly unpredictable. But a crucial historical problematic remains, to the extent that reason can foresee a given development: Will it be freedom or domination that is nourished? I submit that Progress is the advance – and as everyone presumably hopes, the ascendancy – of freedom over domination, which clearly cannot be conceptually frozen in an ahistorical eternity, given the growing awareness of both hopes and oppressions that have come to light in only a few recent generations. Progress also appears in the overall improvement, however ambiguous, of humanity's material conditions of life, the emergence of a rational ethics, with enlightened standards of sensibility and conduct, out of unreflexive custom and theistic morality, and social institutions that foster continual self-development and cooperation. However lacking our ethical claims in relation to social practice may be, given all the barbarities of our time, we now subject brutality to much harsher judgments than was done in earlier times.

It is difficult to conceive of a rational ethics – as distinguished from unthinking custom and mere commandments of morality, like the Decalogue – without *reasoned* criteria of good and evil based on real potentialities for freedom that speculative reason can educe *beyond a given reality*. The "sufficient conditions" for an ethics must be explicated rationally, not simply affirmed in public opinion polls, plebiscites, or an "intersubjective" consensus that fails to clarify what constitutes "subjectivity" and "autonomy." Admittedly, this is not easy to do in a world that celebrates vaporous words, but it is necessary to discover truth rather than work with notions that stem from the conventional "wisdom" of our times. As Hegel insisted, even commonplace moral maxims like "Love thy neighbor as thyself" raise many problems, such as what we really mean by "love."[4]

. . . Minimally, the actualization of humanity's potentialities consists in its attainment of a rational society. Such a society, of course, would not appear ab novo. By its very nature it would require development, maturation, or, more precisely, a History – a rational development that may be fulfilled by the very fact that the society is potentially constituted to be rational. If the self-realization of life in the nonhuman world is survival or stability, the self-realization of humanity is the degree of freedom, self-consciousness, and cooperation, as well as rationality in society. Reduced merely or primarily to scientific "natural law," objectivity is highly attenuated. It does not encompass potentiality and the working of the dialectic in existential reality, let alone its presence as a standard for gauging reality against actuality in the unfolding of human phenomena. . . .

Today, when subjectivism reigns supreme and the common response even to significant events is to erase any meaning and coherence from History, Civilization, and Progress, there is a desperate need for an objectivity that is immensely broader than natural science and "natural laws," on the one hand, and an emphasis on the idiosyncratic, "imaginary," and adventitious, on the other. If vulgar Marxists used "science" to turn the *ethical* claim that "socialism is necessary" into the *teleological* assertion that "socialism is inevitable," today's "post-Marxist" critics repeat a similar vulgarity by mordantly celebrating incoherence in the realm of social theory. The claim of socialism's inevitability was crudely deterministic; the claim of its necessity was a rational and ethical explication. . . .

Dialectic, it should be emphasized, cannot be reduced merely to a "method" on the grounds that such disparate dialectical thinkers as Aristotle, John Scotus Eriugena, Hegel, and Marx comprehended different realms of knowledge and reality in different ways and periods. Humanity's knowledge of dialectic has itself been a process, and dialectical thinking has itself undergone development – a cumulative development, not a so-called "paradigm shift" – just as scientists have been obliged in the give-and-take or sublation of ideas to resolve one-sided insights into the nature of reality and its becoming.

Although the broader objectivity that dialectical reasoning educes does not dictate that reason *will* prevail, it implies that it *should* prevail, thereby melding ethics with human activity and creating the basis for a truly objective ethical socialism or anarchism. As such, dialectic is not simply an ontological causality; *it is also an ethics* – an aspect of dialectical philosophy that has not been sufficiently emphasized. Dialectical reason permits an ethics in history by upholding the rational influence of "what should be" as against "what is." History, *qua* the dialectically rational, exercises a pressing claim, so to speak, on our canons of behavior and our interpretation of events. Without this liberatory legacy and a human practice that fosters its unfolding, we have absolutely no basis for even judging what is creative or stagnant, rational or irrational, or good or evil in any constellation of cultural phenomena other than personal preference. Unlike science's limited objectivity, dialectical naturalism's objectivity is ethical *by its very nature,* by virtue of the kind of society it identifies as rational, a society that is the actualization of humanity's potentialities. It sublates science's narrow objectivity to advance by rational inferences drawn from the objective nature of human potentialities, a society that increasingly actualizes those potentialities. And it does so on the basis of what should be as the fulfillment of the rational, that is to say, on rational knowledge of the good and a conceptual congruence between the good and the socially rational that can be embodied in free institutions.

It is not that social development is dialectical because it is *necessarily* rational, as a traditional Hegelian might suppose, but rather that where social development is rational, it is dialectical or historical. In short, we can educe from a uniquely human potentiality a rational development that advances human self-realization in a free, self-conscious, and cooperative society. Speculative reason here stakes out a claim to discern the rational development (by no means immune to irrational vicissitudes) of society as it *should be* – given human potentiality, as we know it in real life, to evolve from a tribal folk to a democratic citizenry, from mythopoesis to reason, from the submission of personhood in a folklike collectivity to individuality in a rational community – all as rational ends as well as existential realities. Speculative reason should always be called upon to understand and explain not only what has happened with respect to these problematics but why they recur in varying degrees and how they can be resolved.

In a very real sense, the past fifteen or more years have been remarkably ahistorical, albeit highly eventful, insofar as they have not been marked by any lasting advance toward a rational society. Indeed, if anything, they would seem to be tilting toward a regression, ideologically and structurally, to barbarism, despite spectacular advances in technology and science, whose outcome we cannot foresee. There cannot be a dialectic, however, that deals "dialectically" with the irrational, with regression into barbarism – that is to say, a strictly *negative dialectics*. Both Adorno's book of that name and Horkheimer and Adorno's *The Dialectic of Enlightenment*, which traced the "dialectical" descent of reason (in Hegel's sense) into instrumentalism, were little more than mixed farragoes of convoluted neo-Nietzschean verbiage, often brilliant, colorful, and excitingly informative, but often confused, rather dehumanizing and, to speak bluntly, irrational. A "dialectic" that lacks any spirit of transcendence (*Aufhebung*) and denies the "negation of the negation" is spurious at its very core. . . .

Stated bluntly: No *revolutionary* movement can grow if its theorists essentially deny Bloch's "principle of hope," which the movement so needs for an inspired belief in the future; if it denies universal History that affirms sweeping common problems that have besieged humanity over the ages; if it denies the shared interests that give a movement the basis for a common struggle in achieving a rational dispensation of social affairs; if it denies a processual rationality and a growing idea of the Good based on more than personalistic (or "intersubjective" and "consensual") grounds; if it denies the powerful civilizatory dimensions of social development (ironically, dimensions that are in fact so useful to contemporary nihilists in criticizing humanity's failings); and if it denies historical Progress. Yet in present-day theoretics, a series of events replaces History, cultural relativism replaces Civilization, and a basic pessimism replaces a belief in the possibility of Progress. What is more sinister, mythopoesis replaces reason, and dystopia the prospect of a rational society. What is at stake in all these displacements is an intellectual and practical regression of appalling proportions – an especially alarming development today, when theoretical clarity is of the utmost necessity. What our times require is a *social*-analysis that calls for a revolutionary and ultimately popular movement, not a *psycho*-analysis that issues self-righteous disclaimers for "beautiful souls," ideologically dressed in cloaks of personal virtue.

Given the disparity between what rationally should be and what currently exists, reason may not necessarily become embodied in a free society. If and when the realm of freedom ever does reach its most expansive form, to the extent that we can envision it, and if hierarchy, classes, domination, and exploitation were ever abolished, we would be obliged to enter that realm only as free beings, as truly rational, ethical, and empathetic "knowing animals," with the highest intellectual insight and ethical probity, not as brutes coerced into it by grim necessity and fear. The riddle of our times is whether today's relativists would have equipped us intellectually and ethically to cross into that most expansive realm of freedom. We cannot merely be driven into greater freedom by blind forces that we fail to understand, as Marxists implied, still less by mere preferences that have no standing in anything more than "imaginary," "instincts," or libidinal "desires." The relativists of our time could actually play a sinister role if they permitted the "imaginative" to loosen our contact with the objective world. For in the absence of rational objective standards of behavior, imagination may be as demonic as it may be liberatory when such standards exist; hence the need for informed spontaneity – and an informed imagination.

The exhilarating events of May–June 1968, with the cry "Imagination to Power!" were followed a few years later by a surge in the popularity of nihilistic postmodernism and poststructuralism in the academy, an unsavory metaphysics of "desire," and an apolitical call for "imagination" nourished by a yearning for "self-realization." More than ever, I would insist, we must invert Nietzsche's dictum "All facts are interpretations" and demand that all interpretations be rooted in objectivity. We must seek out broader interpretations of socialism than those that cast socialist ideals as a science and strangled its movements in authoritarian institutions. At a time when we teeter between Civilization and barbarism, the current apostles of irrationality in all their varied forms are the chthonic demons of a dark world who have come to life not to explicate humanity's problems but to effect a dispiriting denial of the role of rationality in History and human affairs. My disquiet today lies not in the absence of scientific "guarantees" that a libertarian socialist society will appear – one that, at my age, it will never be my privilege to see – but in whether it will even be fought for in so decadent and desperate a period.

NOTES

1 See James Miller, *The Passion of Michel Foucault* (New York: Simon & Schuster, 1993).

2 See Murray Bookchin, *Re-enchanting Humanity* (London: Cassell, 1995).

3 See Chapter 11 of Murray Bookchin, *The Ecology of Freedom* (1982; reprinted by Montreal: Black Rose Books, 1991).

4 G.W.F. Hegel, "Reason as Lawgiver," in *Phenomenology of Spirit,* trans. A. V. Miller (Oxford: Oxford University Press, 1977), pp. 252–6.

Permissions

Grateful acknowledgment is made to the following for permission to reprint previously published material:

A.K. Press: "Overview of the Spanish Libertarian Movement," in *To Remember Spain* (1995); "After Fifty Years," in *To Remember Spain* (1995); and "Social Anarchism versus Lifestyle Anarchism," in *Social Anarchism versus Lifestyle Anarchism* (1995). Reprinted by permission of A.K. Press.

Black Rose Books: "Ecology and Revolutionary Thought," "Post-Scarcity Anarchism," "Toward a Liberatory Technology," and "Listen, Marxist!" in *Post-Scarcity Anarchism* (1986 rpt.); *The Ecology of Freedom,* second edition (1991 rpt.); "Twenty Years Later . . . ," introduction to the revised edition of *The Ecology of Freedom* (1991); "What Is Social Ecology?" and "Rethinking Ethics, Nature, and Society," in *The Modern Crisis* (1986); *Remaking Society* (1989); "Marxism as Bourgeois Sociology," in *Toward an Ecological Society* (1980); "The New Municipal Agenda," in *Urbanization Against Cities* (1992 rpt.); "Freedom and Necessity in Nature," "A Philosophical Naturalism," "Thinking Ecologically," and "History, Civilization, and Progress," in *The Philosophy of Social Ecology,* revised edition (1994). Reprinted by permission of Black Rose Books.

Cassell: "Biocentrism" in *Re-enchanting Humanity* (1995); "The New Municipal Agenda," in *From Urbanization to Cities,* revised edition (1995 rpt). Reprinted by permission of Cassell.

New Society Publishers: "What Is Social Ecology?" and "Rethinking Ethics, Nature, and Society," in *The Modern Crisis* (1986). Reprinted by permission of New Society Publishers.

South End Press: *Remaking Society* (1990). Reprinted by permission of South End Press.

Index